SETTLING FOR LESS

Settling for Less

WHY STATES COLONIZE AND WHY THEY STOP

LACHLAN MCNAMEE

PRINCETON UNIVERSITY PRESS

PRINCETON & OXFORD

Published by Princeton University Press
41 William Street, Princeton, New Jersey 08540
99 Banbury Road, Oxford OX2 6JX

press.princeton.edu

Library of Congress Cataloging-in-Publication Data

Names: McNamee, Lachlan, 1991– author.
Title: Settling for less : why states colonize and why they stop / Lachlan McNamee.
Description: Princeton : Princeton University Press, [2023] | Includes
    bibliographical references and index.
Identifiers: LCCN 2022026583 (print) | LCCN 2022026584 (ebook) |
    ISBN 9780691237800 (hardback) | ISBN 9780691237817 (paperback) |
    ISBN 9780691237824 (ebook)
Subjects: LCSH: Decolonization—History—20th century. | Indigenous
    peoples–Colonization—History—20th century. |
    Nation-building—History—20th century. | Colonization–Economic
    aspects–History—20th century. | BISAC: POLITICAL SCIENCE / Colonialism
    & Post-Colonialism | SOCIAL SCIENCE / Ethnic Studies / General
Classification: LCC JV185 .M38 2023 (print) | LCC JV185 (ebook) |
    DDC 325/.3–dc23/eng/20220705
LC record available at https://lccn.loc.gov/2022026583
LC ebook record available at https://lccn.loc.gov/2022026584

British Library Cataloging-in-Publication Data is available

Editorial: Bridget Flannery-McCoy and Alena Chekanov
Production Editorial: Nathan Carr
Jacket/Cover Design: Heather Hansen
Production: Lauren Reese
Publicity: Kate Hensley and Charlotte Coyne
Copyeditor: Bhisham Bherwani

Cover image credit: Photograph © Patrick Wack. An unfinished hotel in Turpan, Xinjiang, China (2016).

This book has been composed in Arno

10 9 8 7 6 5 4 3 2 1

My only consolation is that periods of colonization pass, that nations sleep only for a time, and that peoples remain.

—*Aimé Césaire*

CONTENTS

ACKNOWLEDGMENTS

THE PRICE of writing a book is the accumulation of a great many personal debts. David Laitin shepherded this project from its gestation to its completion. He continues to be a source of great inspiration. This book began as a PhD dissertation at Stanford and my committee members there—David, Jean Oi, Jonathan Rodden, Jeremy Weinstein, and Aliya Saperstein—all left their mark on this book in different ways. I am grateful for their individual and collective support. The MERNers in Stanford Sociology, including Aliya, Tomás Jiménez, Jackie Hwang, Jasmine Hill, Beka Guluma, Kim Higuera, Elisa Kim, Marlene Orozco, and Corey Fields, were a fabulous intellectual community and pushed the book to its completion during the dark days of the COVID-19 pandemic. Other Stanford faculty including Ken Schultz, Ken Scheve, Lisa Blaydes, Beatriz Magaloni, Alberto Diaz-Cayeros, Vicky Fouka, and Paula Moya also offered much support. I thank Lisa and Paula for inspiring me to be much more intellectually ambitious, historical, and theory-driven. Felicity McCutcheon and Mark Philp also deserve much credit for my intellectual growth prior to Stanford and so I would like to take this opportunity to sincerely thank them both.

I am also grateful to a number of friends and colleagues for sustaining me through the past few years in California, including Hans Lueders, Mashail Malik, Salma Mousa, Christiana Parreira, Lily Lamboy, Simon Ejdemyr, Artemis Seaford, Dan Masterson, and Anna Zhang. I also had a lovely community in Chicago and so I would like to thank the Brunch Chicks—Kyle Kaplan, Simran Bhalla, Thomas Pringle, Jaime Price, and Tamara Tasevska—as well as Zsofi Valyi-Nagy, Shanti Chu, and Caity Monroe for all the wonderful Summerdale memories.

Much of this book was written in Florence during my postdoctoral fellowship at the European University Institute. I would like to thank Fabrizio Bernardi and Juho Härkönen for their kind welcome. Though all-too-short, I am grateful for the precious time spent with Eleanor Woodhouse, Ari Ray,

Meira Gold, Lola Avril, Luke Sonnet, Victoria Paniagua, Judith Spirig, and Alexa Zeitz. I am also grateful to old friends: Suet Wa Wong, Jonny Lofts, Glen Promnitz, Lizhi Howard, Daivy Babel, Anna Önnered, Ayesha Jhunjhunwala, Marie Lechler, and my LA community including Jasmine Pierre, Allie Morse, Kevan Harris, Wisam Alshaibi, Aziz Sohail, Rohan Advani, Sima Ghaddar, Milan DelVecchio, Muscovado, and Gerry and Linda Sanoff for their friendship.

Many people have kindly read and provided comments on various parts of this book. Special thanks go to Harris Mylonas and Michael Ross for their mentorship. Sincere thanks also go to the participants at my book conference—Dan Posner, Cesi Cruz, Maggie Peters, Claire Adida, Michael Ross, Michael Chwe, Stathis Kalyvas, Dan Treisman, and Anthony Pagden—who read the whole book and helped me sharpen key arguments. Alexa Zeitz and Laurie Anderson generously reshaped some critical first drafts. Others who have provided helpful comments include Nara Dillon, Lynette Ong, Scott Straus, Pradeep Chhibber, Martha Wilfahrt, Adria Lawrence, Jan Pierskalla, Bogdan Popescu, Joan Ricart-Huguet, Kamya Yadav, Macartan Humphreys, Alex Scacco, Miriam Golden, John Gerring, Roger Haydon, John Haslum, Michael Albertus, Dan Mattingly, Benjamin Stefano, Shuhei Kurizaki, Soo Yeon Kim, Mike Tomz, Hannah Waight, Iza Ding, Mayesha Alam, Edward Aspinall, Paul Kenny, Rogers Brubaker, César Ayala, Ron Rogowski, and seminar participants at NUS, Waseda, Nuffield, Yale, Harvard, Berkeley, WZB, EUI, the University of Washington, ANU, the SSHA, the Historical Political Economy group, and UCLA 237.

Parts of Chapter 5 have been published as McNamee and Zhang (2019), "Demographic Engineering and International Conflict: Evidence from China and the Former USSR" in *International Organization*. These are reprinted with the permission of Cambridge University Press. Anna and I were equal partners in the data collection, analysis, and writing of this chapter. Our collaboration, sparked by our shared interest in Xinjiang, was an inspired decision. This book is much stronger for her.

Many thanks go to the editorial team at Princeton University Press, especially Bridget Flannery-McCoy and Alena Chekanov. Bridget provided early and sustained encouragement of the book, and so I would like to offer sincere thanks for all her guidance to a first-time author. Special thanks go to Bhisham Bherwani for careful copyediting and also to two very kind and anonymous reviewers, whose insightful suggestions transformed the book.

My family deserve much of the credit for this book. I am lucky to have you all—Will, Nat, Steph, Pixie, Bruce, Carole, Charlie, Family Christmas, and all of the more recent additions. The Rummikub crew have been and will always be my rock. And I could never have written this book without the support provided by my parents who have been unfailingly encouraging of all my academic endeavors. You instilled in me a love of reading, learning, and global adventure.

This book is dedicated to Scott P. Newman. Meeting you changed my life. I remain, above all, grateful for every day that we have together.

SETTLING FOR LESS

1

Introduction

"WE ARE often told, 'Colonialism is dead.' Let us not be deceived or even soothed by that. I say to you, colonialism is not yet dead."[1] With these words, President Sukarno of Indonesia opened the Asian-African conference in Bandung, Indonesia in 1955. Gathered in the audience were representatives from 29 African and Asian countries, including many of the world's leading anti-colonial activists like Jawaharlal Nehru of India, Gamal Abdel Nasser of Egypt, Zhou Enlai of China, and Ho Chi Minh of Vietnam. The principal aim of the conference was to deepen a sense of political solidarity between the newly liberated nation-states of the Third World. And Sukarno's fiery rhetoric reflected the radical nature of the Bandung conference, which took place in a context when much of the world still remained under Europe's thumb. For how, Sukarno implored, "can we say [colonialism] is dead, so long as vast areas of Asia and Africa are unfree"?

The Bandung conference is often fondly remembered as the moment when the most marginalized peoples around the world joined political forces against European colonizers.[2] Declaring their opposition to the "subjection of peoples to alien subjugation, domination, and exploitation," Bandung's participants vocally affirmed the right of all peoples to self-determination. The Bandung conference essentially heralded the winds of change that would soon sweep away most of Europe's remaining possessions in Africa and Asia. For this reason, Léopold Senghor, the first President of Senegal, later claimed that "since the age of the Renaissance, no event has ever been of such historic significance" (Burke, 2006, 948).

What this romanticized narrative usually omits, however, is that one of Indonesia's primary motives for holding the Bandung conference was to build support for its claim to the western half of the island of New Guinea (West Papua, Figure 1.1). In 1955, West Papua remained under the control of the

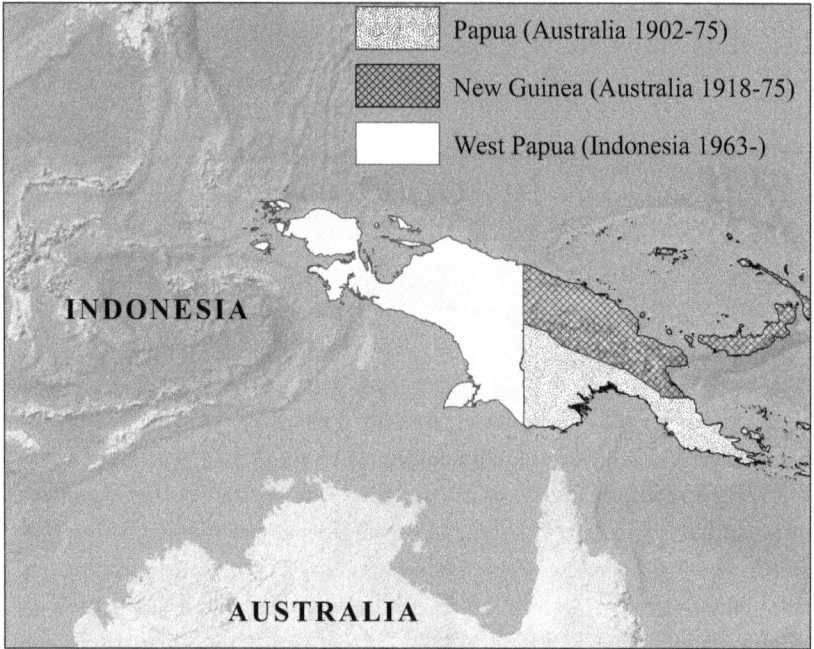

Papua (Australia 1902-75)

New Guinea (Australia 1918-75)

West Papua (Indonesia 1963-)

INDONESIA

AUSTRALIA

FIGURE 1.1. How the island of New Guinea was divided between Australia
and Indonesia over the twentieth century.

Netherlands but was claimed by Indonesia. The Dutch, sensing the winds of
change, were actively preparing to transfer sovereignty to indigenous Papuans.
Sukarno, however, railed against what he regarded as Dutch "trickery" and
attempts to establish a "puppet state" there, calling on all the peoples of Africa
and Asia to help liberate West Papua from Dutch rule.[3] It is in this context,
with Sukarno desperately seeking to prevent an independent West Papua,
that Indonesia invited the world's leading anti-colonial activists to Bandung.[4]
On Sukarno's urging, the Bandung communiqué affirmed that the conference
"in the context of its expressed attitude on the abolition of colonialism, supported the position of Indonesia" in West Papua (Asian-African Conference,
1955, 166).

Chastened and internationally isolated, the Netherlands eventually trans-
ferred sovereignty over West Papua to Indonesia in 1963. If Indonesians
expected to be welcomed as liberators in West Papua, however, they were
sorely mistaken. Since the 1960s, Indonesia has faced a separatist insurgency
there led by the Free Papua Movement (OPM). Seeking to flush out the

OPM, the Indonesian military killed tens of thousands of West Papuan civilians in security operations over the rest of the twentieth century.[5] And, with a view to knitting West Papua permanently to the rest of the Indonesian archipelago, Indonesia resettled 300,000 farmers from its core islands to West Papua between 1984 and 1999.[6] Indigenous Papuans are now a minority in much of West Papua beyond the highlands.

The irony that the Bandung conference was complicit in producing a condition in West Papua that looks distinctly like "alien subjugation, domination, and exploitation" has not been lost on indigenous activists. On the 60th anniversary of the Bandung conference, a leading West Papuan liberation group sent a statement to all foreign embassies in Jakarta, claiming: "It is Indonesia, today, that holds West Papua as a colony. Today, the time has come to end colonial rule and permit West Papuans a genuine act of self-determination."[7] West Papuans, it would seem, agree with Sukarno: colonialism is not yet dead.

The tensions raised by the entanglement of Bandung and West Papua deepen once we turn our attention to the eastern half of the same island. For if West Papuans were seemingly colonized by a state ideologically committed to decolonization in Indonesia, then Papua New Guineans were willingly decolonized by a state ideologically committed to colonization in Australia. Papua New Guinea was at the vanguard of an abortive "Australasian Empire" over the twentieth century. Inspired by the example of the United States, Australian elites in the early twentieth century dreamt of realizing their own "Pacific Ocean destiny,"[8] encompassing the Australian continent, New Zealand, New Guinea, and Fiji. Australia's annexation of Papua in 1902 and New Guinea in 1918 were envisioned as the first steps in a nascent white imperial project in the Pacific.[9]

The centerpiece of Australian colonial rule in New Guinea was a scheme, much like Indonesia's, to resettle farmers onto alienated indigenous land. To entice European settlers to New Guinea, the Australian government ensured that any white male settler that migrated to Papua could have as much land as he wanted for free from 1906. Much to the consternation of Australian officials, however, the promise of free and fertile land in the Papuan highlands proved insufficiently alluring to white settlers. Rather than become farmers in Papua and New Guinea, the hundreds of thousands of Europeans who emigrated to Australia in the early twentieth century flocked to its rapidly industrializing cities like Melbourne and Sydney. White Australia could not make Melanesia white.

Papua New Guineans ultimately gained independence in 1975 as a result of a bizarrely inverted decolonization process. Australia's classification of Papuans as subjects, not citizens, had become increasingly unviable after Bandung, and a delegation from Papua New Guinea requested full Australian statehood and citizenship in the mid-1960s. The Australian government responded by taking statehood off the table and setting Papua New Guinea on the road to independence. Papua New Guinea's decolonization by Australia in 1975 was thus a one-sided affair. There had been no political struggle: no mass rallies demanding independence, no subversive nationalism, no insurgency, no political prisoners, no referendum. Rather, in quite bad faith, Australia's leaders recast Papua New Guinea's independence as a mutually beneficial liberation. For instance, then Prime Minister Gough Whitlam reflected that "Australia was never truly free until Papua New Guinea became free."[10] With Australia determined to decolonize Papua New Guinea, indigenous leaders there could control little but the timing of their own liberation.

The point of starting this book with the history of New Guinea is not to invalidate the Bandung conference, whose spirit of self-determination continues to be a source of inspiration to marginalized peoples around the world. Rather, the point of juxtaposing West Papua and Papua New Guinea is to reveal the hollowness of a Manichean worldview, epitomized by Sukarno, that divides the world into colonized and colonizer based on whiteness. Even the most vocal proponents of decolonization like Indonesia can coercively settle the lands of indigenous peoples. And even white settler states like Australia can, under the right circumstances, become vocal proponents of indigenous sovereignty. In order to understand when and why states colonize indigenous peoples, we should therefore dispense with preexisting assumptions and follow Aimé Césaire's advice "to think clearly – that is, dangerously – and answer clearly the innocent first question: what, fundamentally, is colonization?" (2000, 32).

Innocent yet dangerous like Homer's Sirens, Césaire's question could easily ensnare the unwitting writer in a mess of contradiction. Colonization is a nebulous concept and is used differently in popular, academic, and legal contexts. Lashing myself to the strongest conceptual mast in sight, I draw on its agrarian roots to define colonization as a process of state building involving the displacement of indigenous peoples by settlers. The origins of the word "colonization" in the Latin *colonus*, or farmer, reflects the fact that colonization historically described what happens when groups of farmers coercively settle in and claim a frontier on behalf of a distant state.[11] Let me break this down.

The acquisition of new territory by states is imperialism (Hobson, 1902, 2). Imperialism is distinct from colonialism and colonization, which refer to *how* states govern over frontier lands. Colonialism generally evokes a condition in which states discriminate against certain peoples on the basis of their ethnicity.[12] For this reason, Albert Memmi (2010) suggests that "the idea of privilege is at the heart of the colonial relationship," Partha Chatterjee (1993) calls colonialism "the rule of difference," and for Frantz Fanon (1963) the colonial world "is a world cut in two." Colonial subjects are victims of discrimination and exclusion from certain spaces on the basis of their ethno-racial identity.

But not all forms of colonial rule look the same.[13] For instance, in colonial India, Britain ruled in collaboration with indigenous elites with a view to extracting the resources and labor of its native people. European colonization was severely limited; Charles Cornwallis, the third Viceroy of India, advised his superiors in London in 1794 that "it will be of essential importance to the interests of Britain, that Europeans should be discouraged and *prevented as much as possible from colonizing and settling* in our possessions of India."[14] But in other nineteenth century British colonies, quite the opposite was true. In settler colonies like Australia, Canada, and the United States, colonization was integral to "state making" (Tilly, 1985) or how Europeans eliminated indigenous sovereignty and secured control over frontier territory. Understood as a process of dispossession by ethnically distinct farmers, colonization is analogous to "settler colonialism"; it is a form of state building entailing the coercive redistribution of frontier land to settlers.[15]

I will use the terms settler colonialism and colonization interchangeably and in a descriptive, not normative, way in this book. The identities of settler and indigene, or colonized and colonizer, are contextual and are based on one's relationship to power (the state). Where migrants are gifted expropriated land on the basis of their ethnicity, it is appropriate to speak of them as settler colonists even if these same migrants were also fleeing dispossession and discrimination by another state. In this sense, Edward Said identifies the painful irony that Palestinians since 1948 have been "turned into exiles by the proverbial people of exile, the Jews" (Said, 2000, 178). Refugees can become settlers.[16]

Using the term settler colonialism to refer to resettlement programs within nation-states like Indonesia or Israel does, admittedly, come at the cost of some dissonance. The stereotypical image of a settler is a bronzed white man in Wellington boots, leaning on his shovel, staring into the setting sun (Memmi, 2010). But settlers are simply migrants who partake in projects of territorial conquest. Hence, when migration and land redistribution is non-consensual, undesired and unregulated by a preexisting population, we should speak of settlers and colonization projects even if migrants are non-white. Otherwise, we fall into the trap of using different terms to refer to different resettlement programs based purely on the racial characteristics of those involved or the rhetoric that accompanies them. There are too many similarities in practice between Australia's and Indonesia's attempts to settle New Guinea, for instance, to just dismiss the notion that these two projects may have similar underlying logics.[17]

Alternatively, consider the fact that in 2019 India revoked Kashmir's autonomy to facilitate the migration of Hindus there. Encouraging Hindus to settle in a contested territory prompted considerable international outrage and resistance by native Kashmiris. But as India's Consul General in New York, Sandeep Chakravorty, reasoned: "If the Israeli people can do it, we can also do it."[18] All states can be colonizers.

Having sailed past Césaire's Sirens and found firm conceptual ground, we can now return to the central question of this book: when and why do states engage in colonization?

The conventional answer to this question has remained essentially unchanged since the publication of Karl Marx and Friedrich Engels' *The Communist Manifesto*. This wisdom rests on two key tenets. The first tenet is that colonization is driven by the desire of states to appropriate indigenous land and resources.[19] For instance, in his study of the historically ungoverned zones of Southeast Asia, James C. Scott (2009, xii) echoes Marx and Engels by asserting that states, above all, seek to exploit the labor and land of their peripheries. When faced with mobile indigenes whose forms of subsistence cannot be easily taxed, states forcibly impose more legible agrarian landscapes on the periphery by reallocating land to colonists. As he summarizes:

> Internal colonialism, broadly understood, aptly describes this process. It involved the absorption, displacement, and/or extermination of the previous inhabitants. It involved a botanical colonization in which the landscape was transformed—by deforestation, drainage, irrigation, and levees—to accommodate crops, settlement patterns, and systems of administration familiar to the state and to the colonists.

Colonization is, in other words, a phenomenon "hard wired" into states and the resource needs of capitalism (Scott, 2009, 4–12).

An emphasis on capitalist exploitation also characterizes the writings of prominent anthropologist Patrick Wolfe. Operating with a "logic of elimination," as Wolfe put it in his 2001 essay for the *American Historical Review*, capitalist states kill, deport, incarcerate, and forcibly assimilate indigenous peoples in order to secure land for commercial agriculture.[20] Settler colonialism is, as Wolfe summarizes elsewhere, "an inclusive, land-centered project that *coordinates a comprehensive range of agencies, from the metropolitan centre to the frontier encampment*, with a view to eliminating Indigenous societies" (Wolfe, 2006, 393).[21] The logic of elimination has since become an obligatory point of departure in the historiography of settler colonialism in Australia, Canada, New Zealand, the Pacific, the United States, Japan, and beyond.[22] The logic of elimination, as one historian recently put it, "is now dogma" (Shoemaker, 2015, 29).

The second key tenet of this conventional wisdom is that variation in colonization is driven solely by logistical constraints. After all, if states always prefer to coercively reallocate frontier land to their own colonists, then it follows that indigenous peoples are only spared colonization when settlement is infeasible, indigenous resistance is too fierce, or their land is undesirable. For instance, Scott (2009) emphasizes how mountainous terrain presented hard limits to the viability of commercial agriculture and thus the colonization projects of Southeast Asian states. Acemoglu, Johnson, and Robinson (2001, 1370) emphasize how Europeans extracted native labor only in colonies where mass European settlement was infeasible due to tropical disease burdens.[23] And Wolfe attributes the rise of British settler colonialism in the late eighteenth century to a population boom driven by early industrialization (Wolfe, 2001, 868–870). Iberian colonies like Brazil were largely spared European settlement because Portugal, unlike Great Britain, remained preindustrial and lacked a "surplus" population of willing settlers.

Combined, these two tenets lead scholars to a rather pessimistic conclusion. Since the Industrial Revolution of the nineteenth century, rising population pressure, the suppression of tropical disease burdens and associated settler mortality, and the development of modern infrastructure have made newly possible the penetration of state power into remote lands. Hence, indigenous resistance to colonization is presumably no longer possible. As Scott (2009, xii) laments in Southeast Asia:

Since 1945, and in some cases before then, the power of the state to deploy distance-demolishing technologies—railroads, all-weather roads,

telephone, telegraph, airpower, helicopters, and now information technology—so changed the strategic balance of power between self-governing
peoples and nation-states, so diminished the friction of terrain ...
[that it has] led everywhere to strategies of "engulfment," in which pre-
sumptively loyal and land-hungry valley populations are transplanted to
the hills.

The result is the ultimate triumph of the colonist over the indigene and "the
world's last great enclosure" (Scott, 2009, 282).

This wisdom, though conventional, is incoherent. Take the first tenet. It may
be true that policymakers have generally exploited the people, lands, and
resources of their peripheries for their own benefit. But actively encouraging
the displacement of indigenous peoples by a new population of settlers is an
odd strategy for capitalist exploitation. For why would the metropole seek to
eliminate indigenous peoples and thereby lose a potentially important source
of trade and labor?

   This concern is not merely hypothetical. For instance, in the mid-1830s the
British Parliament established a Select Committee to report on native policy
across the British Empire. Its report was damning of the decision of British
troops in 1811 to clear the Xhosa from the Eastern Cape in order to make way for
settlers. The result of this decision, according to the commissioners, was "a suc-
cession of new wars," the "loss of thousands of good laborers to the colonists,"
and the "checking of civilization and trade with the interior for a period of 12
years," with the only gain "some hundreds of thousands of acres of land, which
might have been bought from the natives for comparatively a trifle."[24] As they
summarized more broadly, indigenous elimination is costly to states:

> The oppression of the natives ... has engendered wars, in which great
> expenses were necessarily incurred, and no reputation could be won; and
> it has banished from our confines, or exterminated, the natives who might
> have been profitable workmen, good customers, and good neighbours.[25]

Similarly, the genocide of the Herero in South West Africa in 1904 by
the German colonial state is often cited as an operative instance of the
logic of elimination. But the Herero genocide led to a sustained recession
in South West Africa, as colonial diamond and copper mines lost most of
their preexisting labor force. The annihilation of the Herero was an "antieconomic" decision that imperiled the economic heart of the German colonial
state (Steinmetz, 2007). Settler colonialism, as a violent process that results

in the loss of indigenous labor, seems to contradict the capitalist imperative of revenue maximization. So, something beyond mere avarice must be driving the calculus of officials when they *do* decide to violently displace or kill indigenous people.

Beyond this underlying theoretical tension, the notion that capitalist states are driven by a logic of elimination also struggles to withstand historical scrutiny. Recall that the logic of elimination is a coordinated, genocidal project connecting the metropole to settlers on the frontier. Examining historical processes as they unfolded, however, reveals that even canonical cases of European colonization—the evidentiary basis of the logic of elimination— were *not* obviously characterized by coordination between settlers and the metropole. For instance, in Victoria, a state that takes up the southeast corner of Australia, almost 80% of the some 10,000 total indigenous population died between 1836 and 1853 following a rush of British settlers (Ryan, 2010). Accordingly, Wolfe claims that the logic of elimination "approximated its pure or theoretical form" in southeastern Australia "resulting, within a short space of time, in the decimation of the Aboriginal population" (Wolfe, 2001, 871).

But the historical record reveals that indigenous elimination in Victoria occurred *against* the wishes of the British government. The first penal colony in Australia was established in Sydney, New South Wales in 1788. Colonial governments in New South Wales subsequently restricted colonization to the extent that by the 1830s European settlement on mainland Australia was limited to a relatively small area in and around Sydney. Chafing at these restrictions, in 1835 a group of settlers formed a consortium with a view to colonizing the southern coast of Australia. Their newly constituted "Port Phillip Association" established a new town at the head of Port Phillip Bay (present-day Melbourne) that same year.

These actions prompted a flurry of letters between Sydney and London. Publicly, the Governor of New South Wales, Richard Bourke, opposed the colonization of Port Phillip Bay, declaring the new settlement "void and of no effect against the rights of the Crown" and the settlers "liable to be dealt with in like manner as intruders upon the vacant lands of the Crown."[26] But privately, Bourke lobbied his superiors in London to relax restrictions on colonization, arguing in October 1835 that "no adequate measures could be resorted to for the general and permanent removal of intruders from waste lands, without incurring a probably greater expense." Bourke pointedly asked the Colonial Office "simply this: How may this Government turn to the best advantage a state of things, which it cannot wholly interdict?."[27] The Secretary of State for the Colonies, Lord Glenelg, accepted Bourke's logic of strategic fatalism and licensed the colonization of "waste land" in Australia in 1836.[28] Expedience and a desire to avoid conflict with settlers lay at the heart of this watershed change in government policy, for as Glenelg put it:

> The motives which are urging mankind, especially in these days of general peace and increasing population, to break through the restraints which would forbid their settling themselves and their families in such situations, are too strong to be encountered [sic] with effect by ordinary means. To engage in such a struggle would be wholly irrational. All that remains for the Government in such circumstances is to assume the guidance and direction of such enterprises, which, though it cannot prevent or retard, it may yet conduct to happy results.[29]

The subsequent, extremely rapid elimination of indigenous peoples in much of Victoria was characterized by a highly decentralized process of killing that is difficult to straightforwardly characterize as official policy.[30] Over the next two decades, settlers, facing at least the nominal risk of arrest and incarceration, progressively eliminated the Aboriginal population when they contested occupation of frontier land.

The absence of metropolitan eliminatory intent or coordination with colonists in southeast Australia suggests that something is amiss with the notion that colonization is driven by a logic of elimination. Rather, the defining paradox of Australian colonial history—one that continues to be debated by scholars and the public today—is that relatively benign metropolitan intentions toward indigenous people coincided with their violent elimination.[31] But lest we think that southeast Australia is a strange anomaly, let us also examine the process through which North America—the other "pure" case of settler colonialism nominated by Wolfe (2001)—was colonized by settlers.

Consider the policy direction of the United States in its earliest stages of independence. In 1783, the United States Confederation Congress, which opened in the last stages of the American Revolution, feared war with the western Indian nations. Consequently, Congress prohibited settlement on Indian lands west of the Appalachias and the purchase of any Indian lands "without the express authority and direction of Congress."[32] But settlers moved into prohibited areas anyway. Over the next year, more than two thousand families migrated to areas of the Ohio valley formally closed to settlement.

Much as in colonial Victoria, American officials, facing a relentless emigration to the backcountry, feared that without any formal incorporation settlers would soon found independent republics. For instance, George Washington told Henry Lee, then President of the Congress, that "the spirit for emigration is great. People have got impatient and, though you cannot stop the road it is yet in your power to mark the way; a little while later and you will not be able to do either."[33] So, in 1784 the Confederation licensed the expansion of the Union west of the Appalachian mountains, ultimately drawing the American state into a long and costly war with the Northwest Indian nations (1785–1795). In this sense, to portray early American expansion "simply as a conflict between the American state and Indian tribes misses the complexity of the relationships of the various groups involved," as White (2010, 420) put it. The violent process of early American colonization was not premeditated or coordinated but rather depended crucially on the agency of settlers.[34]

And lest we think that southern Africa—a third area of the world commonly associated with British settler colonialism—is any different, consider the haphazard series of events that led to the colonization of present-day Zimbabwe in the late 1800s. The 1885 Berlin conference had neatly divided Africa up between competing powers, with only a few areas remaining in dispute. One of the largest disputed areas was the stretch of land that currently makes up Zimbabwe, Zambia, and Malawi, coveted by Portugal, Germany, the Transvaal, and Great Britain. The Berlin Conference had established, however, that European powers could ultimately only acquire territory in Africa through "effective occupation." And effective occupation could only be established in two ways: direct administration by European agents on the ground, or the acquisition of exclusive rights to sovereignty through treaties with local leaders.

The Berlin Conference kicked off a race amongst competing powers to secure a treaty with Lobengula Khumalo, the King of the Ndebele and the leader of the major indigenous kingdom in present-day Zimbabwe. In 1888, the British government wrote to Portugal affirming Lobengula as the "independent King" and "undisputed ruler of Mashonaland and Matabeleland" (Davies, 1989, 31). And Britain signed a treaty with Lobengula in February that year proclaiming that "peace and amity shall continue forever between Her Britannic Majesty, Her subjects, and the Amandebele [sic] people."[35] But by 1894, Lobengula was dead, his kingdom was in ruins, and his lands were being alienated by white settlers. What changed in the intervening six years?

Here, the agency of settlers again mediated imperial expansion and indigenous elimination. Cecil John Rhodes, a leading politician and businessman in the Cape Colony, had recognized that by merely establishing a friendship treaty the February 1888 agreement with Lobengula did not constitute "effective occupation" under the Berlin Conference. So, seeking to secure the reportedly mineral-rich lands in Mashonaland, he pressed his agents to secure from Lobengula the right for British settlers to mine in Mashonaland in return for an annual stipend. Lobengula signed this agreement in October 1888 and his interpreter, Charles Helm, later attested that Lobengula was orally promised Britain "would not bring more than 10 white men to work in his country, that they would not dig anywhere near towns, etc., and that they and their people would abide by the laws of his country" (Brown, 1966, 81). But, no doubt deliberately, the written treaty in fact contained no such limitation.

Having secured this mining concession, Cecil John Rhodes then raced to London to seek the metropole's assent to establish effective occupation over Mashonaland through a private company, the British South African Company (BSAC). The British government was wary of Rhodes' motives, however, and wished to avoid being entangled in costly wars. So, Britain legally limited BSAC to only carrying "into effect divers [sic] concessions and agreements which have been made by certain of the chiefs and tribes."[36] In other words, any effective occupation of new territory in the name of the British Crown was to be done peacefully and with the consent of native authorities.

But Rhodes now had his opening. Recognizing that Lobengula would never agree to a formal renunciation of sovereignty, but with his mining treaty not limiting the number of white settlers allowed in Mashonaland, Rhodes could effectively occupy the area for Britain by sending large numbers of settlers there to "mine." So, in June 1890, he organized a private convoy of 179 settlers to set out for Mashonaland, deftly skirting around the areas most directly controlled by Lobengula's armies. His "Pioneer Column" reached Harare hill in September 1890 and founded a new settlement, Fort Salisbury. A steady stream of settlers from the Cape soon followed, attracted by reports of mineral-rich and easily alienated farmland in the area around Fort Salisbury.

Three years later, a Mashonaland kingdom refused Lobengula tribute, declaring that they were now under the protection of BSAC. Lobengula sent troops to Mashonaland to enforce the tribute but he had fallen into a trap. Rhodes could now claim that Lobengula had broken the terms of the mining treaty and could legally amass BSAC troops in response. A brief war followed that resulted in the complete destruction of the Ndebele kingdom and the capture of its capital, Bulawayo, in late 1893. These actions prompted alarm in the metropole, but a logic of strategic fatalism triumphed once again.[37] The participants in Rhodes' war still got their land bounty. By 1895, more than 1,000 white-owned farms covered more than 10,000 square miles in Ndebeleland and a number of "native reserves" had been established in rough terrain north of Bulawayo to house the displaced Ndebele (Rotberg, 1988).

The point of these cases is not to provide a conservative interpretation of the benevolence of the British Empire. To emphasize the contradictions in state policy does not excuse metropolitan authorities of responsibility for the mass killing of indigenous peoples by their colonists.[38] Rather, the point of examining the intentions of the metropole as European colonization unfolded is to provoke the curiosity of those who want to understand the actual dynamics of settler colonialism. As the elimination of indigenous peoples is an "antieconomic" decision, one would expect that indigenous elimination is rarely viewed as the best outcome by a metropole. And the historical record bears this expectation out. The mass killing of indigenous peoples was triggered by the predation of land by European settlers in Australia, the United States, and Zimbabwe, conducted at critical junctures in explicit contravention of metropolitan authority. Contrary to the notion that there always existed a coordinated project to destroy indigenous peoples and reallocate their land to white colonists, the formative stages of European settler colonialism were characterized by an "illogic of elimination."

We should be wary of studies that ignore such historical complexity and that instead explain colonization with reference to vague abstractions that conflate states and settlers. Consider the central claim by Wolfe that "invasion is a 'structure' and not 'an event' . . . Elimination is an organizing principle of settler-colonial society rather than a one-off (and superseded) occurrence" (Wolfe, 2006, 388). Lorenzo Veracini explains that this "structure persistently pursues a specific end point" (Veracini, 2011, 3) and that "settler colonialism is designed to produce a fundamental discontinuity as its 'logic of elimination' runs its course until it actually extinguishes the settler colonial relation" (ibid., p. 7). This logic manifests itself in a dynamic way as states shift between an array of strategies all with the design to eliminate indigenous peoples. Emblematic of this form of reasoning, Maddison (2016, 425) claims that Australia during the twentieth century "attempted to eliminate the Indigenous presence through policies of protection, assimilation, self-determination, intervention and, most recently, recognition." States are attributed a collective agency and a relentless, unfalsifiable logic in which even the constitutional recognition of indigenous peoples and their ancestral land rights are manifestations of elimination (e.g., Veracini 2007; Moses 2011;

Morgensen 2011; Coulthard 2014; Maddison 2016; Simpson 2016; Strakosch 2016).[39]

It has so far largely fallen to historians, who possess a natural aversion to abstraction, to problematize this understanding of colonial history to date. As Jun Uchida (2011, 396) cautioned in her study of colonial Korea, Japanese settlers far from always furthered the ambitions of the Japanese metropole— rather, much like in Australia, settler "activities and initiatives reveal how colonial power was often dispersed, not simply imposed but mediated and modified at the local level." Likewise, Harris Mylonas (2015, 741) has warned against the tendency of scholars of mass atrocity to infer elite intentions from eliminatory outcomes, emphasizing that policymaker "intentions are not always translated into policy choices, nor do those choices always pro- duce the desired outcome." Perhaps most notably, Frederick Cooper (2005) has admonished the tendency of post-colonial theorists to write "ahistori- cal history." Ahistorical history works backwards, connecting past to present without actually interrogating the way that historical processes unfolded over time. Abstract concepts such as the "logic of elimination" simplify the his- tory of colonialism into a unidirectional narrative, Cooper argues, that ignores contingency and the mediating agency of both colonizer and colonized.

Settler colonial theory at present is characterized by precisely these ahistor- ical tendencies, which has diminished our understanding of colonial history twofold. Firstly, scholars have been overly eager to retrospectively impose a stable, underlying logic to cases of indigenous elimination. Much like teleolog- ical theories of anti-colonial nationalism (Lawrence, 2013), we have lost sight of the paths not taken and the peaceful alternatives for managing ethnically diverse or newly conquered peoples that were once available to the metropole (and that may have once been seen as more desirable). The result has been the creation of historical fables that merely project eliminatory teleologies back- wards in time. And the conflation of all the different means through which states can actually eliminate ethnic difference—assimilation, ethnic cleansing, and genocide—does a disservice to the periods in which indigenous peoples were subject to homicide by state agents. We need to better understand the contingent process through which policymakers shift from one strategy for engaging with indigenous peoples to another (and often back again), and the mediating role of settlers in this process.

Secondly, writing history backwards impedes our understanding of the limits to state power. By only focusing on cases where states ultimately "suc- ceeded" in eliminating native peoples, we have a distorted understanding of the conditions under which colonization occurs.[40] For instance, let's now reconsider Scott (2009)'s claim that modernization and the development of distance-demolishing technologies results in the final victory of the state and settler over the indigene. This conclusion is plausible if we only examine cases where indigenous peoples were actually colonized in recent history. But attending to negative cases reveals that modernization does not necessarily increase the colonizing power of the state. In fact, precisely the opposite might be true.

Consider Portugal's failure to colonize Angola in the late twentieth century. Portugal founded the Angolan capital, Luanda, in 1575 and, except for a brief period in the seventeenth century, Angola remained under Portuguese control until 1975. For the vast bulk of this time, Angola was a canonical "colony of extraction" (Acemoglu, Johnson, and Robinson, 2001); Portuguese rule was primarily oriented toward the coercive exploitation of indigenous labor (through the slave trade) and resources (primarily rubber, diamonds, and coffee).

In 1961, however, Portugal dramatically shifted policy.[41] That year, it founded a provincial settlement board (*Junta Provincial de Povoamento de Angola* or JPP) with the responsibility of facilitating the mass settlement of rural Angola. The Governor General of Angola emphasized in 1961 that he would do everything in his power to attract Portuguese settlers, particularly former soldiers, to the new *colonatos*. With vaulting ambition, the government envisioned securing up to half a million new farmers in the south of Angola alone. Over the next decade, large areas were expropriated from indigenous Angolans for settlers and more than one million people, or almost a one quarter of Angola's population, were ultimately moved off their land (Cain, 2013).[42]

Yet, the *colonatos* were a failure. Not only did few Portuguese settlers actually take up the offer of free transport, land, and income support in Angola, but of those thousands who did, approximately 70% abandoned their farms by the end of the 1960s (Bender, 1978, 131). Reflecting increased metropolitan investment and a brief oil boom, Angola did experience rapid growth in its white population over the 1960s but, much to the consternation of officials, almost all of this growth was concentrated in Luanda. In sum, over the course of a decade, Portugal spent the equivalent today of approximately $200 million dollars on the JPP program to secure an increase in the white population in rural Angola of 840.[43]

The Angolan case raises a number of questions that teleological theories of colonization cannot adequately answer. Echoing the sudden rise in

Indonesian transmigration to West Papua in the 1980s, why did Portugal shift its policy direction so suddenly in 1961 and expend extremely large sums of money encouraging whites to settle in rural Angola? And, echoing Australia's efforts in Papua New Guinea, why were such efforts ultimately a failure? The failure of Portugal to colonize Angola cannot be attributed to lack of population pressure or Portuguese reticence toward emigration. Over the 1950s and 1960s, hundreds of thousands of Portuguese did emigrate but primarily to the Americas and the rest of Western Europe (Penvenne, 2005, 85). Nor can it be attributed to an innate inability of Europeans to live in the tropics. Over the 1960s, over one hundred thousand people did emigrate to Angola from Portugal but, contrary to the intentions of the metropole, almost all of these migrants were drawn to Angola's urban centers (Bender and Yoder, 1974). How is it possible, then, that a relatively wealthy state flushed with the technologies of modernity so spectacularly failed to colonize its periphery?

Faced with historical complexity, the answer is *not* to abandon what Steinmetz (2007) calls the "chimerical" goal of providing general theories of colonial rule. Retreating into the historical detail and warding against every attempt to generalize has the cost of failing to draw out the commonalities in human action that *do* exist across time and place. So, the current additive model of settler colonial studies in history and anthropology—one that provides ever more disconnected case studies of settler colonialism in ever more contexts—has its epistemological limits.[44] We also need theoretical frameworks to help us navigate the morass of history.

Equally, when discerning the common logic behind different cases of settler colonialism, we can do better than rely on ahistorical teleologies like the "logic of elimination" or the "last enclosure." Theoretically, we need to disaggregate the state, clearly distinguishing between the intentions of the metropole and settlers with a view to understanding their conflicts of interest and the limits to state power. We need to attend to the sequencing of historical events, paying close attention to understanding why policymakers in the metropole shift toward encouraging the colonization of particular areas or groups at particular points in time. And finally, we need to track migration flows to discipline our theories and uncover the extent to which they cohere (or do not cohere) with reality. This means that we must insist, above all, that settler colonialism is less an abstract "structure" than a series of concrete migratory events resulting in coercive land redistribution and demographic change.

So, when do states try to colonize the lands of indigenous peoples and when do their efforts prove successful? Colonization projects are characterized by a triangle of actors—settlers, indigenes, and the central state—each with distinct interests (Haklai and Loizides, 2015; Lustick, 2015). Understanding the logic of settler colonialism, I explain in this book, requires attending to the different conflicts of interest within this triangle.

The first and most obvious conflict of interest is between settlers and indigenes. Colonization is, essentially by definition, characterized by a "zero sum" conflict between settlers and indigenous peoples over the control of land. Studies of settler colonialism to date have largely focused on the settler-indigene relation, paying particular attention to the process through which settlers and their descendants legitimate the usurpation of land through racist ideologies.

But states do *not* necessarily have the same zero-sum conflict of interest with indigenous peoples. States seek to control maximal territory at minimal cost, and so the primary goal of states in diverse peripheries is to most economically circumscribe the autonomy of indigenous peoples to facilitate capital accumulation (Sahlins 1989, 117; Tilly 1992, 100; Scott 1998, 82; Hechter 2000, 15). And settler colonialism—unlike other strategies like assimilation or ruling in partnership with indigenous elites—is an "antieconomic" form of state building that exacerbates conflict with indigenes in the short run and results in the loss of capital and labor. This makes colonization a generally unappealing policy. As the Select Committee on Aboriginal Tribes in Great Britain emphasized in 1837:

> One of the two systems we must have to preserve our own security, and the peace of our colonial borders; either an overwhelming military force, with all its attendant expenses, or a line of temperate conduct and of justice towards our neighbours. . . . The choice rests with ourselves.[45]

As an uneconomic strategy for would-be imperialists, states generally license colonization only under two circumstances. The first are circumstances when settler actions force the hand of states. Settlers, responding to population pressure at home and the presence of valuable resources or easily alienated land in the periphery, may push into indigenous territory. Policymakers in the metropole are then faced with the prospect of overextension and frontier war to protect their colonists. But siding with indigenes also creates the fearful prospect that settlers will simply found independent republics outside of central control. Facing population pressure in the core and a seemingly relentless emigration to the periphery, officials—as during the Ohio Valley, Victorian, or Rhodesian migration crises—have often found it most expedient to license the eliminatory actions of their colonists in a laissez-faire way.

But officials do not merely respond to migratory events on the ground; the movement of settlers into a frontier area can also be actively planned and funded by the metropole. State-sponsored colonization schemes like Indonesian transmigration tend to take place under circumstances not necessarily of settler expansionism but when states face a pressing security threat.[46] Colonization improves state security because, in the midst of war and insurgency, states are unable to distinguish between friend and foe in frontier areas. Scholars of political violence have shown how, when states lack information on individual loyalties, they then often use race and ethnicity as an heuristic for individual loyalty.[47] Expelling stereotypically "disloyal" indigenous groups and populating their lands with stereotypically "loyal" settlers is an effective means for the metropole to secure control over a frontier when facing an imminent threat.

This argument, abstractly presented, is best illustrated with reference to some of the cases that I have identified so far. Returning to New Guinea, recall that in the 1980s Indonesia drastically scaled up transmigration to West Papua. In Chapter 3, I detail how this occurred in response to an attempted capture of the West Papuan capital by the Free Papua Movement (OPM) in Februrary 1984. Although the coup failed, heavy fighting continued for several months between OPM and the Indonesian military. OPM's favored tactic during this conflict was "curtain of the masses" (*tirai massa*), a Maoist strategy in which insurgents would launch guerilla attacks on soldiers in rural areas and then quickly melt back into the populace. Unable to distinguish between friend and foe, the Indonesian military responded by treating all West Papuans as potential insurgents and cleansing them from contested border areas. Indeed, the motto of the Indonesian military at the time was "let the rats run into the jungle so that chickens can breed in the coop"—referring to the forced expulsion of indigenous Papuans and their replacement with transmigrants from the rest of Indonesia. By raising the curtain provided by the masses through coercive demographic change, the Indonesian state sought to defeat a separatist insurgency.

The dogs of war also account for shifting Portuguese policy in Angola. In 1961, thousands of Angolan insurgents launched an incursion into northern Angola from their base in Congo-Léopoldville (present-day Democratic Republic of Congo), kicking off the Angolan War of Independence

(1961–1975). This conflict, much like the long-running war of Indonesia against OPM, was characterized by guerilla warfare in which the Portuguese army faced an insurgent group dispersed widely across rural territory whose favored tactics were hit-and-runs. As part of its counterinsurgency campaign, Portugal forcibly relocated over a million Angolans into "protected strategic settlements" (*aldeamentos*) where their movements could be better monitored. This relocation, in turn, opened up a considerable amount of land for new white settlers. The *colonatos*, a demographic buffer through which no indigenous insurgents could pass unnoticed, were envisioned to serve a security buffer between Angola's urban centers and the insurgent-controlled interior.

Warfare, and the use of ethnicity to distinguish between friend and foe, also accounts for many of the cases in which European colonial states *did* actively organize and intend the elimination of indigenous peoples. For instance, consider the fairly well-established series of events that led to the Appin Massacre in 1816, often described as the first state-sanctioned mass killing of indigenous people in Australia.[48] The Governor of New South Wales at the time generally sought to encourage indigenous assimilation with a view to increasing the amount of labor in his colony, exhorting "the Natives to relinquish their wandering, idle and predatory Habits of Life, and to become industrious and Useful Members of a Community where they will find Protection and Encouragement."[49] Governor Macquarie notably supported the establishment of indigenous schools and the allocation of land to indigenes in order to transform them into "civilized," sedentary agriculturalists.

But when facing organized indigenous resistance, Macquarie was also quick to abandon assimilation. In 1814, a chain of tit-for-tat killings between European settlers and the Gandangara started in southwest Sydney following the murder of a youth who had taken maize from a settler farm. This localized conflict escalated in February 1816 when a group of settlers, in pursuit of a group who had stolen some food, was ambushed. During this attack and other similar ambushes over the next month, nine settlers were killed. Facing widespread criticism for his inaction and settler demands for protection, Macquarie ordered a military reprisal aimed at "clearing the Country of [Aborigines] entirely, and driving them across the mountains" and directed "as many Natives as possible to be made Prisoners, with the view of keeping them as Hostages *until the real guilty ones have surrendered themselves*."[50] Lacking information on individual "guilt" or "innocence" for recent attacks, all Aborigines south-west of Sydney were treated as suspect based on their shared ethnicity and subject to collective removal by the colonial state.

This case illustrates how European colonial genocides—like the genocide of the Herero in Namibia in 1904, the genocide of Tasmanian Aborigines in the 1820s, and the genocide of the Yuki in California in the mid-1800s—were preceded by rising conflict between indigenous groups and settlers. Indigenous bands would skirmish settlers in response to settler expansionism and predation of their land, livestock, and people. Facing settler demands for protection and unable to distinguish between combatants and non-combatants, colonial states eliminated indigenous peoples in order to win frontier wars (Madley, 2004). As one *San Francisco Bulletin* editorial during the Yuki genocide summarized: "Extermination is the quickest and cheapest remedy, and effectually prevents all other difficulties when an outbreak [of violence] occurs."[51]

States therefore clearly do sometimes organize and intend the mass displacement, dispossession, and killing of indigenous peoples—from Ireland in the 1600s, to California in the 1850s, or to Angola in the 1960s. But colonization is always the exception, never the rule. Colonization is distinct from policies like forced assimilation or slavery that seek to transform subject peoples into profitable sources of labor. As an "antieconomic" form of violence, one would expect states to only actively displace indigenous peoples during periods of war when there is little information other than ethnicity for states to distinguish friend from foe. In the midst of conflict, states particularly seek control over strategically important areas. So, frontiers endowed with rich natural resources and porous borderlands will both tend to be disproportionately cleansed and colonized by states. Theorizing the decision to colonize relative to the alternatives that exist for exploiting frontier lands sheds clearer light on when states become colonizers.

Finally, and completing the triangle, there is a third conflict between the geopolitical interests of states and the material interests of settlers. This conflict manifests very differently according to a country's level of development. In less developed, agrarian settings, settlers desire frontier land but states seek to avoid costly wars with indigenes. To prevent war with indigenes, it is common for the metropole to demarcate zones of legal settlement for their colonists. But, as I have previously discussed, settlers often do not respect the laws of the center. Facing ongoing skirmishes between settlers and indigenes, states must weigh up the cost of policing their colonists with frontier war.

But in more developed, industrialized settings, states face the opposite problem of settler reticence. Given the high value of land in agrarian states, it has long been easy for states to populate a contested frontier by offering "free land" there to colonists. As countries grow richer and the share of the population engaged in agriculture falls, however, urban areas—not "open frontiers"—attract migrants (Forsyth, 1942; Zelinsky, 1971). Consider the fact that most of Japan today is rapidly depopulating and the only area still growing substantially is its largest urban center, Tokyo.[52] As living standards in the core rise, luring settlers to "backwater" peripheries like New Guinea or Angola through free land or other incentives becomes an ever more expensive and futile task. Hence, states, past a certain threshold of development, ultimately lose the power to colonize indigenous people.

In other words, global history is characterized by the rise and fall of settler colonialism as a technology of state building. As early states developed in Europe and Asia, officials there first harnessed the power to coercively settle contested frontiers. And the logic of state building explains why even formally "decolonized" nation-states like Indonesia and India continue to colonize indigenous peoples today. But, in a somewhat cruel historical irony, European and East Asian states were also the first to *lose* the power of colonization as they grew richer over the nineteenth and twentieth centuries. I detail in this book how even infamous settler states like Australia, China, Portugal, Greece, and the United States ultimately ceased colonizing frontiers not for lack of land but for lack of settlers.

Napoleon's foreign minister, Charles Maurice de Talleyrand, once quipped that empire is "the art of putting men in their place" (Pagden, 2007; Frymer, 2017). But as states modernize, they lose the art of putting men and women anywhere other than major urban centers. Modernization therefore spells the end of empire. For as states are obliged to pay more for settlers, they end up settling for less land.

I am aware that the argument of this book pushes against a number of countervailing intellectual trends in the academy today. Theoretically, the concept of "modernization" has acquired something of a bad name. Influenced heavily by Karl Marx, Max Weber, and Émile Durkheim, historians and social scientists long regarded the countries of Western Europe and North America as the paragons of "modernity," providing a model of political and economic development that the rest of the world would eventually imitate. The notion of a linear, universal process of social change, however, was subject to heavy criticism in the late twentieth century.[53] Since then, understanding generalizable social "transitions" associated with economic development has fallen out of intellectual favor (Smith and King, 2012; King, 2012).

Yet, the baby has been thrown out with the Marxist bathwater. Economic change does prompt political change. Indeed, the durability of Marxist-influenced social science from the mid-twentieth century (e.g., Schumpeter 1942; Williams 1944; Polanyi 1944) is testament to the analytical power of historical materialism. In this book, I account for important changes in the way states engage with indigenous peoples whilst avoiding the discredited assumptions of orthodox Marxism and conventional modernization theory. Economic development does not prevent colonization by making politicians and settlers more humanitarian or less attached to "primordial" ethnic identities.[54] Rather, modernization prevents colonization by reconfiguring the location of valuable economic activity away from the rural-periphery and toward the urban-center. In doing so, modernization reverses the prevailing direction of migration, ending the power of states to colonize contested frontiers—and obliging states to reevaluate their relationships with indigenous peoples. The end of colonization means that decolonization, not imperialism, is actually the highest stage of capitalism (cf. Lenin 2010).

This book also pushes against the prevailing intellectual grain because it does not ascribe great importance to racial ideologies in the global history of settler colonialism. This is not because I think racial ideologies are completely unimportant; racist ideas have certainly helped license violence against indigenous peoples in some historical cases.[55] But recall that I began this book with a contrast between Australia and Indonesia—two countries with starkly different racial ideologies. In the end, the state committed to racial equality (Indonesia) became the violent colonizer and the state committed to white supremacy (Australia) became the willing decolonizer in New Guinea.

What these cases reveal is that notions of racial supremacy are neither a necessary nor sufficient explanation for colonization. Racism is not sufficient because even explicitly white supremacist states like Australia or the United States ceased colonizing indigenous peoples over the early twentieth century. Indeed, Australian and American officials became leading proponents of indigenous sovereignty in Papua New Guinea and the Philippines in the mid-twentieth century in large part *because* both states were committed to maintaining the whiteness of their nations; indigenous independence effectively prevented millions of poor, non-white peoples in these islands from making claims to Australian or American citizenship. Racism is consistent with both colonization and decolonization.

In addition to being insufficient, racism toward indigenous peoples is also not a necessary condition for colonization.[56] At Bandung in 1955, Sukarno declared the dawning of a new day for all the peoples in the world united by "a common detestation of racialism" (Asian-African Conference, 1955, 22). Sukarno would go on to emphasize how Indonesia was a country without ethno-racial oppression, and was instead defined by the principles of "Live and Let Live" and "Unity in Diversity." Indonesia's colonization of West Papua has been difficult for observers to understand precisely because the violent dispossession of West Papuans by settlers appears to contradict Indonesia's core ideological principles. We are confronted by the practice of colonization in a state rhetorically opposed to colonialism.

But just as notions of ineradicable racial inferiority can morph into arguments for decolonization, notions of ethnic equality can morph into rationalizations for colonization. When all ethno-racial groups share the same political rights, after all, no one group has any greater normative claim to a piece of territory than any other group. Equality before the law can therefore be used to rhetorically justify the *denial* of indigenous sovereignty. For instance, to justify the presence of Han settlers in ethnic minority areas like Tibet and Xinjiang, China's President Xi Jinping recently emphasized how "Ethnic equality is the prerequisite and basis for achieving national unity . . . the Han cannot be separated from the ethnic minorities, and the ethnic minorities cannot be separated from the Han."[57] Martono, Indonesia's Minister for Transmigration, similarly emphasized how settling people in frontier areas like West Papua would "realize what has been pledged: to integrate all the ethnic groups into one nation, the Indonesian nation."[58] The rhetoric of national equality was also recently used by Indian Prime Minister Narendra Modi to justify the abrogation of Kashmiri autonomy. Modi emphasized how scrapping Article 370, which long prevented non-Kashmiris from emigrating to Kashmir, would help foster equality by removing the special legal privileges in Kashmir previously held by indigenous Kashmiris.[59]

Racial ideologies are malleable things, easily twisted to rationalize the interests and actions of those in power. By way of analogy, consider how white Americans today resist policies like affirmative action that would affect their material standing by using the rhetoric not of racial supremacy but of racial equality and color blindness (Bonilla-Silva, 2006). Indigenous autonomy can be similarly delegitimated by those in power, like Sukarno, Modi, and Xi, for purporting to give special rights over a piece of territory to a particular ethnic group. "Ethnic equality" and "national development" then become codes for denying the territorial claims of indigenous peoples and flooding their lands with co-nationals.

The only necessary and sufficient condition for colonization is the existence of willing settlers. This is what makes economic development the most powerful force for ending the subjection of peoples to "alien subjugation, domination, and exploitation." For if we are to understand why—exactly contrary to the expectations of Bandung's participants in 1955—Indonesia colonized West Papua and Australia decolonized Papua New Guinea, then we must understand why Indonesians and not Australians were willing to emigrate to New Guinea for free land. By constraining the practice of colonization, economic development creates the demographic space for decolonization. I develop these and other implications of my findings further in the conclusion.

Following custom, I will now end this introduction by briefly summarizing the rest of the book. In the next chapter, I outline in much greater detail my theory of colonization. I take a shamelessly interdisciplinary approach, borrowing insights from anthropologists, historians, economists, political scientists, geographers, and demographers. My object of study demands this interdisciplinarity, as to understand settler colonialism we need to understand the intersection of land, migration, race, and state power. My aim in this chapter is to provide a toolbox of concepts for understanding the contingent place of coercive migration in state building. Throughout, there is a concern with distinguishing the logic of state-sponsored colonization from the logic of colonization initiated and led by private settlers.

The later chapters are then devoted to exploring how well my theory makes sense of different colonization schemes around the world by drawing on rich, newly collected historical data. My first two empirical chapters compare Indonesia's and Australia's colonization of West Papua and northern Australia, encompassing the Northern Territory and Papua New Guinea. Historical comparison illuminates the causes of settler colonialism that might not be evident when examining particular cases in isolation.[60] Comparing Indonesia and Australia in New Guinea allows me to control for other factors that we might think are important, like geography or resources, and better uncover how economic development shaped the success of these two countries at colonizing the same island.

These cases were also chosen for their historical importance. Indonesia's transmigration program was the world's largest voluntary resettlement scheme during the twentieth century and involved the assisted migration of over five million people (Whitten, 1987). Any theory of settler colonialism worth its salt should help make sense of this important case. Likewise,

Australia has long been regarded as an example of a state governed by a teleological logic of elimination. If Australia—the canonical "settler colony"— ceased colonizing indigenous peoples, then it is important that we understand precisely when and why.

In Chapter 3, I provide the first analysis of Indonesian transmigration using an unexplored archive of government statistical data. I have compiled detailed data on the yearly numbers of state-sponsored transmigrants and Muslims in every regency (county) in West Papua after 1964. Consistent with my theory, I find that Indonesia colonized its borderland with Papua New Guinea after 1984 in order to defeat secessionist insurgents based along its border. I secondly find that Indonesian transmigration in West Papua during this conflict is best explained by the location of valuable gold and petroleum resources. Drawing on the first comprehensive data on transmigration, I provide quite strong evidence that Indonesia's colonization of West Papua was driven by the twin logics of resource extraction and counterinsurgency.

In Chapter 4, I contrast Indonesia's "success" in colonizing West Papua with Australia's failure to colonize its unsettled north. Australia attempted to colonize Papua New Guinea and the Northern Territory in the early twentieth century for a combination of ideological and security reasons. To understand why this failed, for Papua New Guinea I have compiled new data tracking the number of settlers both over time between 1906 and 1938 and within each district. There was almost no increase in the white population in Papua New Guinea over this period. Drawing on diverse archival sources, I find that the closure of Australia's frontier can be attributed to the state's inability to overcome the forces drawing Europeans to mainland cities. I then turn to examining Australia's struggle to colonize its Northern Territory in the interwar period in response to the rising threat posed by Japan. I draw on archival sources to show how, as in Papua New Guinea, Australia was unable to settle its north due to countervailing forces drawing labor and capital to its more developed urban centers. Together, this chapter demonstrates that economic change, not normative change, is key to understanding why Australia ceased colonizing indigenous peoples during the twentieth century.

The next two chapters focus on the dynamics of settler colonialism in China. China has long occupied a central place in the study of frontier colonization. This is for good reason. As Scott (2009, 142) points out, "The nearly two-millennia push—sporadic but inexorable—of the Han [Chinese] state and Han settlers . . . has surely been the single great historical process most responsible for driving people into the hills [of Southeast Asia]." The perceived inexorability of Han Chinese expansion, particularly after the adoption of modern transportation technologies, also makes China a hard case to corroborate my argument. For, as Owen Lattimore stressed in the mid-twentieth century: "wherever a region of frontier colonization is served by a railway there is no longer any doubt of the ascendency of Chinese over the tribesman" (Lattimore, 1962, 316). But what if China's rapid development over the late twentieth century instead reduced the power of the state to settle Han in minority areas?

Chapter 5, co-authored with Anna Zhang, uncovers the contingent origins of Han dominance in China's frontiers by examining demographic change in northwest China. We compiled confidential internal statistical data tracking yearly Han Chinese settlement and ethnic minority expulsions in every county in the northwest province of Xinjiang since the early 1950s. We find that conflict with the former USSR over the Sino-Soviet split (1959–1982) explains why Han Chinese only predominate in certain areas of Xinjiang. China responded to the Sino-Soviet split by colonizing non-natural border areas, oil rich areas, and Russian-populated areas with Han Chinese. We also draw on Soviet census statistics to show that the USSR similarly responded to conflict by cleansing and settling strategically important border areas with China. International conflict and geopolitical strategy, not inexorable historical forces, reshaped the demography of much of Central Asia in a very short period of time.

In Chapter 6, I use the same demographic data to examine China's struggle to colonize Xinjiang since the emergence of an Islamist insurgency there (1990–present). I find that, despite Beijing's spending remarkable amounts of money trying to colonize Muslim-majority and border areas of Xinjiang with Han since 1990, very few Han Chinese have migrated to these areas. With the exception of the few oil-rich areas of Xinjiang, almost all internal migration over this time has been toward China's rapidly industrializing eastern seaboard. By comparing China's attempts to colonize the same region at two different times during the twentieth century, these two chapters show how China's rapid development since the 1980s ultimately closed its western frontier.[61] Consistent with the patterns from New Guinea, I show how *less* developed states actually have much *greater* power to colonize their frontiers. Given the economic forces drawing migrants to cities and away from rural areas, even wealthy and strong states such as Australia or China today have little power to settle contested peripheries.

To demonstrate that my theory applies more widely than these specific cases, in Chapter 7 I look at global patterns of colonization. This chapter is based on data that I have compiled on the incidence of settler colonialism and ethnic cleansing in the late twentieth century across all countries from a number of sources. Consistent with my argument, I find that settler colonialism tends to occur in less developed and territorially insecure states like Indonesia, Iraq, Bangladesh, and Myanmar. Such states tend to colonize rebellious and resource-rich minorities like the West Papuans, the Tamils, the Kurds, and the Rohingya, as well as minorities inhabiting contested border zones. There is little evidence that democratic institutions or international norms explain these patterns. Together, these chapters establish that that colonization is a highly patterned form of violence outmoded by economic development.

In the final chapter, I reflect on what the end of colonization means for our understanding of modernization and the politics of decolonization. Both the individual chapters and the conclusion are relatively self-contained, and the reader is free to peruse as she wishes.

2

A Theory of Settler Colonialism

GREECE PERHAPS does not naturally spring to mind as a modern settler colony. Scholars of migration typically draw a distinction between nation-states like Australia, Canada, and the United States whose histories have been shaped by immigration and frontier colonization and the "older established populations" of Europe like Greece (Castles, 1992, 562). But this distinction, plausible at first, struggles to withstand historical scrutiny. For much of Greece as we know it today was actually colonized by settlers over the past century.

Following its victory over Bulgaria and the Ottoman Empire in the Balkan Wars of 1912–13, Greece annexed Macedonia and Thrace and consequently doubled in size. Greek nationalists led by Prime Minister Eleftherios Venizelos maintained, of course, that Macedonia and Thrace had been "Greek" since the time of Philip of Macedon and Alexander the Great. But ethnic Greeks were a demographic minority in Greek Macedonia in the early twentieth century, outnumbered by Turks and Bulgarians. How, then, did Macedonia become Greek?

Macedonia was "Hellenized" over the next two decades through ethnic cleansing and colonization. After a disastrous military defeat at the hands of Turkey in 1922, Greece struck a deal in which both countries agreed to exchange their national minorities—Greeks in Turkey for Turks in Greece. Greece, with a population of little over 5 million, quickly confronted a wave of over 1.2 million displaced Greeks from across the Aegean Sea. The massive influx of impoverished and traumatized refugees threatened to overwhelm the Greek state. But, amidst crisis, Venizelos also spied geopolitical opportunity. By allocating land to Greek refugees in depopulated areas of Macedonia, he argued, the state could both provide refugees with a sustainable livelihood and secure control over Greece's contested border areas. Greece subsequently spent over 40% of its national budget preparing and parcelling out land to hundreds of thousands of refugees in "New Greece" (Kontogiorgi, 2003, 74). By 1926, Greek Macedonia had become 90% Greek and one of the most ethnically homogeneous areas of the Balkans (Voutira, 2003, 147).

Thrace, however, still possessed large enclaves of non-Greeks. As part of its peace agreement with Turkey, Greece had exempted Muslims in Western Thrace from expulsion. The presence of some 100,000 Muslims along Greece's only land border with Turkey would become a thorn in the side of Greek nationalists for the rest of the twentieth century. Greek suspicions that Turkey had lingering designs on Western Thrace were only heightened when, in the mid-1970s, Turkey invaded and partitioned the island of Cyprus in order to "protect" enclaves of Turks there. Greek policymakers in the 1970s and 1980s fretted at the prospect of Western Thrace becoming a "second Cyprus" (Demetriou, 2004, 107).

It must have seemed like demographic manna from heaven, then, when the state was suddenly confronted by a second wave of new Greeks from across the sea. As the Soviet Union collapsed in the late 1980s, ethnic Greeks scattered across the Eastern Bloc sought "repatriation" to the Greek homeland. The Greek government established a new body in January 1990 to manage and resettle these newcomers.[1] The National Settlement Plan provided subsidies to Greek repatriates who elected to live in rural Thrace and eastern Macedonia, including interest free loans and one-off payments of 11 million drachmas (approximately $75,000 USD today). Greek parliamentarians stressed how the influx of new Greeks could settle the demographic imbalance in Thrace, just as the wave of Greek refugees from Asia Minor in the 1920s settled Macedonia (Mylonas and Žilović, 2019, 624). And officials were full of optimism that these new Greeks, given their poor background, would find life in the borderland appealing.

Such optimism was, however, entirely misplaced. Of the 140,000 ethnic Greeks who emigrated from the former Soviet Union in the early 1990s, only 14,000 actually took part in the rural resettlement program (Voutira, 2003, 151). Once inside Greece, repatriates were drawn to the bright lights of Athens and Thessaloniki. The failure of the National Settlement Plan and the formation of Russian-speaking ghettos in Greek cities created much consternation inside the government (Pratsinakis, 2014). By the mid-1990s, the state began to limit the influx of foreign Greeks because, as the former Greek Secretary of State lamented:

> When we planned their resettlement we thought that these people [from the former Soviet Union] would be appreciative of all the material assistance and the training programmes we were devising for them. But unfortunately we found them to be choosy and ungrateful towards the Greek state.[2]

Greece is far from the only country to have its grand geopolitical plans stymied by reluctant colonists. Russia, for its part, also struggled with choosy and ungrateful settlers after the fall of the Soviet Union. In March 2006, President Vladimir Putin's envoy to the Far East announced plans to resettle 18 million people there, primarily along the border with China (Larin, 2013, 15). These plans took a concrete form in 2016 when the Russian government announced that any citizen could apply for a free hectare of land in the Far East so long as they committed to live there for five years. This homesteading program was explicitly inspired by Catherine the Great's success in drawing European settlers east of the Urals through the promise of free land in the eighteenth century. This time, however, the demographic results were desultory; between 2016 and 2020, only 83,000 people applied for a plot of land.[3] And most of these applicants were residents of Vladivostok—the largest city in Russia's Far East—who just wanted land for a vacation home.[4]

These cases, cursorily presented, alert us to the fact that colonization is a process over which states exert imperfect control. In a very general sense, colonization can be defined as a form of state building involving the displacement of indigenous peoples by settlers. Frontier migration that is coercive—undesired by an indigenous population or foreign claimant—is a form of state building because such migration reshapes patterns of sovereignty. As Mamdani (1998) nicely put it: settlers are made by conquest, not just by migration. But, as highlighted in the previous chapter, the coercive settlement of frontier regions can be led by settlers in the absence of or even contrary to directives by officials. And, as evinced by the cases of contemporary Greece and Russia, state-sponsored colonization schemes often fail for lack of settlers.

This suggests that we need to differentiate instances of settler colonialism based on whether they are characterized by state or settler participation (Table 2.1). In the bottom-left quadrant of Table 2.1 are instances of settler-led colonization,[5] like the colonization of Victoria, Hawai'i, Zimbabwe, and the

TABLE 2.1. A typology of different logics of colonization.

Conditions	Not directed by officials	Directed by officials
No settler participation	None	Failed colonization
Settler participation	Settler-led colonization	State-led colonization

Ohio Valley. Officials are involved insofar as they decide whether to license the actions of their colonists in a laissez-faire fashion and incorporate newly settled areas into the state. An analogy here can be made to the case of rape during war. Scholars increasingly question the claim that rape, when frequent, is ipso facto military policy (e.g., Wood 2010; Baaz and Stern 2013; Wood 2018). Rather, rape can be frequent in war without having been purposefully ordered by officials. Much like wartime rape, the displacement of indigenous populations by settlers can be a practice that is (1) implicitly tolerated and (2) driven by settler opportunism, rather than being the result of official direction.

On the other hand, much like wartime rape, frontier colonization can also be a form of violence purposefully adopted by the state for its own objectives. In the bottom-right quadrant are cases like Greece's colonization of Macedonia in the 1920s or Indonesia's colonization of West Papua in the 1980s. These colonization schemes were clearly led by the state as bureaucrats played a central role in selecting settlers, financing their relocation, and designating particular sites for settlement. Such cases are straightforwardly characterized as official policy.[6]

"Null" cases, where a frontier region is spared colonization, can be similarly decomposed into two forms. In the top-left quadrant of Table 2.1 are the large number of cases like Angola prior to the 1960s or West Papua prior to the 1980s in which neither states nor settlers attempt to colonize an area. But there are also a considerable number of cases where officials *do* try to colonize frontier areas but their plans fail for lack of settlers. Greece's failed colonization of Western Thrace in the 1990s or Russia's failed colonization of the Far East today both fit this bill.

Table 2.1 clarifies how historical outcomes that look the same—the presence or absence of people coercively settling a frontier—can have very different underlying causes depending on the configuration of state and settler interests. So, to understand the logic of colonization, it is to these different interests that we must now turn.

Place yourself in the position of a newly arrived repatriate in Greece in the early 1990s, faced with a number of different options for where to make a home. In general, you would only find settling in a periphery like Thrace appealing when the expected quality of life is clearly greater than elsewhere. As Memmi (2010, 48) put it: "the change involved in moving to a colony, if one can call it a change, must first of all bring a substantial profit . . . you go to a colony because jobs are guaranteed, wages high, careers more rapid and business more profitable." So, the first assumption I make follows neoclassical models of migration, as I assume that all settler migration is voluntary and economically driven (e.g., Ravenstein 1885; Lee 1966; Todaro 1969).

This means that the decision of settlers whether to colonize a periphery can be reduced to a number of "pull" and "push" factors. On the "push" side, economic desperation exerts a major effect on the willingness of people to emigrate to a frontier. It is always worth remembering that most people do not leave home, with all of their familial networks and comforts, entirely willingly. Rather, people often have to be pushed whether through violence or material necessity. And as agricultural production has historically been the major constraint on population growth, famine—or the threat of it—has historically been a major factor in driving settler colonialism.[7] For instance, the great willingness of Greek refugees to settle in Macedonia in the 1920s cannot be divorced from the fact that they had been recently forced to flee from Asia Minor with little more than the clothes on their back.

On the "pull" side, frontiers characterized by (i) easily alienated land, (ii) fertile land, and (iii) rich natural resources will disproportionately tend to be colonized. Taking these factors each in turn, land that is controlled by a militarily strong indigenous group tends not to be subject to colonization as settlers fear being entangled in a grisly war. Repeated attempts by the British state to colonize Ireland during the late 1500s failed, for instance, because Ireland had a reputation for being a dangerous place for settlers. As one newly arrived English "planter" in Ireland in 1610 fretted:

> Since my coming to Dublin . . . I think I have been asked 16 several times what I thought of this plantation and whether it were possible that this laborers and workmen that are sent now for the building could save their throats from cutting, or their heads from being taken from their shoulders before the work was finished.[8]

The deterrent effects of Irish insurrections continued to imperil the success of British plantations there well into the 1600s.[9]

Beyond ease of alienation, fertile land is also a major draw for settlers. Port Phillip (present-day Victoria) was colonized extremely rapidly in the 1830s and 1840s in part because it had already gained a reputation as "Australia Felix." Victoria has a milder climate and more reliable rainfall than the rest of the Australian mainland. And a long drought had afflicted eastern Australia between 1824 and 1830, creating a great deal of desperation on the part of farmers in and around Sydney. Initial settler excursions into Victoria in the early 1830s had returned with wondrous depictions of rolling grasslands free from drought (Barta, 2008). The rapacious colonization of Victoria by Europeans over the subsequent two decades was thus due, in large part, to its relatively mild climate and suitability for pastoralism relative to the rest of the Australian continent.

Thirdly, natural resources are a major draw for colonists. Mineral discoveries have exerted major effects on migration. Indeed, the history of European colonial settlement in the 1800s is, in many ways, the history of alluvial gold. In the six years following the discovery of gold in California in 1848, more than 300,000 people migrated to the new state. Then, in the decade following the discovery of gold north of Melbourne in 1851, more than 400,000 people migrated to Victoria. Reflecting these successive rushes, the nickname for San Francisco in Chinese is "Old Gold Mountain" (*jiu jinshan*) and the nickname for Melbourne is "New Gold Mountain" (*xin jinshan*). Other gold rushes, like the Queensland gold rush centered in Gympie in the 1860s, the Witwatersrand gold rush centred on present-day Johannesburg of the 1880s, or the Rhodesian gold rush of the 1890s centered on present-day Kadoma, led to dramatic increases in settler numbers in otherwise remote areas.

Settler-Led Colonization

Because settler-led colonization is driven entirely by the private interests of settlers, the combination of these push and pull factors—population pressure in the core combined with mineral wealth or easily alienated land in the periphery—account for most such cases of colonization. For instance, on the push side, the rapid British settlement of North America and Australia during the 1700s and 1800s coincided with an unprecedented British population boom and the enclosure of formerly communal lands in Britain, forcing destitute British peasants to emigrate elsewhere.[10] And, on the pull side, it has also been shown that such settlers tended to emigrate to salubrious areas of the New World where agricultural land could be easily alienated from indigenous peoples (Acemoglu, Johnson, and Robinson, 2001; Engerman and Sokoloff, 2002; Lange, Mahoney, and Vom Hau, 2006; Gerring et al., 2011; Hariri, 2012).[11]

These same factors drive the few notable cases of settler-led colonization after World War II. For instance, the island of Mindanao in the southern Philippines was internally colonized after 1945. Mindanao, a relatively sparsely populated island where migrants could claim "empty" land (much to the consternation of indigenous Moros), became a major destination for rural Filipinos eager to secure their own farms. Between 1948 and 1960 alone, more than a million people migrated to Mindanao from the rest of the Philippines (Wernstedt and Simkins, 1965). This rapid internal redistribution of population, facilitated in a laissez-faire way by the central government, was prompted by extremely fast population growth in the northern island of Luzon and the Visayas (Krinks, 1970).[12]

Cases of settler-led colonization are characterized by ambiguity over official intent. The metropole is likely to be wary of overextension and of entangling themselves in a costly war to protect their colonists. So, when facing organized indigenous resistance, policymakers will often be tempted to simply forbid frontier settlement. For instance, over the seventeenth and eighteenth centuries a large number of Han Chinese settlers emigrated to Taiwan and coercively alienated indigenous land. Following a major uprising by indigenous Taiwanese in 1721, which succeeded in briefly suspending central rule over the island, the Qing court established a internal wall cutting Taiwan in half. Han settlers were expressly prohibited from crossing the Tu Niu wall to farm in indigenous territories. Similarly, in 1905 following the Herero uprising, the German colonial state established an internal border prohibiting further European settlement in Southwest Africa (present-day Namibia). The German Reichstag was irked by the cost of colonization and mandated that protection of settlers was to "be restricted to the smallest possible area focusing on those regions where our economic interests tend to coalesce." (Lechler and McNamee, 2018, 1865)

However, too forcefully restricting settlement also creates the prospect that settlers will found republics outside of the center's realm of control. For instance, after its victory over France in North America in 1763, Britain legally restricted American settlement on Indian land over the Appalachias in order to conserve military expenditure. This policy led to conflict with land-hungry speculators like George Washington and was a major contributing factor to the American Revolution a decade later.[13] Publicly siding with indigenes against the settlers may also do little to change the situation on the ground. For instance, United States President Grover Cleveland steadfastly refused to annex Hawaii in 1893, pitting him and Hawaiian Queen Lili'uokalani against the white settler population in Hawaii that had recently seized power there. The settlers nonetheless did not return power to Lili'uokalani but instead declared an independent Hawaiian republic on the Fourth of July 1894—an Independence Day of remarkable pique. When facing a relentless land hunger on the part of their colonists, policymakers are forced to navigate the Scylla of frontier war against indigenes and the Charybdis of settler independence.[14]

Policymakers, looking to manage these competing threats, usually follow the path of least resistance. And the path of least resistance is to post hoc incorporate land already colonized by settlers. This can be accomplished reactively through simply changing the border of legal settlement. For instance, the Tu Niu wall in Taiwan repeatedly failed to prevent the intrusion of settlers into prohibited territories. Facing settler demands for protection of new farmland, the Qianlong emperor was compelled no less than four times—in 1750, 1760, 1788, and 1790—to redraw the border between Han and indigenous territories of Taiwan (Ye, 2017). Similarly, Cleveland's admirable stance against American imperialism in the Pacific only temporarily delayed Hawaii's fate. Just two years after Cleveland's replacement by William McKinley in 1896, the United States formally annexed Hawaii to the delight of the American settlers there.

But legally incorporating newly colonized land can also be achieved proactively through homesteading. For instance, Thomas Jefferson's "Plan for the West," formulated in the midst of the Ohio Valley migration crisis of 1784, established the contours of American settlement policy over the next century (Berkhofer, 1972). Jefferson's Ordinance of 1784 set clear criteria for the creation of future American states and counties based on the number of white settlers in an area. Frontier land rights would be assigned not by the state but through individual right of possession. The principle that American state authority followed settler volition would define America's westward expansion and its ultimate limits over the nineteenth century, as America generally only granted statehood to areas where whites already predominated (Love, 2005; Frymer, 2017).

Similarly, after the crisis prompted by the unlicensed settlement of Port Phillip (Victoria) in 1835, the British colonial government began to authorize the grazing of livestock on "waste land" in Australia. As Australian Aborigines were denied the right to sell land, the only claim that settlers could have to particular plots of land was common-law right of possession. This form of

Australian homesteading created an incentive for settlers to claim parcels of frontier land as quickly as possible. The legal limitation of grazing to "waste land," designed in part to protect Australia's indigenous peoples from dispossession, also perversely created an incentive on the part of settlers to displace Aborigines; the legal possession of land in Port Phillip in the 1830s and 1840s required that the land be unoccupied. These two incentives combined created a genocidal land rush. As one Tasmanian periodical reported following the proclamation of this new land policy on 24 September 1836:

> Within twenty-four hours coming to Hobart Town numerous persons of every grade were contriving how to get to Port Phillip. . . . the only feeling existing among men of capital here appears to be that of jealousy who shall have the first and best hold of land and stock at Port Phillip. (Boyce, 2011, 232)

Policymakers often frame settler-led colonization in a fatalistic way, as if they had no choice but to accept the rush of colonists into the frontier. But policymakers always have a choice—at certain critical junctures, they simply found avoiding conflict with their colonists more expedient than standing in their way. For this reason, I suggest that settler-led colonization is characterized by a logic of "strategic fatalism".

The fact that the underlying causes of settler-led colonization may seem somewhat mechanical, driven by factors like population pressure and carrying capacity, has meant that social scientists have largely focused on the lasting effects of settler colonialism rather than its causes.[15] Settler-led colonization is also a largely historical phenomenon as border controls and the widespread availability of guns has made it difficult for farmers to coercively move into frontier areas of their own volition, as was once quite common. However, colonization is not always settler-led—the movement of colonists into a frontier area can also be actively planned, funded, and facilitated by officials. And, unlike settler-led colonization, state-led colonization is still prevalent across the world today. To recover the logic of state-led colonization, we must therefore turn to the competing interests of the metropole.

State-Led Colonization

Now place yourself in the position of a policymaker in the metropole, deciding whether to actively send colonists into a frontier like Thrace. The "benefits" to doing so have long been recognized by geopolitical strategists. Colonization improves state security because frontier areas are vulnerable to incursions and insurgencies (Lee, 2018). As a remedial response, it has been commonplace for states—from the Roman Empire to twentieth century Indonesia—to ask demobilized soldiers to actively farm border zones (McGarry, 1998).[16] Even when civilians are being resettled to the border, a common precondition of resettlement is that settlers actively maintain arms. For example, Han Chinese settled on China's northwestern frontier during the 1960s and 1970s were actively given paramilitary training and were expected to pacify restive minorities in the event of a Soviet invasion. Colonization improves a state's military capacity as it anchors an armed co-ethnic population in a contested region that can be called upon to defend the state.[17]

The reader may query at this point why the ethnicity of settlers is so important to the state. Ethnicity is important only insofar as ethnicity is stereotypically linked to political allegiance. Unlike other social identities such as class or gender, ethnicity—understood as a composite category based on individual language, phenotype, and cultural traits—varies predictably across space (Bulutgil, 2016). As such, all states since antiquity have been stereotypically associated with the languages, religions, and modes of life that characterize their core. And in situations of conflict with an insurgent group or foreign power, states are faced with the challenge of quickly identifying friend and foe. Out of expediency, ethnicity quickly morphs into an *heuristic* for political loyalty.[18] Emptying frontiers of people stereotypically associated with political disloyalty (like Turkish Muslims) and populating them with stereotypically loyal ethnic groups (like Orthodox Greeks) is one way for states to rapidly secure control over contested frontiers.[19]

Of course, settling a frontier region with stereotypically loyal ethnic groups has somewhat more limited military value in an age of missiles and military sophistication. But populating a borderland with a core ethnic group in the contemporary world still furthers a state's geopolitical interests. By changing the demographic "facts on the ground," settler colonialism can change a state's normative claim to territory. Due to the norm of self-determination, state boundaries since the dissolution of empires are determined in part by the distribution of ethno-national groups (Wimmer, 2002). Hence, periods of imperial collapse, like that of the Ottoman Empire in the Balkans in the early twentieth century, were characterized by particularly rapid demographic change as emergent nation-states—Greece, Turkey, Bulgaria and Serbia— sought to populate contested areas with their core ethnic groups. Coercively moving people in space can ensure that the distribution of ethno-national groups reflects a state's desired territorial borders (Lustick, 1993; O'Leary, 2001).

Somewhat more subtly, colonization also signals to competitors the commitment of a state to the defence of a region. States signal credible commitment through colonization by both (i) "sinking costs" by making costly financial investments in a frontier, and (ii) "tying their hands" to the defence of a region that now contains a substantial proportion of the majority ethnonational group.[20] As an example, consider the debate in Australia over whether the state should settle the Northern Territory—a lightly populated area on the northern Australian mainland whose major city had been razed by Japan in World War II. A prominent opponent to this scheme, Member of Parliament Kim Beazley, pointed out that:

> If we intend to speak realistically about defence in an atomic age, we should understand that the best defence we can possibly have is an empty north in which rocket bases could be concealed. An atomic attack in such an area would not matter. To congregate a large population in an area does not constitute a defence in an atomic age.[21]

Yet, proponents of this scheme responded by highlighting how the presence of large numbers of settlers in the Northern Territory would send a message of commitment to Communist powers.[22] Even in an age when soldier-farmers have limited military value, the settlement of a frontier has strategic value insofar as it signals to potential competitors the commitment of the state to the defence of a frontier.

Despite these manifold security benefits, not all states colonize frontier regions and even those that do are highly selective as to when and where they resettle people. This is because colonization is *costly*. Unlike passively licensing the colonization of a frontier—as in cases of settler-led colonization—actively spending money resettling people has opportunity costs. Consider the fact that Greece ultimately went bankrupt in 1932 in large part due to the enormous debt accrued from resettling hundreds of thousands of refugees to Macedonia over the previous decade.[23] Or consider the case of Papua New Guinea. After World War II, the Australian government debated settling Papua New Guinea with demobilized soldiers. A government commission closely weighed up Australia's competing objectives, which sought to prevent a future Japanese invasion from the north whilst avoiding the waste of taxpayer funds. After totalling the likely investment in roads, hospitals, ports, and schools needed to make migration there economically attractive for European settlers, the commissioners concluded:

> [It is] unwarrantable to expend public money to the extent of 30,000 pounds (or more probably 50,000 plus) per settler, with dubious economic and more than dubious social prospects, unless there were a clear over-riding necessity for some such type of development. Some have indeed proclaimed this necessity, on the grounds that the defence of Australia needs a "large" population in this its northern bulwark. . . . [But] settlement on this scale could not be attained without such a disruption of native life . . . that the allegiance of the natives would be forfeited to us. . . . Once more, why buy a rather doubtful good at the price[?][24]

Following the publication of this report, Australia did indeed abandon its plans to settle former servicemen in Papua New Guinea. Australia could settle Papua New Guinea and remain solvent but the opportunity costs of doing so were simply too great.

The commissioners also highlighted the fact that settling a frontier region has the potential to backfire and lead to a costly war. In this sense, colonization is *not* a first-best strategy for maintaining control over a periphery. Although settlement can help to shore up control over a border zone, it also has the potential to radicalize a displaced indigenous population and lead to a more protracted conflict in the medium term. Examples are not hard to find. For instance, the colonization of the Eastern Cape by Britain in 1811 led to a long-running war with the Xhosa whose cost fully outweighed the value of the land obtained.[25] And the settlement of Mindanao in the mid-twentieth century by Christian Filipinos led to a long-running insurgency by indigenous Moros. The conflict is estimated to have cost the Philippines $2–3 billion and killed approximately 120,000 people since 1969 (Schiavo-Campo and Judd, 2005). In light of this extreme loss of labor and capital, it was clearly a mistake for Manila in the 1950s and 1960s to have granted police protection to squatters in Mindanao.[26] A key risk entailed in settling a frontier is that such schemes can backfire and radicalize displaced indigenes, in turn creating the conditions for a protracted insurgency.

These are merely the possible domestic costs. Colonization is also a hostile act that may provoke retaliation by foreign actors. For example, after India announced the revocation of Kashmir's autonomy in 2019—widely seen as a precursor to mass Hindu migration because it removed restrictions on non-Kashmiris owning land there—Pakistan announced the expulsion of India's

top diplomat in Islamabad, the withdrawal of its ambassador, and the cessa-
tion of all trade.[27] Sanctions may also be directed against countries like Israel
that settle contested regions in defiance of international law. Given these significant domestic and international costs, the real question is perhaps not
why settler colonialism *doesn't happen* in the midst of so much territorial
conflict but rather why states ever decide that it's worth colonizing frontier
regions at all.

Threat Perceptions and Demographic Engineering

To uncover the conditions in which policymakers will elect to colonize a
frontier, I follow the rationalist tradition in international relations by assuming that states are principally concerned with balancing wealth and security.
Just like individuals, policymakers in the metropole have numerous priorities
and must make trade-offs between different objectives rather than pursu-
ing one goal, such as land accumulation, at the expense of all others. And,
just like individuals, policymakers make choices from among alternatives.
Instead of trying to hold on to a frontier at all costs, the metropole can always
cede control over territory. And there are a myriad of strategies available to
policymakers if they *do* want to engage in "state making" (Tilly, 1985) by eliminating challenges to their rule over a frontier. The key question from the
perspective of a metropole seeking to exploit a frontier region at minimal
cost, then, is the question of strategy. When is colonization likely to be the
most cost-effective strategy for ruling over a diverse frontier relative to its
alternatives?

Let us now fully consider the various strategies that states can use to rule
over indigenous peoples. In a broad sense, states can tolerate indigenous difference and autonomy by ruling "indirectly" and in partnership with indigenous
elites. And, if policymakers do want to eliminate indigenous autonomy, they
can do so in three main ways.[28] First, by encouraging an indigenous population, forcibly or otherwise, to change their ethnic identity (assimilation).
Second, through migration (settler colonialism and/or ethnic cleansing). And
finally, through killing (genocide). Under what conditions is settler colonialism chosen over these alternatives?

In the absence of a perceived threat posed by a minority group, empires
historically sought to garner the loyalties of frontier minorities by allowing
for a degree of indigenous sovereignty. For example, China under the Qing
Dynasty (1644–1912) governed frontier areas like Tibet, Taiwan, or Xinjiang

in partnership with local elites, granting indigenes substantial autonomy in exchange for tribute and loyalty to the emperor (Elliott, 2001). Since the rise of nationalism in the 1800s, states have more commonly sought to assimilate minority groups into a common national identity.[29] For instance, following Greece and Turkey's joint accession to NATO and a lessening of geopolitical tension over the mid-twentieth century, Greece tried to assimilate its Turkish minority by launching a campaign "proving" that Muslims in Thrace were Islamized Christians of Greek descent (Antoniou, 2005). As the least coercive options, the assimilation and accommodation of indigenous peoples are generally the baseline policies that policymakers use to manage ethnic diversity (Mylonas, 2012).

Even empires, however, did not accommodate the presence of indigenous groups whom they viewed as a pressing threat. For instance, the Qing were hardly always accommodating to frontier minorities. After the Qing defeated the Dzungars in Central Asia in 1759, for instance, it eliminated all remnants of the Dzungar state by massacring approximately 500,000 Dzungars and settling their lands with Han (Perdue, 2009; Clarke, 2004). The perception of threat is generally critical for understanding when and why states seek to eliminate ethnic outsiders (Davenport, 2007; Butt, 2017).

Assimilation also has two major strategic downsides from the perspective of policymakers. First, assimilation requires a substantial period of time to be successful. Ethnicity is slow to change *within* generations but can be remarkably quick to change *between* generations (Laitin, 1998, 22). Assimilationist policies like national schooling or conscription can lead to significant intergenerational change in ethnic identity but, given the amount of time necessary to be successful, is an ill-suited strategy to pursue in response to a pressing threat.

Second, assimilation—if heavy-handed and coercive—can backfire, hardening ethnic minorities against the center. Policymakers, especially during periods of conflict, can be tempted to speed up assimilation by restricting the use of minority languages, religious practices, or cultural symbols. But a number of studies have shown that such policies—from the anti-Catholic Penal Laws in colonial Ireland (Hechter, 1975), to the shuttering of German schools in the United States during World War I (Fouka, 2016), or France's recent headscarf ban (Abdelgadir and Fouka, 2020)—rebound on the metropole by fostering resentment against discrimination and reducing minority integration on average. Polarized settings in which minorities face rising pressure to choose between different identities are precisely the conditions under which assimilation is most likely to fail. For these two reasons combined, trying to coercively assimilate "disloyal" minorities in the midst of conflict is risky.

As such, we should expect that states would generally seek to rule in partnership with indigenous elites or engage in assimilation when perceived threats to the state's territorial integrity are low.[30] Coercive migration, on the other hand, is more effective at quickly improving a state's control over a contested region. So, territorial conflict, by creating a short-term need to secure control over a frontier, increases the likelihood of colonization. The importation of a new population into a frontier is usually accompanied by the expulsion of indigenous persons (ethnic cleansing). Cleansing restive frontiers of "disloyal" or "violent" minority groups, as the Qing did to the Dzungars in 1759, as Macquarie did to Sydney's Gandangara in 1816, and as Greece did to the Turks of Macedonia in 1923, can quickly eliminate a threat when the state is otherwise unable to distinguish between friend and foe (Valentino, Huth, and Balch-Lindsay, 2004; Downes, 2008a).[31]

Equally, when the danger posed by external or internal competitors to the state is immediate, extremists are empowered to undertake more radical policies designed to quickly and with finality eliminate a perceived threat. So, rather than the displacement of a minority group—which can gift an enemy potentially highly motivated conscripts and turn them into "refugee warriors" (Stedman and Tanner, 2004)—genocide tends to take place amidst clashing armies in existential conflicts like the Rwandan civil war (Valentino, 2004; Downes, 2006).

Taken together, I expect that state-led colonization and ethnic cleansing tend to occur in settings of neither geopolitical harmony nor outright war (Figure 2.1). In this middle ground of uncertain peace like Macedonia in the 1920s or the China-Russia borderland today, states are motivated to consolidate control over contested areas in the short run through coercive migration whilst avoiding escalatory mass killing.[32] In other words, colonization and ethnic cleansing tend to be policy choices in states characterized by territorial insecurity but not existential war.[33]

Now that the idea has been introduced that colonization is a strategy used by states when facing a pressing threat, we can begin to think about the areas where states would disproportionately redirect settlers. We can also parse out when settlement happens in conjunction with ethnic cleansing and when it happens alone.

Degree of territorial insecurity

Low   Medium   High

Assimilation

Colonization & ethnic cleansing

Genocide

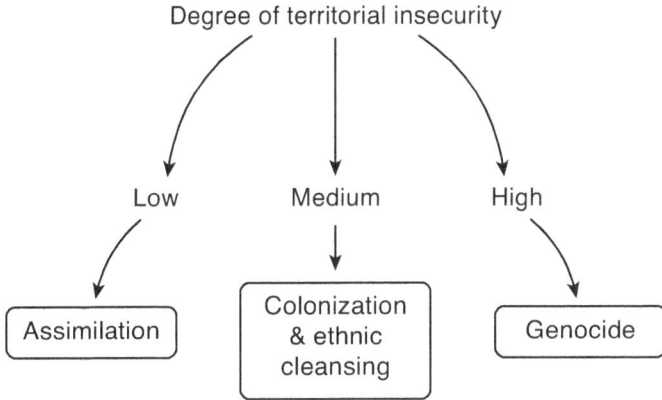

FIGURE 2.1. The selection of demographic engineering strategies.

Colonization only tends not to happen in conjunction with ethnic cleansing when the state is responding to an *external* threat by settling a contested borderland, and that area is already inhabited by the majority ethnic group or by a minority seen as stereotypically loyal. For example, Indonesia and Malaysia share a long, porous, land border on the island of Borneo historically populated by an indigenous group, the Dayak, stereotypically allegiant to neither state. In May 2005 the Indonesian Minister of Agriculture announced the creation of a 200-kilometer-long plantation corridor (*Kawasan Agropolitan*) that would span the length of the border and employ half a million migrants. One high-ranking military officer claimed that this scheme would fill Indonesia's frontier with loyal subjects who could police incursions from Malaysia (Eilenberg, 2014, 12). Settling a border region with a hostile state, even in the absence of ethnic cleansing, still usefully signals commitment and increases a state's capacity to police a porous frontier.

But colonization tends to happen in conjunction with ethnic cleansing when states are seeking to secure control over areas populated by "disloyal" minorities. To be sure, the perception that a minority is stereotypically disloyal is necessarily somewhat subjective. But two kinds of minorities are most prone to being viewed as threatening by state officials: rebellious minorities and so-called "fifth column" minorities.

Fifth column minorities are minority groups who are co-ethnics with policymakers in a hostile power, such as Greeks in Turkey, Turks in Greece, Somalis in Ethiopia, and Muslims in Indian Kashmir. Because they share ethnicity with elites in hostile external powers, fifth column minorities are often viewed by the metropole as potential threats to internal security (Mylonas, 2012). So, ethnic cleansing and colonization tends to be targeted at minorities who are co-ethnics with elites in a hostile state.[34] For example, following its acquisition of territory in eastern Germany after World War II, Poland cleansed the area of approximately eight million Germans and repopulated it with five million Poles resettled from the east (Charnysh, 2019).

Second, states tend to colonize and cleanse minorities whose co-ethnics are actively engaged in civil war against the state. To be sure, only a minority of rebellious minorities are subject to colonization. For instance, Myanmar has been consistently embroiled in warfare with a number of minority groups such as the Kachin, the Shan, and the Karen since the 1950s. Relative to Myanmar's Rohingya minority, such groups have been spared collective violence. Myanmar's military has instead tended to tolerate and even co-operate with minority militias in its highlands. More generally, and contrary to classic models of European state-building (e.g., Tilly 1975), states do not always seek to monopolize violence and coercively eliminate indigenous challengers— rather, states often strategically outsource governance to militias (Reno, 1997), incorporate bandits into the center (Barkey, 1994), and share sovereignty with regional militias (Staniland, 2012). Only certain types of indigenous rebellions result in repression.

Colonizing and cleansing a minority is anti-economic and so we should expect states to seek to strike bargains over autonomy with rebellious minorities. In this vein, recurrent clashes and bouts of negotiation over shared sovereignty have characterized Myanmar's relations with its highland minorities since independence. For states to embark upon colonization, there must be some additional factor that prevents the state and an indigenous group from coming to a peaceful accommodation. In other words, a necessary condition for settler colonialism during civil war is persistent bargaining failure between the state and a minority rebel group over zero-sum issues like independence.

This kind of bargaining failure is most likely in two types of situations. The first situation is when a minority group has support from and can access a base in a neighboring state. Rebellious minority groups subject to colonization and ethnic cleansing such as the Rohingya of Myanmar, the Jumma of Bangladesh, the Papuans of Indonesia, and the Malays of Thailand tend to have access to a transnational sanctuary. External support is important because it converts simmering secessionist tensions into full-blown insurgencies by providing militants with an external haven, funding, and military training, and international legitimacy (Salehyan, 2009). Reflecting the increased likelihood of successful secession, such minorities tend to demand independence over autonomy (Jenne, Saideman, and Lowe, 2007). External support means that it is much harder to end a conflict peacefully and that states will accordingly seek to "resolve" secessionist conflicts through coercion (Butt, 2017). So, one would expect that states tend to colonize and cleanse rebellious minorities with foreign support and a transnational sanctuary.[35]

The other kind of civil war likely to result in bargaining failure is resource conflicts. Resources increase the likelihood that secessionist tensions explode into conflict as resource wealth encourages demands for independence (Ross, 2013). For example, following the discovery of natural gas in Aceh, Indonesia, Acehnese separatists claimed that Indonesia's "Javanese" elite were stealing Aceh's wealth and that independence would allow Acehnese to benefit from their own resources (Ross, 2004). Resource-based separatism is hardly unique to the Global South, of course. After oil from the North Sea came on tap in the 1970s, for instance, the Scottish National Party campaigned with great success around around the notion that "it's Scotland's oil." Resource wealth strains the bonds of nationalism and tightens those of regionalism.

Resources also raise the economic stakes of a territorial conflict and accordingly make it less likely that the central state would ever agree to minority secession. This is particularly true in developing countries. In countries that lack industry or advanced services, the vast bulk of export and tax revenue is derived from natural resource extraction. Given the high economic stakes, developing countries facing demands for independence in resource-rich areas have a strong incentive to try to stand their ground and defeat secessionists through violence.[36] The combination of minority and state intransigence in resource-rich areas has been central to producing some of the most violent instances of forced migration around the world in the late twentieth century: Iraqi Kurdistan, Indonesian East Timor and West Papua, Papua New Guinea's Bougainville, the Bangladeshi Chittagong Hills, Moroccan Western Sahara, Nigerian Biafra, Chinese Xinjiang, Pakistani Balochistan, among others.

So, to briefly summarize my expectations for where states are willing to pay the not inconsiderable costs of settler colonialism and ethnic cleansing, I expect states to generally try to settle borderlands with hostile foreign states. I also expect that they will try to colonize and cleanse disloyal minorities: fifth column minorities and rebellious minorities. This is particularly true if a rebellious minority has a foreign sanctuary or is endowed with natural resources, which, by reducing the prospect of a bargain over autonomy, increases the likelihood that states will seek to defeat indigenes through violence.[37] As the axes of such conflicts revolve around control of the border and natural resources, we should expect that states generally seek to colonize and cleanse borderlands and resource-rich areas populated by rebellious minorities.

But recall that states are constrained in their use of colonization by the economic interests of their settlers. In order to colonize a contested area, states must ensure that migration is consistent with the material interests of individual settlers.[38] Otherwise, as in the cases of contemporary Greece and Russia, few settlers will take up the state's offer of resettlement and those that do will soon abscond.

The notable exception to this rule is Communist states. Communist states are exceptionally effective colonizers as people have no ability to live independently from the state. For instance, China comprehensively settled parts of Xinjiang in the 1960s by simply rusticating youths to state farms and factories in the periphery. In market economies where individuals *do* have outside options, however, people generally require material inducement to remain in frontier areas, if only in the form of free land.[39] So, Communist states aside, when and where are the interests of states and settlers likely to be aligned?

States are in luck when it comes to colonizing resource-rich areas, which, by definition, offer lucrative economic opportunities to settlers. For example, during the 1970s, the Iraqi government sought to "Arabize" Kirkuk—the site of the largest oil deposits in northern Iraq. It did so in part by transferring Kurdish oil and industrial workers in the Northern Oil Company to southern Iraq and replacing them with Arabs. Industrial centers of Kirkuk like Yaychi quickly became predominantly Arab (Knights and Ali, 2010). Similarly, when Indonesia took control over West Papua in the 1960s, it dismissed most of the indigenous Papuan workforce in the petroleum industry.[40] As migrants were drawn in to replace Papuans, oil-rich areas of West Papua such as Sorong or the Cenderawasih Bay quickly became predominantly non-Papuan.[41] Given the alignment between state and settler interests, we should expect that resource-rich areas populated by disloyal minorities are subject to particularly extreme levels of settlement.

Less fortunately for states, however, not all borderlands are appealing to settlers. Borders that follow natural boundaries[42]—those that are difficult to traverse due to the presence of geographic partitions such as deserts, mountain ranges, or bodies of water—are generally characterized by less settlement. Agricultural profitability is determined by the suitability of land for crop production and the costs of shipping produce to the market. Frontiers characterized by deserts and mountains are unattractive destinations for farmers because they are both less productive and less accessible. For instance, no transmigrant farms in Indonesia were possible in areas with a slope greater than 8 percent due to erosion (Bazzi et al., 2016), ruling out transmigration to much of the Papuan highlands and producing a lasting demographic division between the highlands and lowlands. It is no coincidence, then, that—as in West Papua—geographic borders so often neatly coincide with ethnic borders. As James C. Scott (2009, 20) quipped: "civilizations can't climb hills."

Borderlands characterized by mountains and deserts are also less strategically important. All skilled military tacticians throughout history have necessarily taken into account terrain and climate in warfare (Keegan, 1993). And borders delimited to follow natural features are easier to defend from aggressors because bodies of water and mountains present obstacles to communication, trade, and transport between states (Pounds, 1972).[43] As natural borders independently bolster a state's territorial defences, settlement schemes tend to focus on relatively porous low-lying border areas where insurgents can easily cross into the state. So, natural border regions tend to be spared colonization whereas non-natural border zones, along with resource-rich areas, experience the greatest amount of colonization.

The Settler Colonial Transition

Finally, consider how the interests of the metropole and settlers change as a country modernizes economically. Let us start with the metropole. As long as humans have lived in states, most economic value has been tied up in land, and states have derived the bulk of tax revenue from agriculturalists (Barkley, 1990). Consequently, policymakers in pre-modern states were preoccupied with territorial annexation (Markowitz, Fariss, and McMahon, 2018). Pre-modern states were dependent upon land rents and so territorial expansion has historically constituted the chief spoil of war.

However, territorial conflict is increasingly rare in the modern world (Holsti, 1991). A primary reason for the decline in global territorial conflict is the rise of services and manufacturing. Economic modernization severs the link between territory and state wealth as most economic value is produced in industry and services, both of which are concentrated in major cities (Hardt and Negri, 2000). Industrial wealth, crucially, cannot be conquered or looted.[44]

Reflecting the declining value of territory to states, a large literature in international relations has shown that as states develop they are less and less likely to initiate territorial disputes (Rosecrance, 1986; Frieden, 1994; Brooks, 1999, 2005; Gartzke and Rohner, 2010). Rather than conquer new territory, industrialized states are more likely to invest in military capabilities such as navies that allow them to project power around the globe and compel policy change in competitors at a distance (Gartzke and Rohner, 2011; Markowitz, Fariss, and McMahon, 2018).[45]

Consider the example of the United States. The United States aggressively sought to expand its territorial remit in the first half of the nineteenth century, most notably acquiring over half of Mexico's territory after the Mexican-American war of 1848. At this time, agriculture constituted 50% of the American economy and America quickly moved to consolidate control over its newly annexed territories (Markowitz, Fariss, and McMahon, 2018). But by the early 1900s, agriculture had fallen to less than 10% of America's GDP. Even as America continued to rise economically and militarily during the twentieth century, it did *not* seek to further expand its territorial remit. Rather, American foreign policy emphasized the projection of military power from afar and the protection of America's trade interests.[46]

The shrinking of American manifest destiny was undoubtedly shaped by a number of factors, but the importance of economics is borne out when attending to policymaker debates. For instance, between 1912 and 1916 there was much debate in Congress over the future of American presence in the Philippines, a territory that America had acquired from Spain in 1898. William A. Jones, a Democratic member of the House of Representatives, authored the bill that successfully declared the intention of the United States to one day allow Filipinos independence. Jones' push for Filipino independence was driven by American self-interest (Beadles, 1968). When introducing the bill in 1913, Jones refrained from making any humanitarian arguments about self-determination and rather questioned whether "the American people are ever to be relieved of the enormous financial burdens that their retention [of the Philippines] yearly entails."[47] Jones then contended that it was in the self-interest of America to free the Filipinos because the cost of maintaining and defending the islands was far too high relative to any benefits from trade or taxation. Jones' arguments proved persuasive to his previously retentionist peers; modernizing economies, such as early twentieth century United States, derive relatively little benefit from poor, agricultural frontiers like the Philippines. Economic development in the core makes it more likely that states will peacefully cede control over frontier areas to indigenes.[48]

Of course, states do not always behave so rationally. As Snyder (1991, 8–9) puts it, "all the industrial great powers have at times expanded past the point where marginal costs equals marginal benefits, in terms of both economic and security interests." Due to capture by sectional interests and nationalistic ideologies, relatively developed states such as Germany in the interwar period or China and Israel today can waste enormous amounts of resources seeking to consolidate control over peripheral and economically marginal territory.

Yet, even when highly developed states do seek to retain control over contested frontiers for ideological reasons, their *power* to do so through colonization is very limited. Economic development, crucially, also reduces the willingness of settlers to migrate to a frontier. The central way that states have historically made the colonization of frontier areas compatible with the interests of settlers is through the provision of land. In less developed states, the bulk of economic value is derived from farming. So, it has been historically quite easy for elites with access to advanced weaponry to manipulate the direction of internal migration by offering free land. In pre-modern and early modern settings, officials need only clear land of its prior inhabitants for there to be a sufficient incentive for individuals to relocate permanently from the core. Even otherwise weak states such as the Qin dynasty in the second century BCE, the British state in Ireland in the early 1600s, the Greek state in the 1920s, and Indonesia and Myanmar today have been able to effectively colonize frontier regions precisely because "empty" land has long been a valuable asset.

The availability of settlers, however, dries up with development. As states develop, the relative value of farm labor declines rapidly as high-wage jobs are increasingly centered in large cities. And rural-to-urban migration is highly responsive to the relative wages of farmers and nonfarmers (e.g., Barkley 1990; Sicular and Zhao 2004; Breustedt and Glauben 2007). Consequently, economic development leads to a *reversal* in the prevailing direction of migration as already dense areas, rather than "open" frontiers, become magnets for migrants (Forsyth, 1942; Zelinsky, 1971). Highly developed states actually experience severe depopulation in rural areas as families abandon the land for the better job opportunities and services in cities. For instance, almost 11% of Japan's previously productive farmland now lies fallow, unwanted, and unclaimed.[49]

Developed countries may still seek to colonize contested frontiers but, given high living standards in the core, they are unlikely to be successful in attracting settlers. Consider again the case of the United States in the Philippines. Leonard Wood, the American Governor of the southern province of Mindanao (Moro) between 1903–1906, sought to suppress widespread indigenous unrest there. In tandem with his violent counterinsurgency campaign, Wood's administration widely publicized Mindanao to American settlers and promoted the area as "a new West" (Charbonneau, 2019). The local chronicle, the *Mindanao Herald*, was scarcely less optimistic about the prospects for European colonization, declaring in 1905 that:

> The Moro Province is a white man's country and will remain so. The native population is infinitesimal. . . . The white population here is increasing rapidly, and as time goes on will multiply. Opportunities in great abundance are here for hustling white men in almost every walk of life.[50]

But the rush of hustling white men never eventuated and only eighty whites remained in Mindanao by the 1920s (Abinales, 2000, 78).

Instead, much to the consternation of American authorities, a wave of Japanese settlers colonized Mindanao in the interwar period. As part of its strategy of *nanshin-ron*, or southward advance, Japan in the early twentieth century encouraged Japanese peasants to migrate across Asia-Pacific (Lu, 2019). And, unlike the United States, which was already a medium-income country by contemporary standards in 1913, Japan was still quite poor and had a large reserve of peasants willing to emigrate to distant frontiers.[51] In the 1920s and 1930s over 20,000 Japanese farmers, streetwalkers, and tradesmen emigrated to Mindanao, making it the largest Japanese community in southeast Asia (Shiraishi and Shiraishi, 2018).[52] By the early 1930s, the American officials in the Philippines began to fret at the "potential menace to the security of the Islands" (Goodman, 1967, 27) and the *New York Times* ran articles condemning the "peaceful economic invasion" of Mindanao by Japan.[53]

In this somewhat perverse way, Japan's relatively low level of development in the interwar period was actually a source of strategic strength that facilitated its imperial expansion. Officials in both Japan and the United States adopted a laissez-faire approach that licensed the colonization of frontiers like Mindanao in the Asia-Pacific by their co-nationals. But only Japan succeeded in doing so. Japan's comparative success placed it in an extremely powerful position vis-à-vis the United States during World War II, when it was able to easily secure control over Mindanao by invading and absorbing the Japanese community into its wartime administration. Less developed states are much more effective colonizers.

To be sure, wealthy states have ample financial resources at their disposal that they can use to bribe settlers. States can fix the price of agricultural produce artificially high to subsidize farming in the periphery. They can also try to create high-paying jobs in the periphery by encouraging industry to relocate through generous tax breaks or grandiose infrastructure schemes. Consistent with this logic, for instance, Australia throughout the twentieth century did far more than just offer free land to encourage whites to settle in the Northern Territory. It also constructed new roads and rail to ameliorate freight costs and abolished income taxes for any company in the Territory involved in agriculture, mining, or fishing.[54] Together, these concessions and investments amounted to billions of today's US dollars.

Despite their immense wealth and capacity, however, developed states struggle to redirect investment and labor to contested frontiers. Businesses invest in an area when production can be maintained at a lower cost base relative to its geographic *alternatives*. And peripheral areas are expensive production sites due to transportation costs. It is all well and good to produce something in a peripheral area but widgets need to be shipped to urban markets to be consumed. Agricultural and industrial producers located close to cities in the core therefore possess a considerable commercial edge over their more distant competitors.[55]

The opportunity costs faced by capital in the periphery are matched by the opportunity costs to labor. Destitute peasants may emigrate far and wide for small parcels of land or mineral wealth, but not wealthy urbanites who value quality of life and proximity to friends and family. Peripheral areas, after all, often lack high-quality schools and hospitals, diverse retail, entertainment and sporting facilities, or modern services. As one Russian settler recently lamented after discovering that it would cost the equivalent of $61,000 to connect electricity to his new plot of land in the Far East: "The hectare itself is free, but everything else is a headache. . . . It's too expensive and too tiring to come so far for just a barbecue and a swim."

The obvious exception to this general pattern is, of course, Israel (Lustick, 1987). Israel's success in settling the Palestinian West Bank over the past half century would appear to contradict the notion that developed states have little power to engage in colonization. But it is worth clarifying the ways in which Israel is, and is not, exceptional. Israel's use of settlers to secure control over a contested area is *not* exceptional. A vast array of states during the the twentieth century—from Greece, Indonesia, Morocco, China, India, and Iraq—have displaced ethnic minorities and colonized their lands on the basis of dubious "ancestral" or nationalistic claims. And nor is Israel exempt from the struggle to make colonization compatible with the interests of its settlers. Over two-thirds of the Israeli settler population live in East Jerusalem today (Handel, Rand, and Allegra, 2015), in large part because the government has struggled to push settlers outside Jerusalem's metropolitan belt (Allegra, 2013, 509). Survey after survey has shown that the bulk of Israelis who move to East Jerusalem and the West Bank are primarily driven not by Jewish nationalism but by material considerations, lured to the area by tax breaks and subsidized housing, and so have largely remained within commuting distance to the urban core.[56]

Israel is therefore only exceptional because, unlike almost every other developed country, it has had some success in luring migrants to a contested periphery. But this success is largely due to Israel's idiosyncratic geography; unlike most other contested frontiers, East Jerusalem and the West Bank are extremely close to Israel's urban centers. This means that Israel can colonize the West Bank by simply expanding its urban commuter belt. For instance, when Israel opened Route 398 or the "Lieberman Road"[57] to the southern West Bank in 2007, it slashed the driving time to Jerusalem from 40 minutes to just 10 minutes.[58] The number of settlers in the area subsequently doubled in the next six years. By linking settlements in the West Bank to Jerusalem via highways that skirt around Palestinian towns, Israel can create affordable, safe suburbs that are appealing options for Israeli urbanites.

Israel failed to similarly colonize the Gaza Strip because of Gaza's relative distance to Israel's urban core. Israel's main Jewish settlement bloc there, the Gush Katif, was established shortly following Israel's annexation of Gaza in 1967. But the number of Jewish settlers in Gush Katif never exceeded 10,000. Despite Israel's efforts to lure settlers to Gaza, the sheer distance from Gush Katif to Tel Aviv and Jerusalem—exceeding two hours by highway—and the fact that Gush Katif was subject to almost daily attacks during the 1990s, meant that it was an unappealing residential option for most Israelis. As one commentator derided: "Most Israelis cannot grasp . . . why anyone would live in a hot, sandy, bombarded enclave, surrounded by barbed wire and watchtowers, much less put their children in such danger."[59] Israel's inability to attract Jewish settlers to southern Gaza, and the fact that the settlers were completely outweighed by the million-strong Arab population there, is ultimately what prompted Sharon to betray his settlers and cede the territory in 2005. For, as Sharon lamented as he presented his plan for Israel to "disengage" from Gaza that year: "Disengagement recognizes the demographic reality on the ground specifically, bravely and honestly" (Rynhold and Waxman, 2008, 25).

Israel's partial success at what I call "commuter colonization" in East Jerusalem and the West Bank is therefore best understood as the exception that proves the rule. Because states in the Global North are largely unable to redirect labor away from the urban core, this means that they are unable to colonize all but the most geographically proximate areas to their major cities. Development makes colonization infeasible, obliging states—whether America in the Philippines, Australia in New Guinea, or Israel in the Gaza Strip—to settle for less land.

Hence, as they grow richer and denser, I propose that all states go through a transition in which they lose the power to colonize. The notion that all countries go through a number of standard social transformations with modernization is well known in demography (Zelinsky, 1971; Skeldon, 2012). The most prominent such concept—the *demographic transition*—captures the fact that all developing states progressively shift from a pre-modern equilibrium characterized by high maternal fertility and high infant mortality to a modern equilibrium in which both fertility and infant mortality are low (Notestein, 1945; Chesnais, 1993).

Yet, what has been less appreciated is that modernization—a process encompassing urbanization, rising living standards, and the ascent of services and manufacturing—also produces a *settler colonial transition*. Settler and state-led colonization are evolutionary phases in human history. As states develop, they derive increasingly little economic benefit from territorial expansion, which reduces their willingness to fund colonization. Development also reduces the value of farm labor and so reduces the willingness of migrants to settle in a periphery. Together, economic development shifts states from a *colonizing equilibrium* characterized by both territorial expansionism and pliant settlers to a *decolonizing equilibrium* characterized by little territorial expansionism and "choosy and ungrateful" settlers.

Two key implications follow. First, developed states should be less likely to engage in colonization. Without the power to manipulate the direction of migration, policymakers in developed states must either forgo contested frontiers or use other strategies to mollify restive minorities. Second, those developed states that *do* nonetheless seek to colonize frontier areas face a conflict of interest with individual settlers. Middle- and high-income states should therefore be less effective at colonizing frontier areas relative to their

TABLE 2.2. Hypotheses explaining the incidence of settler colonialism.

Variation across countries
H1: Settler colonialism and ethnic cleansing tend to occur in less developed states
H2: Settler colonialism and ethnic cleansing tend to occur in territorially insecure states
H3: As states develop, they lose the power to settle frontier regions

Variation across ethnic groups
H4: States tend to colonize minorities in contested border zones
H5: States tend to colonize and cleanse fifth column and rebellious minorities

Variation across space
H6: Within contested areas, states tend to colonize and cleanse resource-rich areas
H7: Within contested areas, states tend to colonize and cleanse non-natural border areas

less developed counterparts. They will have to pay much more in order to colonize much less.

Table 2.2 summarizes these and other hypotheses above.

Alternative Explanations

Understanding colonization as a transitional phase in state building prior to modernization is not the conventional wisdom. As discussed in the previous chapter, leading theories—drawing on Marx and Engels—tend to explain colonization with reference to elite interests in land accumulation. Other perspectives on state violence against indigenes also exist, however, and can be summarized as: (i) institutional and (ii) ideational.[60] It is worth briefly digressing from my argument in order to understand these alternatives.

With respect to political institutions, scholars have suggested that liberal democracies are less likely to engage in settler colonialism and ethnic cleansing (e.g., Rummel 1995; McGarry 1998). For example, McGarry (1998, 624) hypothesizes that "one reason why state-directed movements of ethnic minorities have not occurred in much of western Europe or North America since the nineteenth century is that these countries have usually been centrist liberal democracies" because liberal democracies are less susceptible to capture by political radicals.[61] If regime type does indeed affect the state's propensity to commit violence against minorities, we should expect that a state's propensity to engage in settler colonialism and ethnic cleansing declines after democratization.

Scholars of international relations have also argued that a new norm against violence against civilians emerged in the late twentieth century after the horrors of Rwanda and the Balkans (e.g., Preece 1998; Walling 2000; Gurr

2000; Bannon 2005; Ther 2014). For example, at the turn of the millennium Ted Gurr (2000) famously contended that there has been a marked decline in state violence against minorities in the 1990s due to rising accommodation of minority rights. This norm has been enshrined in statements at the United Nations committing the international community to the protection of vulnerable minorities.[62] If these norms have been broadly effective, then we should expect that ethnic cleansing declined over the late twentieth century.

But the more common approach to understanding settler colonialism, particularly among historians, anthropologists, postcolonial theorists, and sociologists, is ideational/discursive. This approach, unlike Marxist or rationalist approaches to history, does not begin with the assumption that states or leaders act on the basis of "objective" economic or political interests. Rather, scholars in these fields tend to assume that state interests are the product of particular ideas, and so settler colonialism is the result of socio-legal discourses that make indigenous elimination and territorial expansion appear desirable to elites.[63]

One particular set of interrelated ideas, which Lu (2019) calls "Malthusian expansionism," has been identified as important in past settler colonial campaigns. Following the publication of Malthus' *Theory of Population* in 1798, it became widely accepted in Europe that food production was a binding constraint on population growth. To avoid the Malthusian nightmare of overpopulation and mass starvation, officials advocated the creation of new settler colonies beyond Europe that could absorb "excess" population and become new sources of state power.[64]

The idea that a state must have extra land abroad in order to alleviate population pressure at home has indeed been a recurrent feature of settler colonial campaigns. Most notoriously, perhaps, in this vein of thought is the notion of *lebensraum* ("living space"). The idea, popular in Germany in the early twentieth century, asserted that the German people needed overseas colonies and more land in eastern Europe in order to reduce internal overpopulation and, ultimately, increase German national power. Based on the prevalence of this kind of discourse among Japanese officials during the Meiji era, Lu (2019, 10) contends that Malthusian expansionism "lies at the center of the logic of settler colonialism in the modern era." The postmodern turn has meant that historians today tend to explain settler colonialism with reference to these rationalizing discourses rather than structural factors like population density.

The issues with discursive explanations for settler colonialism are twofold. First, discourses should not be treated as *causa sui*.[65] It is true that policymakers have sometimes justified settler colonialism through fear of "overpopulation" and by emphasizing that territorial expansion is central to state power. And it is also no doubt true that, as Snyder (1991, 6) puts it, "imperial overexpansion correlates closely with the prevalence of these concepts in a state's discourse on national security." But correlation is not causation. A full theory must also ask: why were expansionist ideas appealing to officials in some countries and not in others?

For instance, to account for why officials were so committed to expansion in interwar Japan and Germany but less so in Britain and the United States, Snyder (1991, 49-55) emphasizes that Japan and Germany were both authoritarian states. Democracy, Snyder argues, presents checks on concentrated interests that promote territorial expansion at the expense of all other objectives, as well as allowing for the free diffusion of information that can dispel inaccurate myths (such as land being the key to power in the modern era). In this sense, a rereading of Snyder's framework indicates that the underlying cause of imperialism is actually autocracy, and discourse the "mere" causal mechanism.

Similarly, to account for why the German colonial state engaged in violence against some minorities and not others, Steinmetz (2008, 590) emphasizes the importance of racial ideologies and that "at the moment of imperialist conquest, a plurality of possible framings were available for characterizing the colonized." But to account for variation in official policies toward indigenous peoples across the German Empire, Steinmetz has to appeal to other factors. Consistent with my framework, he finds that German perceptions of the colonized were shaped by indigenous actions (rebellions or collaboration) and geopolitics (whether indigenes were co-ethnics with an ally or enemy state).[66] So, racist German discourses that represented particular ethnic groups as threatening and requiring elimination were not constructed in a vacuum. Rather, elite ideas are malleable and are shaped in systematic ways by conflict. In other words, even theories that take the causal importance of ideas seriously still rely on structural factors—such as regime type or indigenous rebellion—to explain why some ideas resonate and take hold.

Second, because settlers have their own interests and agency, we cannot solely explain settler colonialism with reference to the discourses of elites. As I have emphasized, the metropole may have little control over the actions of settlers on the ground, precisely because metropolitan ideas may not be aligned with the economic interests of individual settlers. And it is ultimately the decision of settlers to comply or not with metropolitan directives that proves decisive.

Reconstructing elite reasoning remains extremely important for understanding when and why states shift toward encouraging the colonization of frontier areas, and will be often be drawn upon in this book to judge whether particular instances of mass migration constitute state policy. But to most parsimoniously explain variation in settler colonialism across different contexts, I abstract away from discourse and instead focus on the structural factors that make colonization an expedient and effective tool for state building generally. Elite ideas may still matter at the margin. But competitive state building, modernization, and the changing value of frontier land to settlers are central to understanding the rise and fall of settler colonialism around the world.

Conclusion

In 1848, Karl Marx and Friedrich Engels published their landmark *The Communist Manifesto*. One of Marx and Engels' most enduring theses is that European colonization was driven by the desire of its mercantile class to secure new resources for trade. As they put it:

> The need of a constantly expanding market for its product chases the bourgeoisie over the whole surface of the globe. It must nestle everywhere, settle everywhere, establish connexions everywhere.

Drawing on Marx and Engels, social scientists continue to explain settler colonialism with reference to elite interests in securing land for commercial agriculture (e.g., Wolfe 1999; Veracini 2010; Scott 2009; Brown 2014; Coulthard 2014; Hirano 2015; Glenn 2015; Lloyd and Wolfe 2016). But teleologies like the "logic of elimination" or the "last enclosure" do not account for the costs of colonization to the metropole and so overpredict its occurrence. As a process that creates conflict and displaces indigenous labor, settler colonialism is far from necessarily an effective strategy for economic exploitation. Settler colonialism is always the exception and never the rule.

In this chapter, I sought to place the study of colonial history on a more solid theoretical footing by carefully specifying the conditions under which colonization is likely to be chosen by the metropole as the best strategy for engaging with indigenous peoples. The foundational move I made was to clearly distinguish between the interests of states and settlers. Following the influential works of Patrick Wolfe, it has been common in studies of settler colonialism to attribute a collective agency to settler colonies, as if states were persons. But colonization can occur in the absence of, or even contrary to, state directives. And, even when they do operate with a "logic of elimination," states are far from omnipotent; as settlers have their own interests, state-sponsored colonization schemes frequently fail. Settler colonialism is fundamentally a process of migration—a phenomenon over which states exert imperfect control.

I theorized that cases of "settler-led colonization," like Australia, the United States, and Rhodesia, occur largely in response to the private economic interests of settlers. Settlers respond to both push factors, like population pressure, and pull factors, like the presence of valuable resources or easily alienated land, by coercively settling frontier regions. In these cases, the metropole is faced with trying to balance territorial over-extension and frontier war with the prospect of settler independence. So, cases of settler-led colonization are generally characterized by a logic of strategic fatalism, as policymakers license the eliminatory actions of their colonists in a laissez-faire way.

On the other hand, in cases of what I call "state-led colonization" such as Greece's colonization of Macedonia and Indonesia's colonization of West Papua, the metropole determines the areas that are to be settled. Settlement is but one of a number of strategies that the metropole can use to secure control over an ethnically diverse frontier. Given the trade-off between the immediate security benefits of colonization and its economic cost, I theorized that settling a frontier would only be an appealing policy choice when the metropole faces a pressing threat. Officials would tend to cleanse and settle areas where state control is most contested: porous border zones and areas populated by fifth column and rebellious minorities. This is particularly the case if a rebellious minority has foreign support or natural resources which, by reducing the scope for a bargain over autonomy, increases the likelihood of coercion.

But even when states do elect to become colonizers, colonization schemes are only successful when they align with the material interests of individual migrants. In developed countries the value of land to potential settlers is negligible, meaning that settlers are less likely to spontaneously emigrate to frontier regions and that any colonization schemes are much less likely to be successful. Modernization in the core closes the frontier.

My framework has the strength of parsimoniously explaining the history of colonization at multiple levels: across different countries, across different time periods, across different indigenous groups, and across different areas. The proof of any theory is, however, in the data pudding. So, let us now see how well the theory can make sense of past colonization projects in different areas of the world.

3

Hit the Road, Jakarta: Indonesia's Colonization of West Papua

BETWEEN 1972 and 1999, the proportion of the Indonesian province of West Papua (*Irian Jaya*) that was Muslim rose from 6 to 21%. This rapid demographic shift was largely the result of a central government policy of "transmigration," which relocated approximately 300,000 people to West Papua in less than thirty years[1]—the vast majority of whom were landless Muslims from the island of Java, attracted by the promise of free land and transport by the Indonesian government.

Indonesia's settlement projects in West Papua have been the subject of substantial debate. On the one hand, particularly in activist circles, it is commonly asserted that transmigration has been used strategically by the Indonesian state to "Javanize" West Papua. By populating restive areas of West Papua with Javanese settlers, Jakarta has arguably prevented the secession of West Papua and permanently secured control over West Papua's rich resource base (e.g., Budiardjo 1986; Fearnside 1997; Webster 2001; King 2004; Singh 2017).

Yet, beyond suggestive evidence for an underlying geopolitical motive, like the clustering of transmigrant sites near resource-rich areas, harder evidence has proven difficult to come by. Official Indonesian sources maintain that the primary purpose of transmigration is to foster development and redistribute farmers from land-scarce Java to less densely populated outer islands (Indonesia, Ministry of Transmigration Staff, 1991). And factors such as soil quality and land availability have undeniably also played a central role in the selection of transmigrant sites within targeted localities (e.g., Whitten et al. 1987; Manning and Rumbiak 1989; Bazzi et al. 2016). As such, many scholars remain skeptical of an underlying geopolitical motive to Indonesian transmigration. For example, Barter and Côté (2015, 71) contend that the "fact that almost all transmigrants were resettled in relatively peaceful areas challenges the claim that transmigration focused specifically on trouble spots in an effort to dilute rebellion."

The source of this ongoing dissensus is the paucity of data on Indonesian transmigration. If we had detailed data on the timing and location of Indonesian transmigration in restive areas like West Papua, we would be able to test competing explanations for the incidence of state-sponsored migration. However, given its political sensitivity, data on transmigration is difficult to obtain—indeed, one recent study on West Papua asserted that "it is impossible to locate accurate official statistics on the number of transmigrants" (Anderson, 2015, 13).

These data challenges are, fortunately, overstated. In this chapter I draw on an unexplored trove of internal government documents to reconstruct a panel of all Indonesian transmigration, ethnic cleansing, and religious composition change in each regency of West Papua between 1964 and 1999—the first and last years that West Papua was subject to transmigration. I find, consistent with the claims made by West Papuan activists, that Indonesian settler colonialism in West Papua over the twentieth century was primarily driven by the twin logic of resource extraction and territorial consolidation. I show that there was very little transmigration to West Papua until an aborted uprising by West Papuan insurgents in 1984. Exploiting the timing of this uprising and using statistical methods to rule out alternative explanations, I show that Indonesia then ethnically cleansed and settled its most porous borderlands with Papua New Guinea in order to prevent cross-border insurgent activity. Together, the timing and location of Indonesian colonization patterns provide strong evidence that transmigration has indeed been used by the Indonesian state to create a demographic *cordon sanitaire* with Papua New Guinea and thereby defeat Papuan insurgents.

Yet, not all transmigrants in West Papua were resettled to border areas controlled by insurgents; approximately half of all transmigrants in West Papua were resettled to areas far from the border. To credibly demonstrate that transmigration has also been used to secure control over West Papua's natural resources, I leverage a "natural experiment" of history—the discovery of the largest gold deposit in the world, the Grasberg mine, in the late twentieth century. I show that there was no transmigration to the area around Grasberg prior to the mine's opening in 1990. However, I show that immediately after 1990 there was a substantial increase in transmigrant settlement and ethnic cleansing of indigenous Papuans in the area around the mine. Settler colonialism was used to secure a pliant workforce in the area around Grasberg and prevent indigenous Papuans from accessing the mine. By reconstructing the timing and location of all state-sponsored migration in West Papua over the late twentieth century, I provide the strongest evidence to date that Indonesia's colonization of West Papua has indeed been driven by the twin goals of resource extraction and coercive state building.

The Origins of Settler Colonialism in West Papua

In order to understand the logic of settler colonialism in West Papua, it is important to first understand how territorial conflict emerged there over decades of shifting constellations of political authority. West Papuans were first conquered belatedly. The island of New Guinea is geographically defined by its low-lying swamps, remote highlands, and fast-moving rivers. Given its impassibility, West Papua[2] promised little in the way of riches to Europeans who first explored the area during the sixteenth and seventeenth centuries. On the other hand, the island of Java, a fertile, easily navigable island perfectly suited to rice cultivation, soon became the jewel in the crown of the Dutch East Indies Company. Eager to protect the eastern approach to Java from rival European powers, the Netherlands claimed the western half of New Guinea from 141 degrees east longitude in 1828.

Having achieved their goal of strategic denial, the Dutch exercised only notional control over West Papua over the nineteenth century. West Papua was at the economic, political, and geographic margins of the Dutch colonial state centered in Java. Government extended to only selected settlements along the coast. Indeed, even by the 1930s, fewer than 200 Europeans lived in West Papua the bulk of whom were missionaries. Christian missions set up the first schools and hospitals across the island. By the mid-twentieth century, Catholic and Protestant missionaries had together converted much of the indigenous population to Christianity.

World War II (1939–45), however, fundamentally altered the political dynamics of the Asia-Pacific. Japan's brief takeover of the Dutch East Indies as it expanded southward toward Australia provided an opening to Indonesian nationalists such as Sukarno who quickly began to replace the Indies Dutch in political leadership. With the assistance of US soldiers, the Netherlands managed to reestablish military control over the East Indies after the war's conclusion. However, colonial hegemony was irreparably lost. Sukarno declared the independence of Indonesia two days after the surrender of the

Japanese emperor on 17 August 1945. A bitter civil war subsequently dragged on between Indonesian nationalists and the colonial state until the Netherlands, under international pressure, ceded the independence of Indonesia in 1949.

The peace agreement between Indonesia and the Netherlands, however, contained a poison pill. The Netherlands ceded control over the entirety of the East Indies with the singular exception of West Papua. The reasons were twofold. First, Europeans viewed Papuans as racially distinct from the rest of the archipelago. Indigenous Papuans are Melanesian, meaning they are stereotypically associated with dark skin and curly hair. Papuans have historically been seen as racially distinct from other Indonesians, who are stereotypically associated with straight hair and fair skin. Second, the Netherlands sought to prevent a total victory for Indonesian nationalists and to retain a regional haven for Dutch settlers in the rest of the archipelago, their mixed-race descendants, and other supporters. The racial distinctiveness of Papuans became a useful justification for the Dutch to retain a political foothold in the region.

Indonesian independence in 1949 transformed West Papua from a backwater into the very center of Dutch presence in southeast Asia. The new Indonesian state, however, retained a territorial claim over West Papua. Eager to legitimate their tenure in the eyes of the international community, the Netherlands began to heavily invest in education, health, and infrastructure on the island. The Dutch also began the aggressive recruitment of newly educated Papuans into the colonial bureaucracy as part of a broader policy of "Papuanization." By 1961, there were over 16,000 Papuans employed in wage labor and 9,000 in government service (McGibbon, 2004). A popularly elected national council even took office from 1960 in preparation for self-government. The 1950s thus represented a period of rapid development in West Papua and led to the emergence of an educated and politically active indigenous elite.

Indonesian nationalists led by Sukarno viewed these developments with rising frustration. Negotiations with the Netherlands over the status of West Papua at the United Nations failed and so, over the course of the 1950s, Indonesia retaliated by nationalizing Dutch companies and expelling hundreds of thousands of Indies Dutch from the archipelago. In December 1961, Sukarno escalated the territorial dispute by establishing a People's Triple Command (Trikora)—a military command with the sole objective of taking over West Papua by force by January 1963. A number of skirmishes between the Dutch and Indonesian militaries ensued over the course of 1962. The Netherlands' allies in the region, Australia and the United States, were chiefly concerned with preventing Indonesia from falling further into the orbit of the USSR. Not wishing to see Indonesia suffer a politically disastrous defeat by a NATO power, they abandoned their support for the Netherlands. Internationally isolated, the Netherlands signed an agreement in New York in 1962, transferring sovereignty of West Papua to Indonesia in 1963.

So began Indonesian rule in West Papua. As part of the New York agreement, Indonesia had formally committed to holding a popular plebiscite or Act of Free Choice in 1969 to determine whether West Papuans would prefer self-determination or to remain part of Indonesia. The period between 1963 and 1969 was an uneasy one, defined by preparations for the Act of Free Choice. Ultimately, rather than provide a vote to the some 800,000 indigenous Papuans, the Indonesian government hand-picked approximately 1,000 Papuan leaders to declare their choice publicly in the presence of Indonesian soldiers. Perhaps unsurprisingly, the vote in 1969 was unanimous in favor of accession to Indonesia. West Papuan independence had been sacrificed at the altar of Cold War geopolitics.

Yet, Indonesia's political triumph in 1969 served only to mask more deep-seated issues in West Papua. Without the substantial investment provided by the Dutch, previously abundant goods and services had become scarce in West Papua over the 1960s (Hastings, 1969). Prior to the vote, there was also an influx of new officials from Java to replace indigenous Papuans—whose loyalties were politically suspect—in the civil service (McGibbon, 2004). The de-Papuanization of the state in the 1960s sowed the seeds for lasting disillusionment toward Indonesia among educated Papuans. Indonesia inherited a province in 1969 characterized by economic decline, extremely low state capacity in highland areas, political repression, and deep-seated mistrust toward the state amongst the indigenous elite. The conditions were ripe for an insurgency. A number of indigenous Papuans had actually first launched attacks on Indonesian garrisons in 1965. Disparate insurgent groups subsequently coalesced into the umbrella Free Papua Movement (OPM), which launched a number of low-level attacks against Indonesian soldiers throughout the 1970s.

Papua New Guinean (PNG) independence in 1975 from Australia provided a significant boost to the nascent Papuan insurgency. Not only did West Papuans now have a symbolic model for Melanesian self-government to draw upon, but OPM now had free reign in the long and porous borderland between PNG and West Papua. Australia, keen to maintain good relations with anti-Communist Indonesia, had been quite effective at using its military force to prevent OPM from operating and recruiting in Papua New Guinea before 1975. However, after independence, Papua New Guinean forces had almost no effective presence in the borderland. As King (2004, 179) summarized, "with the defence force more or less out of the picture . . . the OPM has had a fairly free hand in the PNG border region." OPM guerillas could use the Papua New Guinea borderland as an extended sanctuary from which they could resupply and recruit Papuan insurgents for attacks across the border.

Ongoing skirmishes between OPM and the Indonesian military along the border would come to a head in early 1984. A number of OPM factions had joined forces during a covert meeting in the Papua New Guinea capital, Port Moresby, in April 1983. In a December meeting of that same year, the newly unified OPM planned a widespread uprising for February 1984. As Elmslie (2002, 45) put it, this "was to prove the largest and most concerted operation ever undertaken by OPM." The plan involved mass Papuan defections from the Indonesian military and the capture of the regional capital, Jayapura. The uprising began when the OPM raised the West Papuan flag in front of the regional assembly on February 13. In the days that followed, over 100 Papuan members of the Indonesian military did ultimately defect. The defectors broke into the arms depot of the local military batallion and seized automatic rifles, ammunition and sub-machine guns (Osborne, 1985, 100). Heavy fighting ensued in the area around Jayapura. However, the military coup failed.[3]

Stunned by the organizational sophistication of OPM and the defection of its own soldiers, Jakarta escalated repression in West Papua after 1984. The governor of West Papua that year dramatically called for up to 12 million new, "straight-haired" settlers to replace "curly-haired" indigenous Papuans (Gietzelt, 1989).[4] And after 1984, Indonesia indeed drastically scaled up transmigration to West Papua (Figure 3.1).

Transmigration refers to a policy of resettlement that originated in the Dutch colonial state. The Indonesian archipelago is characterized by substantial variation in population density. Its geographic core (Java-Madura-Bali) is highly suitable for rice cultivation and is densely populated, and its periphery (Borneo-Sumatra-Papua) is far less fertile and is very scarcely populated. For example, although Madura-Bali-Java make up only approximately 10% of Indonesia's landmass, they contain 90% of its entire population (Osborne, 1985, 128).

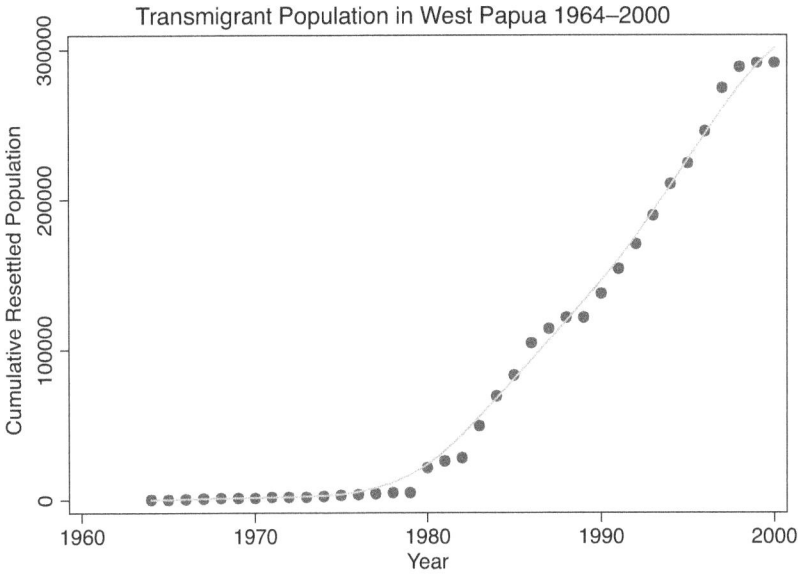

FIGURE 3.1. The total population resettled to West Papua as part
of the transmigration program (1964–2000).

The Dutch colonial policy of sending landless Javanese to the outer islands
to increase the amount of land under cultivation was repurposed by the post-
colonial state as a strategy for knitting the fractious new Indonesian nation
together. After independence, Sukarno and his successor Suharto increased
dramatically the amount of transmigration.[5] In Java and other core islands, the
state widely advertised free plots of land and free transportation to the outer
islands. Those who elected to resettle would receive title to 3.5 hectares of
land, agricultural training, and subsidized income support over their first year.
Sukarno's initial plans in 1949 would have redistributed over 48 million people from the core. The costs involved necessitated a reduction in scale but, by
1990, over five million people had indeed been moved to Indonesia's peripheral islands (Fearnside, 1997). And the evidence suggests that transmigration
has been an effective tool for nation-building—for instance, areas of Indonesia settled by transmigrants are characterized by substantially more fluency in
the Indonesian national language today (Bazzi et al., forthcoming).

Preventing the secession of the outer islands through transmigration was
a critical national imperative for material—as much as ideological—reasons.
As then Vice President B. J. Habibie emphasized in 1992, "the future of our

nation is very much dependent on our ability to exploit the potential of *Irian Jaya*" (Elmslie, 2002, 73). The Indonesian state was desperately strapped of revenue for most of the twentieth century. The outer islands, richly endowed with timber, oil, gold, and copper, have been a financial boon to the state. The main source of revenue from West Papua has been from mining. In 1967, President Suharto signed a contract with the American mining company, Freeport McMoRan, to explore the potentially rich copper and gold resources in the remote Cartensz Range. The first-discovered gold deposit proved disappointing and was largely depleted by the mid-1980s. In 1988, however, Freeport found their El Dorado—the Grasberg reserve, which is the world's largest known deposit of gold and second largest deposit of copper. The mine opened for operation in 1990 and Freeport quickly became the country's largest taxpayer. By the mid-1990s, the mine was responsible for over 50% of West Papua's gross domestic regional product (GDRP) and 90% of its export revenue, with annual output in the billions of dollars (Leith, 2002).

Such revenues have assisted with Jakarta's finances. Freeport alone provided over $1.6 billion in direct payments to Jakarta in the decade between 1991 and 2000 (Leith, 2002, 70). But the diffuse financial interest of the Indonesian state in preventing West Papua's secession was arguably less important than the financial interests of its elites. President Suharto was the most egregious kleptocrat in the world in the late twentieth century according to Transparency International (2004), which estimated that he looted some US $15–35 billion over his tenure. And Grasberg, as the largest mine in Indonesia, was a prime target for Suharto's avarice. Freeport's financial affairs over the 1990s reveal a dizzying web of payouts to many of Indonesia's most influential figures. For instance, two months after Suharto was forced to resign in 1998, an Indonesian periodical revealed that Freeport had paid at least $50 million dollars to the president and his notorious charities in "tribute" over the preceding seven years (Leith, 2002, 90). Freeport had also gifted approximately 5.5% of its shares or some $160 million US dollars to prominent Indonesian businessman Aburizal Bakrie in 1992, who was a member of Suharto's notorious "Team 10" (Leith, 2002, 79). In total, between 1991 and 1997, Freeport provided some $673 million in financial assistance to three Indonesians with close ties to Suharto or his ministers.[6]

Grasberg has also been a financial boon to the Indonesian military. As McCulloch (2003, 112) details, Grasberg "is viewed by the military as a lucrative business venture from which they have 'demanded'—quite successfully— a 'share' of the profits." Freeport maintained (and still maintains) strong financial ties with the security forces in West Papua (Global Witness, 2005). In exchange for "protection," Freeport has supported a small army in and around Grasberg. These maintenance costs amounted to tens of millions of US dollars annually in the early 2000s (Ballard and Banks, 2003, 169). Retaining West Papua's mineral wealth generally and Grasberg specifically has been a key contributor to Indonesia's hard line on secession.

Given the ongoing secessionist conflict and the discovery of the lucrative Grasberg mine, West Papua was the largest single provincial target for Indonesian transmigration throughout the late 1980s and 1990s. However, transmigration to West Papua ceased abruptly in the late 1990s. Indonesia was hit hard by the Asian financial crisis of 1997. Facing widespread protest and a collapsing currency, Suharto was unable to maintain the support of the military. Following his resignation, Indonesia liberalized substantially and it held its first free and fair elections in 1999. Given the unpopularity of transmigration, provincial governments in the outer islands across Indonesia took advantage of this political opening to lobby for an end to mass resettlement (King, 2004). By 2000, formal transmigration to West Papua had ceased.

Economic migration to West Papua from the rest of Indonesia, however, continued unabated into the new millenium. Throughout the 1990s, the state had complemented transmigration with a broader suite of policies designed to encourage economic migration to West Papua. The "Go East" program led to ambitious expansion in roads, airports, hotel, and tourism infrastructure across the province (McGibbon, 2004). Many economic migrants followed, and Papua continued to receive substantial government infrastructure investment throughout the 2000s. Unlike transmigration, which was predominantly rural, economic migration during the 1990s and 2000s was directed toward West Papua's urban centers and migrants tended not to come from Java but from Sulawesi (Barter and Côté, 2015). As a result of substantial economic migration and the movement of transmigrants into towns, West Papua today is characterized by a demographic division that maps neatly onto a geographic division. Its highland and rural areas remain predominantly Papuan whereas its towns and industry are settler dominated.

Uncovering the Logic of Indonesian Transmigration

Recall that in the theory chapter I predicted generally that the *timing* of colonization projects is shaped by the onset of violent conflict and the *location* of colonization is shaped by the location of valuable natural resources and

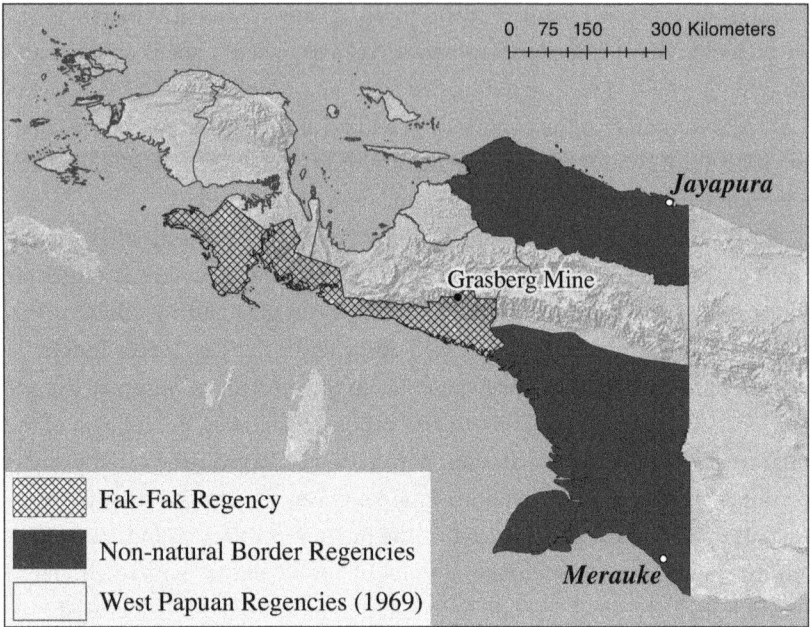

FIGURE 3.2. The province of West Papua (*Irian Jaya*), its non-natural border regencies with Papua New Guinea, and the location of the Grasberg mine in Fak-Fak regency.

non-natural borders. States in the midst of territorial conflict generally seek to shore up control over porous, low-lying land border areas as well as areas that contain resource wealth. But do patterns of Indonesian settler colonialism in West Papua actually reflect the importance of these factors? Translated to this context, the 1984 Jayapura uprising constitutes a key escalation of the secessionist threat in West Papua. The PNG-Indonesia border is highly mountainous in the middle of the island but is otherwise low-lying. The two regencies of Jayapura and Merauke share this low-lying and non-natural border with PNG, and so I hypothesize that transmigration and the ethnic cleansing of indigenous Papuans were focused on these regencies after the 1984 uprising (Figure 3.2).

The discovery and opening of the Grasberg mine in 1990 also provides a uniquely powerful setting to test whether Indonesian colonization has been shaped by the presence of valuable natural resources. So, second, I hypothesize that transmigration was focused on the area around the Grasberg mine after 1990. Grasberg and the major mining town immediately south of the mine, Timika, are both located in Fak-Fak regency (Figure 3.2).

To recover the history of Indonesian colonization, I compiled a new panel dataset capturing all transmigration and demographic change in West Papua's nine regencies between 1964 and 1999—the period in which West Papua was subject to state-sponsored transmigration. These data have never been compiled before and are based on the internal statistical yearbooks for West Papua.[7]

These yearbooks contain information on both transmigration numbers and the religious composition of each regency in each year. These data were intended for internal use alone.[8] Given its political sensitivity, publication of statistical data on religion and ethnicity was prohibited in Indonesia during the Suharto and Sukarno regimes (Ananta, Utami, and Handayani, 2016). Data on transmigration numbers is also extremely sensitive. As a further complication, the data on transmigrant numbers report only the total number of *new* settlers in each regency in each year. So, only by compiling the entire set of yearbooks between 1964 and 1999 are we able to calculate the total number of transmigrants resettled to West Papua over the twentieth century. From these data, I find that the total number of transmigrants resettled to West Papua was 297,026.

These data constitute the best available data on historical population changes in West Papua and, because they were never intended for public release, there is little evidence of deliberate manipulation.[9] For example, the data reflect politically sensitive changes in population such as the precipitous fall in the indigenous Papuan population in the West Papuan borderland following the Indonesian military's ethnic cleansing campaign in 1984, and its estimates of religious composition are consistent with publicly available data on ethnicity collected after the fall of the New Order in 1998.

The main outcomes of interest are the number of transmigrants and the proportion of the population that is Muslim in each year. As indigenous Papuans are 96% Christian (McGibbon, 2004) and over 95% of transmigrants to Papua were Muslim,[10] the percentage of the population that is Muslim is a useful proxy for the demographic predominance of settlers relative to indigenous Papuans.[11]

Transmigration was controlled by the Indonesian state and its incidence therefore clearly reflects state intentions. But by also measuring the change in the proportion of Muslims in West Papua, I am also capturing the incidence of "spontaneous" or economic migration to West Papua from the rest of Muslim-majority Indonesia. More than half of the settler population in West Papua today are actually spontaneous migrants not transmigrants (Barter and

Côté, 2015), meaning that they were not given free transportation, nor were they recorded as part the transmigration program. Yet, we should be wary of simply presuming that spontaneous migration is apolitical. Transmigration, by creating new infrastructure and investment in frontier lands, begins a process of chain migration that the relatives and friends of initial transmigrants often follow to farm the newly profitable land immediately around the transmigration sites (Arndt, 1984). For this reason, Hardjono (1977, 30) finds in her landmark study that "the ultimate goal in transmigration is to set up a flow of 'spontaneous' migrants" who will more comprehensively settle targeted areas at no additional cost to the state. Spontaneous migration was an intentional indirect effect of state-sponsored transmigration.

Moreover, not all settler colonialism occurs through the provision of free land—rather, as detailed in the previous chapter, states often seek to colonize contested regions indirectly by investing heavily in new infrastructure and encouraging labor and capital to relocate to the periphery. Consistent with this logic, the Indonesian government has sought to encourage economic migration to West Papua through programs such as the Go East program of the 1990s. By examining patterns of change in the proportion of Muslims, we are therefore usefully capturing both transmigration and "spontaneous," but nonetheless political, migration to West Papua. In any case, I present my results using both the proportion of Muslims and transmigrant numbers alone. Finally, to measure the incidence of ethnic cleansing, I also measure the change in the number of non-Muslims in each regency in every year.

Patterns of Indonesian Settler Colonialism

Figure 3.3 illustrates the rise in Muslim demographic predominance between 1972 and 1999[12] as well as the geocoded locations of Indonesian transmigration sites. As is immediately apparent, the areas with both the greatest increase in Muslim predominance and the largest amount of transmigration are the two non-natural border regencies of Jayapura and Merauke. Otherwise, transmigration sites tend to be located around the petroleum-rich Cenderawasih Bay and the town of Timika south of the Grasberg mine. This provides suggestive evidence that Indonesian colonization has indeed been driven in part by the imperatives of securing natural resources and securing a demographic *cordon sanitaire* with Papua New Guinea.

But the timing of this demographic shift in the borderland is much more revealing. If we compare patterns of demographic change in the two

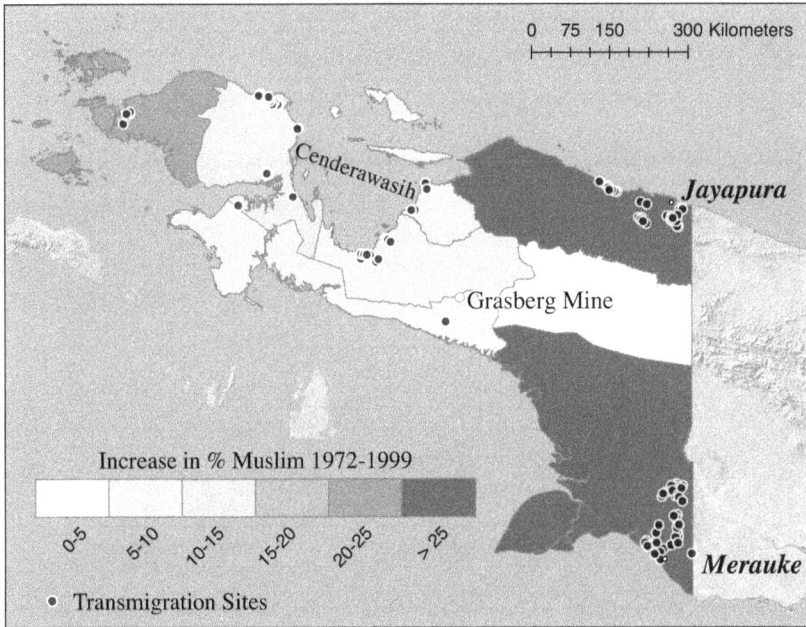

FIGURE 3.3. The province of West Papua (*Irian Jaya*), its transmigration sites, and the increase in the percent of the population that is Muslim by regency (1972–1999).

non-natural border regencies with the rest of West Papua over time we can see that actually, prior to 1984, Jayapura and Merauke looked very much like the rest of the province—they experienced only small increases in Muslim demographic predominance in the decade prior to 1984 (Figure 3.4). However, after the uprising of 1984, the percentage of Muslims in West Papua's non-natural borderland jumped precipitously from 15% to 25% and continued to rise steadily. Statistical estimations bear out the disproportionate rise in Muslim demographic predominance in Merauke and Jayapura after 1984 relative to the rest of West Papua (Table 3.1 column 5).

This precipitous rise in Muslim presence after 1984 was driven by both the ethnic cleansing of indigenous Papuans and a substantial rise in transmigration to Jayapura and Merauke. The data reveal that, in total, approximately 13,000 indigenous Papuans were displaced in each regency as a result of this ethnic cleansing campaign—over 2% of the entire indigenous population of West Papua (Table 3.1, column 3).[13] The motto of the Indonesian military at the time was "let the rats run into the jungle so that chickens can breed in the coop" (Anderson, 2015, 15)—referring to the cleansing of indigenous

Demographic change in West Papua and the 1984 uprising

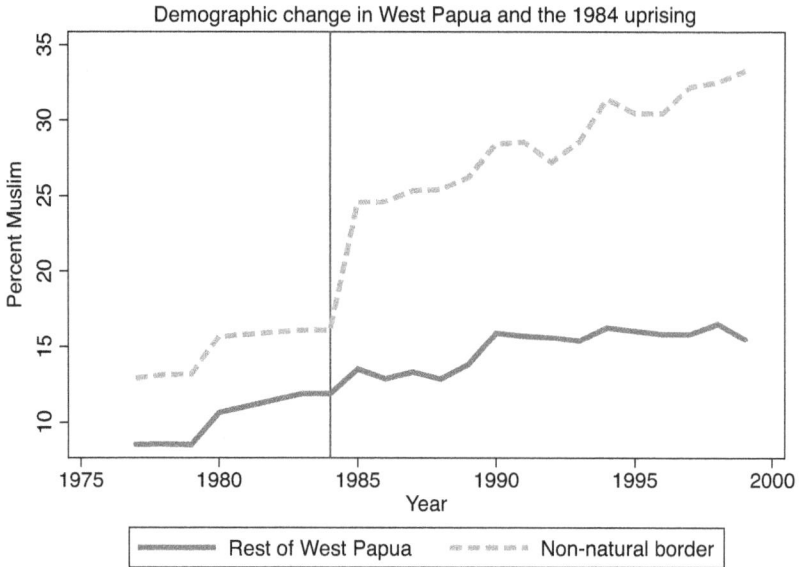

FIGURE 3.4. The change in Muslim predominance within the two non-natural border regencies (dashed) and the rest of West Papua (solid) (1972–1999).

Papuans in order to make way for new migrants. The favored tactic for OPM was "curtain of the masses" (*tirai massa*) in which guerrillas would launch attacks on Indonesian soldiers and subsequently melt back into the population (Osborne, 1985, 77). Unable to distinguish between combatants and non-combatants, Indonesian troops carried out a number of brutal clearance operations (*operasi turun*) following the February 1984 uprising to remove indigenous Papuans from the borderland. For example, between April 18 and April 20, Indonesian soldiers entered the villages of Woropko and Tinika, close to the Papua New Guinea border, and indiscriminately shot people hiding in the church and on school grounds. The villages were emptied of people and their domestic animals killed in a scorched earth policy designed to deter any future return (International Commission of Jurists, 1985, 37).

These clearance operations paved the way for Indonesia to settle the borderland with new, non-Papuan, and so politically "loyal," migrants. The 1984 uprising is estimated to have led to an additional 25% increase in transmigration to Merauke and Jayapura regencies (Table 3.1, column 1), whilst it had no effect on transmigration to the rest of West Papua. The strategic logic of the clearance operations was clear to its victims at the time. For example, the village of Ninati near the border was cleared of its some 700 residents following

TABLE 3.1. Models 1, 3, and 5 are regency-level difference-in-differences specifications where secessionist conflict (the years after 1984) is interacted with regency contiguity with a non-natural border (Merauke and Jayapura). Models 2, 4, and 6 examine demographic change in all the regencies of West Papua relative to Fak-Fak regency in the years after the Grasberg mine opened (1990–). Standard errors are clustered at the regency level using Arellano's covariance matrix.

	Log transmigration		Non-Muslim pop.		Percent Muslim	
	(1)	(2)	(3)	(4)	(5)	(6)
Secessionist conflict (1984–)	0.03 (0.02)		1818 (1607)		1.59 (1.00)	
Secessionist conflict: Non-natural border	0.25*** (0.07)		−13588*** (4702)		6.64*** (2.15)	
Grasberg mine open (1990–)		0.08*** (0.03)		2363** (1184)		2.22*** (0.77)
Grasberg mine open (1990–): Fak-Fak		0.63*** (0.03)		−10364*** (1185)		2.36*** (0.76)
First Differences	Yes	Yes	Yes	Yes	Yes	Yes
Regencies	9	9	9	9	9	9
Observations	333	333	198	198	198	198

Note: $^{*}p < .1$; $^{**}p < .05$; $^{***}p < .01$.

indiscriminate shooting by the Indonesian military on April 13. As a panel of Australian jurists who conducted interviews with these refugees in PNG in 1985 summarized:

> The people [from Ninati] related the troubles to the February flag-raising in Jayapura . . . [and] there was a rumour that Javanese transmigrants were to move into the now empty villages. (International Commission of Jurists, 1985, 39)

In essence, the data merely confirm that this rumour was very well founded. After clearing the border zone of indigenous Papuans, Indonesia used transmigration to create a demographic bulwark along the border with Papua New Guinea.

Although the Indonesian state was clearly effective at colonizing its border with Papua New Guinea after 1984, we should not presume that the Indonesian state could settle absolutely anywhere at will. Jakarta faced great difficulty in making farms along the border profitable for new migrants as the farms were located in areas far from existing markets and regular transport.[14] Even Salor, a relatively close transmigrant site some 60 kilometers from Merauke, was completely cut off to vehicles from the town during the wet season as the road flooded. This presented a major challenge for the Javanese transmigrants relocated to Salor as rice is harvested during the wet season. The farmers could walk over two days to Merauke to sell their produce but, as they complained to investigative reporter George Monbiot, they could not carry any meaningful quantity of rice to sell (Monbiot, 1989, 29). So in what was actually quite a common phenomenon, most of the transmigrants in Salor had abandoned their plots by the late 1980s and left to become fruit sellers or minibus conductors in Merauke.

These infrastructural challenges were, of course, even greater in the highlands of West Papua. Indeed, these areas simply could not be settled in the first place—sedentary farming is impossible in areas with steep slopes due to erosion. Accordingly, there was almost no transmigration in the highlands of West Papua. For example, the hilly area of Senggi on the Papua New Guinea border south of Jayapura was initially slated to receive almost 10,000 households after 1984. However, the state was forced to ultimately abandon this site after surveys revealed that the area was unsuited to sedentary agriculture (Manning and Rumbiak, 1989, 48). Transmigration along the geopolitically sensitive Papua New Guinea borderland occurred only in the non-natural border areas that could sustain commercially viable agriculture.

In sum, internal statistics reveal that transmigration in the Indonesia-PNG borderland over the twentieth century clearly had a counterinsurgency logic. The substantial rise in Muslim demographic predominance in West Papua's non-natural borderland only occurred after the 1984 uprising and was driven by the tandem expulsion of the indigenous Papuan population and the mass resettlement of Muslim transmigrants who quickly took their place. Indonesia's transmigrant program has been used to defeat insurgents and secure control over West Papua.

Transmigration for Resource Extraction

Yet, not all transmigration occurred in Jayapura and Merauke—approximately half of transmigrants settled elsewhere in West Papua. Between 1980 and 1984, most transmigration was actually directed to the regency of Sorong, the heart of West Papua's oil and gas industry. It is difficult, however, to move

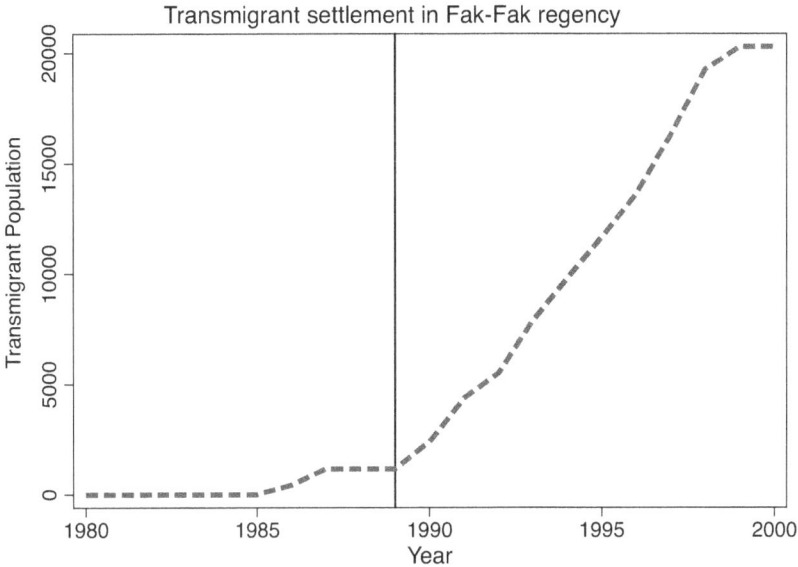

FIGURE 3.5. The total population resettled to Fak-Fak as part of the transmigration program (1980–2000) and the opening of the Grasberg mine in 1990.

beyond suggestive evidence and prove more definitively that Indonesian transmigration has been used to secure control over resources in West Papua. The discovery of the enormous Grasberg gold and copper deposit in the 1980s and the opening of this mine in 1990, however, provides a kind of "natural experiment" to see whether Indonesian transmigration was responsive to the location of valuable natural resources.

The data reveal that, indeed, after the opening of the Grasberg mine in 1990, transmigration to the regency of Fak-Fak increased dramatically (Figure 3.5). There was almost no transmigration to Fak-Fak prior to 1990. However, after the opening of the mine, transmigration to Fak-Fak increased by over 60% (Table 3.1, column 2) and Fak-Fak became one of the leading recipients of transmigration in the whole of Indonesia, receiving almost 20,000 transmigrants in the 1990s alone. Although Fak-Fak was a large regency, the only transmigrant site in Fak-Fak was the site south of the mine (see Figure 3.3). So, all this recorded transmigration in Fak-Fak occurred in the area around Grasberg. Statistical estimations bear out the disproportionate increase in transmigration and Muslim demographic predominance in Fak-Fak after 1990 relative to the rest of West Papua (Table 3.1, columns 2 and 6).

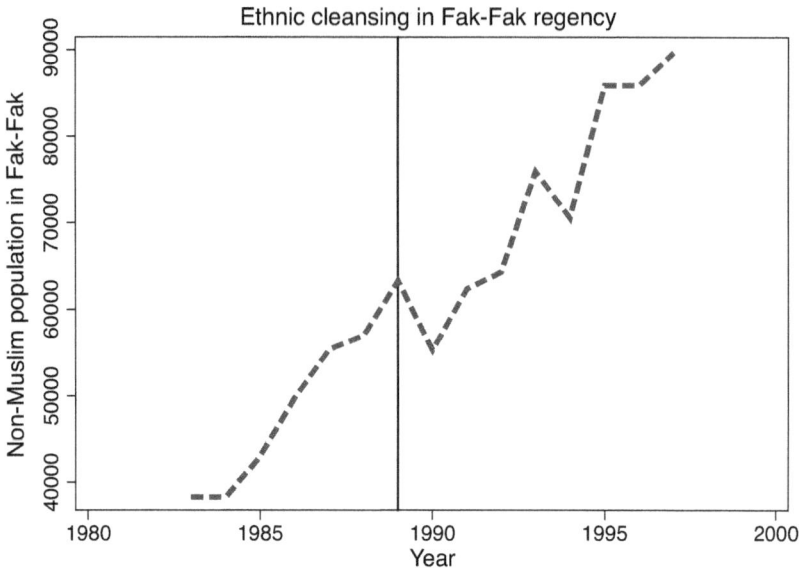

FIGURE 3.6. The total non-Muslim population in Fak-Fak and the opening of the Grasberg mine in 1990.

Transmigration was used to secure a pliant workforce for Freeport and lock potential indigenous saboteurs out of the mine. OPM had notoriously disabled the main Freeport pipeline in 1977. To prevent future attacks, indigenous Papuans were not to access the mine. As one Freeport employee put it, "Freeport was told it must employ staff from other parts of Indonesia. Say, 300 from Menaldo, 300 from Ujung Pandang, 2,899 from Java" (Leith, 2002, 199). Freeport secured a cheap and pliant workforce whereas the Indonesian government secured a loyal population in a site of national importance subject to attacks by minority insurgents. As such, the vast bulk of the workforce at Freeport were settlers—of the 3,500 mine workers at Freeport in 1990, only 20 were indigenous Papuans (ibid.).

The opening of the mine also led to substantial displacement in the surrounding area. Unlike transmigrant settlement data, which we can geolocate to a specific project, we have no ability to know where ethnic cleansing occurred within Fak-Fak. Yet, it is highly suggestive that after 1990, the number of indigenous Papuans in Fak-Fak (as proxied by the non-Muslim population) fell by over 10,000 (Figure 3.6, Table 3.1 column 4). This is much higher than the oft-quoted figure of 400 displaced persons from Freeport McMoRan. The reasons are twofold.

First, to maximize profit, Freeport McMoRan did not bury or dam the waste (tailings) from the mine. Rather, it diverted its tailings—on average over 200,000 tonnes of runoff every day—into local river systems. Less than a year after the mine began operation, these tailings overran the Aikwa River and resulted in mineral waste being disgorged over a 30-square-kilometer area of lowland forest (Mealey, 1996). The opening of the mine irreversibly contaminated local forests, turned once-pristine waterways into turgid swamps, and created a copper-enriched wasteland stretching all the way to the coast.[15] Since the opening of the mine, indigenous Papuans have had to abandon their contaminated hunting and fishing grounds in the area downstream of Grasberg.

Second, the mass contamination led to widespread unrest, which in turn prompted the Indonesian military forces to conduct clearance operations in surrounding villages—killing, detaining, and torturing Papuans suspected of being insurgents (Ballard, 2002). It is difficult to obtain information on violence by the military given that outsiders had almost no access to the area at the time. However, detailed and cross-checked eyewitness reports during the second wave of violence in 1994 (see Figure 3.6) have been carefully recorded by the Australian Council for Overseas Aid (1995).

In one instance, they report that approximately 300 villagers protested against Freeport in the village of Tembagapura[16] on Christmas Day, 1994, and raised the OPM flag. Not long after the demonstration started, the Indonesian military and Freeport security surrounded the villagers and began indiscriminately shooting into the crowd. As the "rebels" fled into the forest, the military began to round up and search nearby villages for suspected participants. For example, the soldiers broke into the congregation of the nearby church in Waa and stopped the Christmas service. Operating with a logic of associative guilt based on ethnicity and proximity, the commander warned the congregation that:

> "It is impossible for those 300 rebels to have been here this morning in Tembagapura and raise the Papuan flag if there was no food supply to them. . . . If we find out there'll be no forgiveness. Don't try to cooperate with those in the forest." (Australian Council for Overseas Aid, 1995, 6)

Seven members of the congregation were then killed or disappeared following the service, and dozens more rounded up in the surrounding area. Those detained were brutally tortured with electric shocks, cut with razor blades, stabbed with knives, and repeatedly beaten until they signed a letter accepting that they had "cooperated" with the rebels.

Although this incident is but one of the few eyewitness reports of violence that have been well documented, it vividly demonstrates how the opening of the mine led to unrest by indigenous Papuans followed by indiscriminate retaliatory violence by the Indonesian military. After 1990, the area around Freeport quickly became the most heavily militarized area in one of the already most heavily militarized provinces in Indonesia (Kirksey, 2012). Many indigenous Papuans have been killed, detained, or forced to flee, contributing to the significant rise in enumerated Muslim predominance in and around Grasberg since 1990.

Thus, patterns of transmigration and ethnic cleansing in West Papua as recorded by internal statistical data are quite unambiguous in their revealed logic. Indonesia's colonization of West Papua over the late twentieth century was driven by the twin imperatives of resource extraction and counterinsurgency. There was relatively little transmigration and ethnic cleansing in West Papua until the start of a coordinated indigenous uprising in 1984. Since that time, Indonesia has colonized and cleansed its porous nonnatural borderlands in order to forestall cross-border insurgent activity from Papua New Guinea. It has also secured control over West Papua's natural resources—most notably, gold and copper around the Grasberg mine after 1990, but also petroleum around Sorong and the Cenderawasih Bay—by settling resource-rich areas with transmigrants and displacing indigenous Papuans. Together, these policies brought immense riches to Suharto and his cronies and immense destruction to the Papuan people and environment.

Conclusion

West Papua remains poorly understood. Popular stereotypes represent the province as a changeless land of pristine highlands populated by isolated tribes. Yet, few areas of the world have been so brutally "modernized" through rampant resource extraction, military repression, and settler colonialism in recent history. This enigmatic quality is due in part to an effective government blackout on information. Over the past fifty years, nearly all foreign journalists, researchers, non-government organizations and humanitarian agencies have been prevented from entering West Papua. As such, primary sources are rare; social science and contemporary history rests largely on titbits relayed from trusted government confidantes and informants, local media, and second-hand reports from the Papuan diaspora.[17] Given the absence of a shared evidentiary base, discussion of even basic research questions—such as the causes and consequences of Indonesian transmigration in West Papua—is characterized by much heat but very little light.

In this chapter, I have sought to overcome these challenges by taking advantage of a rich government archive to reconstruct all Indonesian transmigration and demographic change in West Papua between 1964 and 1999. From these detailed panel data, I find that Indonesian transmigration in West Papua is best understood through a logic of resource extraction and territorial consolidation. There was little transmigration to West Papua until a major indigenous uprising in 1984. Since that time, Indonesia has ethnically cleansed and settled its non-natural borderland in order to prevent further attacks by insurgents based in Papua New Guinea. Leveraging the timing of the Grasberg mine opening in 1990, I also show that Indonesia has ethnically cleansed and settled resource-rich areas in order to secure a loyal workforce in industries critical to the national finances. Together, the revealed logic of Indonesian transmigration in West Papua largely supports the claims made by Papuan activists—Indonesia colonized West Papua in order to defeat secessionist insurgents and to secure control over its rich resource base.

Reviewing this sordid history, one cannot help but be struck by the contrast between the ideological and practical manifestations of state rule. Indonesia's nation-builders like Sukarno were rhetorically committed to decolonization, Afro-Asian solidarity, and the elimination of racial oppression (Bandung). Yet, given its extreme levels of racial stratification, violent repression of indigenes, and resource alienation, West Papua represents one of the purest cases of settler colonialism in the world today. On the other hand, the Dutch were long committed to European racial supremacy and resource extraction in the East Indies. Yet, the Netherlands ruled West Papua with benign neglect and even belatedly promoted Papuan self-rule in the mid-twentieth century.

This disjuncture between practice and ideology is, if anything, even more striking when comparing West Papua and Papua New Guinea. Australia administered Papua New Guinea for most of the twentieth century, at a time when its leaders were explicitly committed to racist ideals and to maintaining a homogeneously White Australia. Yet, Australia failed to make Papua New Guinea white. Rather, and much like the Dutch, Australia ultimately pushed for Papuan self-rule in the 1960s and 1970s. The next chapter explains why.

4

White Australia or White Elephant? Australia's Failed Colonization of Papua New Guinea and the Northern Territory

AUSTRALIA HAS long been regarded as a canonical "settler state." The standard historical narrative is as follows. In the century following the landing of the First Fleet in Sydney in 1788, the Australian continent was relentlessly colonized by Europeans. As a result of new diseases, clashes with settlers, and forced deportations, Australia's indigenous population was almost entirely wiped out. By the early twentieth century, Australia had become one of the most racially homogeneous states in the world and almost entirely predominated by whites.

This narrative, like all conventional histories, has much truth to it. But a perhaps deeper truth is that there have always been two Australias: North and South (Rowse, 2014). The South fits the narrative.[1] The North, however, does not. In particular, the Northern Territory and the Territory of Papua were long Australia's unsettled frontiers (Figure 4.1). Europeans were a vanishingly small minority in both territories at Australia's Federation in 1901 and were outnumbered even by Chinese and Japanese. Australia's white, southern elites in the early twentieth century were faced with a challenge familiar to their Indonesian, Chinese, and Russian counterparts: how were they to exert control over vast tracts of a continent in which state presence was non-existent and which was overwhelmingly populated by groups—Asians, Melanesians, Aborigines, and Torres Strait Islanders—who were racially other?

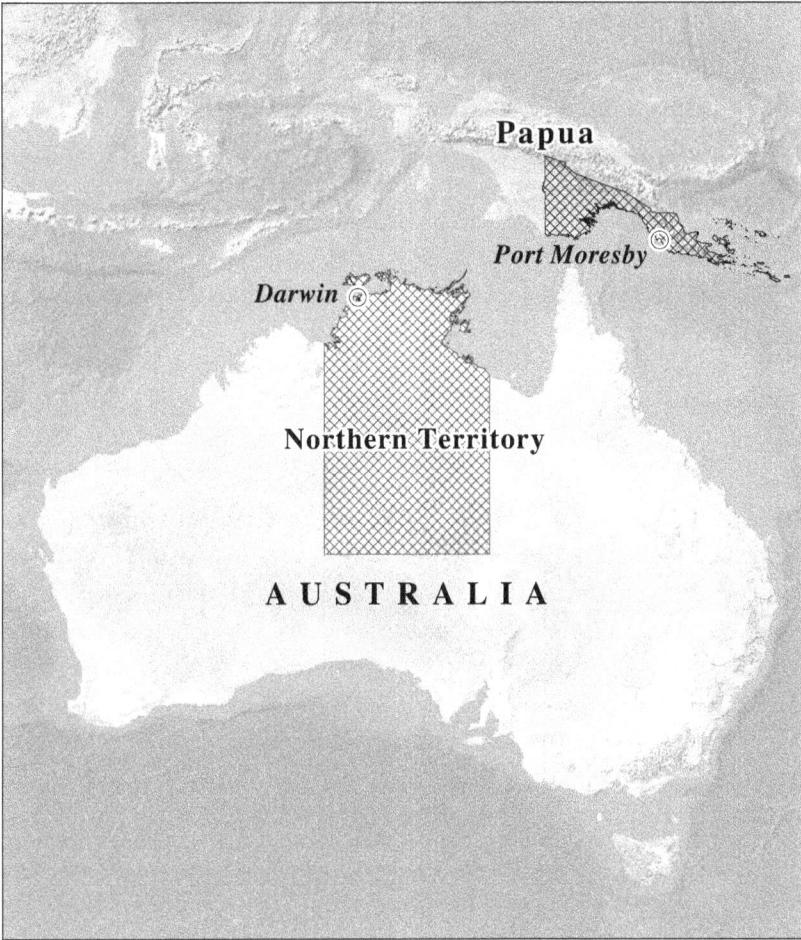

FIGURE 4.1. Australia's Northern Territory and Territory of Papua (1902–1975).

In the first half of the twentieth century, the South attempted to colonize the North. This history is not well known and I am unaware of any other study that examines this settlement program in detail.[2] Motivated first by greed and racism, Australia encouraged Europeans to settle in Papua and exploit its rich resource base. Then, motivated by fear, Australia spent enormous sums of money trying to encourage Europeans to settle in the Northern Territory in order to provide a line of defence against a rising Japan. In both cases, European colonization failed. Why, then, did one of the world's canonical settler states prove so spectacularly ineffective at colonization?

Papua: Australia's Unmanifested Destiny

Almost immediately after Federation in 1901, Australia had assumed control over Papua from Great Britain as part of its aspiration to create an "Island Empire" in the Pacific.[3] Australia's northward expansion was motivated primarily by avarice (West, 1957; Joyce, 1971). The oft-echoed assertion at the time was that Papua was richly endowed with gold and well suited to the cultivation of any number of tropical crops: cotton, tobacco, sugarcane, rubber, timber, coffee, rice, and coconut palm.[4] Papua was expected to become a rich and profitable addition to Commonwealth coffers.[5]

There was an obvious tension, however, between Australia's territorial incorporation of some 300,000 indigenous Melanesians in Papua and the ideological commitment of its officials to keep Australia as purely white as possible. The solution to this demographic dilemma was to whiten Papua. Australia's second Prime Minister, Alfred Deakin, established a Royal Commission in 1906 to report on the prospects for white settlement in Papua. The commissioners were extremely enthusiastic upon their return from the island, reporting plainly in 1907 that "hour has struck for the commencement of a vigorous forward policy, as far as white settlement [in Papua] is concerned" (Mackay, Parry-Okeden, and Herbert, 1907, x). The commissioners were pessimistic about whether mining could ever provide a basis for long-term white settlement given the transient nature of mining labor. But they were optimistic about the suitability of Papua for more durable white farmers:

> [The present absence of whites] is in no sense due to a want of proper natural advantages, for the soil of Papua is rich, virgin, and easily worked, whilst its infinite variety makes the successful cultivation of almost all tropical products possible. . . . Your Commissioners have no doubt as to the practicability of converting Papua into an agricultural and pastoral asset of great value to the Commonwealth. (Mackay, Parry-Okeden, and Herbert, 1907, x–xii)

However, foreshadowing what would become a frequent refrain from Australian administrators in Papua over the twentieth century, transportation costs were identified as the main obstacle to profitable agriculture. Accordingly, the commissioners recommended a massive expansion in road construction:

> Many parts of the country (and in large tracts) are second to none in Australia, and only require an energetic European population of settlers

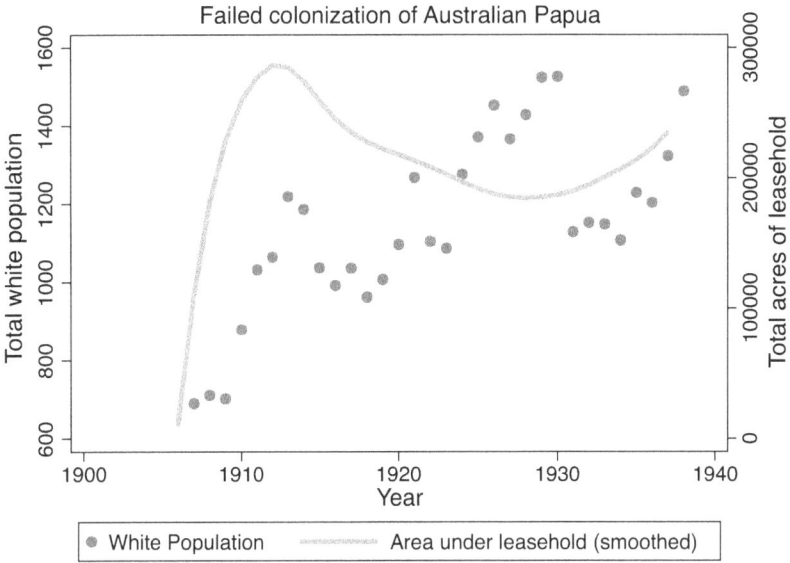

FIGURE 4.2. The total white (European) population in Australian Papua 1907–1938
and the total area under leasehold (lowess smoothed).

to successfully work it. This cannot be done without roads. (Mackay,
Parry-Okeden, and Herbert, 1907, xxxvii)

Following the Royal Commission's report, an ordinance was passed to make it
straightforward for white male settlers to obtain land through 99-year leases in
Papua.[6] The leases were extremely generous. There were no survey fees and
no legal fees, and, in the cases of leases longer than 30 years, there was even
no rent charged for the first decade.[7] From 1907, white men in Papua could
effectively have as much land as they wanted, anywhere they wanted, with no
deposit or rent.

As a result, there was an initially rapid expansion in both agricultural production and the overall white population in Papua. In just six years to 1913,
the area under lease in Papua more than quadrupled to 363,425 acres and the
white population almost doubled to approximately 1,200 (Figure 4.2). Official
reports, flushed with these early indicators of success, were optimistic about
the prospect that the territory would soon need no financial assistance from
the rest of Australia.[8] A White Melanesia appeared within reach.

However, during the global downturn in trade generated by World War I
(1914–1918), both the total land under lease and the overall white population

in Papua markedly declined (Figure 4.2). The first wave of settlers, sustaining losses, began to scale back planting and forfeit unimproved land to the administration.

Germany's defeat in 1918 offered renewed hope to Australia's policymakers. Soon after the war's conclusion, Australia received a League of Nations mandate over German New Guinea, meaning that Australia now administered both Papua and New Guinea. Prime Minister William Hughes was bullish about the prospects about Australia finally extracting a return from its island empire. As he explained to Parliament in 1920:

> In all human probability there is oil [in New Guinea]. It will grow sago. It will grow such things as coffee and rice, and it will grow rubber. It is probable that its metalliferous wealth is considerable. . . . New Guinea is quite a different country than Papua, and is, I believe, an incomparably better country. The possibilities of trade, and what that trade will mean to Australia in wealth and opportunity, can hardly be exaggerated.[9]

Agricultural development in New Guinea, however, proved just as unsuccessful as in Papua (Thompson, 1990).

The root of Australia's troubles in Papua and New Guinea remained stubbornly high transportation costs.[10] The Lieutenant-Governor of Papua (1908–1940), Hubert Murray, had long identified the high cost of shipping produce to the mainland as the main impediment to agricultural development. For example, Murray warned in 1920 that: "under the present system of high freights and scanty shipping it is improbable that agriculture either in Papua or in German New Guinea can ever be as profitable as in other tropical countries" (Murray, Hunt, and Lucas, 1920, 71).[11] And in 1922, Murray correctly predicted that "the present post-war period, I think will be a period of almost complete stagnation. . . . At the root of the whole matter are the difficulties of shipping."[12]

To be sure, we should be wary of taking Murray's rationalization of Australia's failure to colonize Papua and New Guinea at face value. But we can triangulate the importance of transportation costs with data on European settlement. In summarizing where European farmers had settled in Papua, Murray had contended that:

> The main centers of settlement . . . have, no doubt, been recommended to a large extent by their comparative proximity to Samarai and Port Moresby respectively, and their consequent greater convenience of access. Equally good land is, of course, available elsewhere.[13]

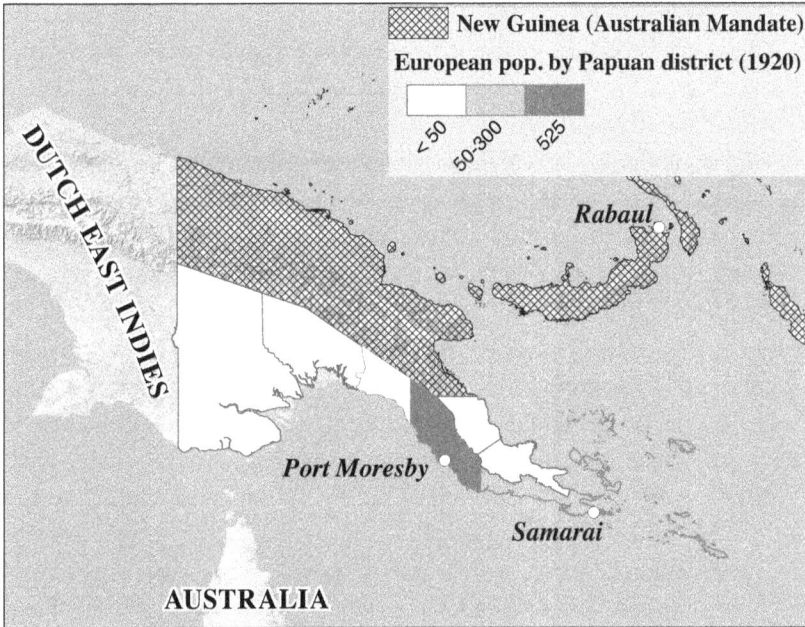

FIGURE 4.3. Papua and New Guinea in 1920 with the total European population by district in Australian Papua.

Consistent with the primary importance of transportation costs, the vast bulk of the European farming population in Papua in the 1920s remained clustered in and around Port Moresby and Samarai—the two principal ports (Figure 4.3). Even though the Papuan highlands were generally more fertile and less malarial than the lowlands, very few Europeans farmed in the highlands. And even in the lowlands, the unreliability and high cost of shipping made Papuan producers uncompetitive relative to their mainland competitors. Transportation costs were critical in explaining the success and, mostly, failure of European farmers in Papua.

Desperate for some kind of success story, the local administration in Papua over the interwar period nonetheless tried to find a sufficiently lucrative agricultural product that might overcome high transportation costs and sustain European settlement.[14] In conjunction with the British New Guinea Development Co. Ltd., officials experimented with tobacco and tobacco manufacturing. Yet, in the wake of heavy losses, the corporation was forced into voluntary liquidation in 1922. Subsequently, the administration experimented with rice agriculture. It sent an officer to India to learn best practices for growing rice and sought to ameliorate freight costs by building a domestic rice milling plant. Yet again sustaining large losses, the government rice scheme was abandoned by the late 1920s. Sugarcane, cotton, and cocoa production were similarly attempted and abandoned over the 1920s.[15]

With mass European settlement an increasingly distant possibility, Murray advocated developing Papuan agriculture with indigenous labor. On his urging, a law was passed in the 1920s compelling Papuan villagers to plant cash crops in communal plantations and work on these plantations for sixty days a year. The Papuan administration provided the seed, tools, and training and in return took a share of the proceeds that were paid into a Native Education Fund (McKillop and Firth, 1980). However, the administration failed to achieve any meaningful success with this program. As for farms run by Europeans, the returns on these indigenous plantations were generally poor.[16]

By the early 1930s, with little prospect of any profitable agriculture and in the midst of a seemingly interminable global depression, despair set into the administration. Murray, with characteristic understatement, summarized the grim state of affairs in his annual report to Canberra in 1933: "As things are now we grow various products and sell them for less than they cost to produce, a form of commercial activity which cannot be regarded as satisfactory."[17] The only profitable agricultural products were copra[18] and rubber, and Papuan rubber only remained sustainable because of a subsidy not available to other Australian producers. Seeking to protect this subsidy from mainland opposition, Murray emphasised to Canberra that as soon as "the rubber leaves the plantation, the Papuan planter loses ground, for freights, especially local freights, are high."[19] Only rubber producers in Papua who avoided the costs imposed by horrendous local roads by staying close to ports could even remain afloat.

A nascent economic recovery in Papua over the late 1930s was interrupted again by war. During World War II (1938–1945), Port Moresby was an important Allied military station and the island of New Guinea was one of the central theatres of the war. As Japan expanded southward over 1941 and 1942, it took control of New Guinea and made Rabaul its central military base in the entire South Pacific. However, Japan was blocked from seizing Port Moresby by the American navy at the Battle of the Coral Sea in May 1942. So, Japan launched a major overland military offensive from New Guinea, seeking to capture Port Moresby by crossing the Papuan highlands. Heavy fighting ensued between Allied and Japanese forces in the highlands and, after a series of bitter clashes over late 1942, Japanese forces were forced into their first retreat of the war. Papua and New Guinea had proved the buffer that saved Australia from an invasion from the north.

The devastation wrought by World War II produced a "New Deal" for Papua and New Guinea (Hunt, 2017). The Australian government, filled with a renewed awareness of Papua and New Guinea's strategic importance, committed to spending much more in developing the newly amalgamated territory (May, 1998). Between 1945 and 1950, the Australian government allocated 13 million pounds in direct grants to Papua New Guinea compared to 212,500 pounds in the five years before the war (Griffin et al., 1979, 102). Canberra was keen to use some of these funds to settle ex-servicemen in Papua New Guinea. As then Minister for External Territories Percy Spencer put it to Parliament in 1950: "During the course of my visit [to Papua New Guinea] numerous representations were made to me that some scheme of land settlement for ex-servicemen should be formulated for the territories. I favor such a proposal and it will be examined in consultation with the appropriate Commonwealth authorities."[20] Three leading academics at the Australian National University (ANU) were subsequently commissioned to undertake an expert review of Papua New Guinea's settlement prospects.

This report had the effect of finally killing off the prospect of white colonization, with the authors plainly advising the government that "of all possible methods for developing New Guinea, it seems that 'soldier settlement' is the most hopeless" (Belshaw, Swan, and Spate, 1953, 21). Consistent with the long-held view of Murray, the central issue identified by Belshaw et al. preventing colonization was transportation costs. As they summarized:

> At every point in the investigation of the economy of the Territory one is brought up against the absolute inadequacy of the transportation available; it would be an abuse of language even to call it a transport system. . . . The high costs of air freighting, and still more the unreliability . . . impose a heavy toll on any bulk commercial production, and on the import of necessities, at any distance from a port. (Belshaw, Swan, and Spate, 1953, 5–6)

They went on to state quite plainly:

> The climate is not an absolute bar to European settlement, but it does impose costs, heavy if not precisely measurable. Difficulties of terrain and accessibility render the provision of adequate services for Europeans very

expensive in most areas. . . . This completely precludes a de novo rural occupation of the land as took place in Australia itself. (Belshaw, Swan, and Spate, 1953, 58)

In order to make European settlement in Papua New Guinea viable, the authors estimated that the government would have to spend upwards of 50,000 pounds *per settler* (or approximately $1,000,000 today) on amenities and infrastructure. European settlers simply had better options in mainland Australia.[21] A White Melanesia was not to be.

The Abandonment of Papua and New Guinea

Australia did ultimately abandon its attempts to colonize Papua New Guinea following this report and, over the 1950s and 1960s, government policy evolved to set Papua New Guinea on a path to independence. In 1960, the international campaign against colonialism reached its climax in the form of the abolitionist Declaration on Colonialism adopted by the UN General Assembly. The rising tenor of self-determination, as well as Indonesia's coercive expulsion of the Dutch from West Papua in 1963, vividly demonstrated to Australian policymakers that it might not be long before their rule in Papua New Guinea was contested (Nelson, 2000). The Indonesian invasion also demonstrated that, in the event of a territorial conflict in New Guinea, Australia would not necessarily be able to rely on support from the United States. With Papua New Guinea's legally subordinate status quickly becoming politically unviable, Australia was faced with a stark choice for Papua New Guinea: statehood or separation.

Inverting the standard logic of decolonization, Papua New Guineans pushed for statehood whereas mainland Australians ultimately pushed for separation. Australia's policymakers were initially divided after World War II over the future of Papua New Guinea (Nelson, 2000). Papua, after all, had been a core part of Australia since 1902. But given its relatively low level of development, statehood for Papua New Guinea could only come at immense cost. Approximately half of the Papua New Guinean budget over the 1960s was provided directly by grants from Australia (Garnaut, 1976) but living standards there still lagged far behind the mainland. So statehood, and an equal claim to government welfare for Papua New Guineans, was not acceptable to Australia's policymakers. As government MP Henry Turner put it in 1962:

To my mind, [statehood] is a completely misguided notion, because I cannot conceive that state-hood would be in the interests of this country. . . .

There [are] continual demands for more public works, more services, and the expenditure of more money in a hundred and one ways; and just as we are not able to meet all these commitments on the mainland itself, so it would become increasingly impossible to meet them in New Guinea, particularly when you consider that New Guinea is even far less developed than is the mainland of Australia.[22]

The ambiguous future of Papua New Guinea would only be clarified in 1966 when a delegation from the island asked the government that it become Australia's seventh state. The Cabinet recoiled from this vision, which would have entailed the abandonment of the White Australia policy and enormous levels of redistribution (Nelson, 2000; Denoon, 2012). Australia formally killed off the possibility of statehood in 1968 when the Governor-General presented to Parliament the new government position that "the destiny of Papua and New Guinea is to become a self-governing country developed for independence."[23] Papua New Guineans could control little except the timing of decolonization. Australia was henceforth to end at the Torres Strait.

The reader may question whether Australia simply lacked sufficient motivation to settle Papua New Guinea. As discussed in the theory chapter, states often need a pressing threat to fund colonization. And one of Belshaw et al.'s central arguments against colonization was indeed that there was no "clear over-riding necessity" for placing tens of thousands of soldier-settlers in Papua New Guinea (Belshaw, Swan, and Spate, 1953, 21–22). However, the next section shows that even in the face of grave territorial insecurity, Australia still had little power to settle threatened areas. Mainland Australia faced a rising threat of invasion from Japan over the interwar period. And, relative to Papua New Guinea, Australia's southern elites had a pressing security interest in settling the Northern Territory given the absence of any natural sea border to protect them from an invader. Yet, despite substantial effort and financial investment, Australian efforts to colonize the Northern Territory also proved a remarkable failure. The next section explains why.

Australia's Unsettled Northern Territory

Ever since the early days of European settlement, northern Australia has been the focus of Australian defence anxieties. The Northern Territory—a vast and largely arid expanse in the middle of the continent (see Figure 4.1)— had just 864 white residents at Federation in 1901, constituting less than 0.02% of Australia's white population.[24] The Territory still held the largest surviving population of indigenous Australians. Aborigines, however, were not accorded much importance by the Australian state because, according to the prevailing racial orthodoxy, they were soon destined to die out (McGregor, 1997). Australia's population density in the early twentieth century was also markedly lower than that of its near neighbors to its north in Asia. This substantial imbalance in population density became the basis of apocalyptic invasion fears in the new nation, as white settlers fretted that the Australian continent would be colonized once again. For example, Dr. Richard Arthur, founder of the Immigration League of Australia, warned darkly in 1910 that:

> Asia will begin to pour her millions into Australia through the unpopulated and unguarded entrance of the north. And those myriads of yellow and brown men will not tarry there, but will spread as the lava of a volcanic eruption all over Australia, submerging completely the organized society that has been so painfully built up here during the last hundred years. Believing this as I do, it is small wonder that I regard all other political questions of infinitely little moment compared to it.[25]

The imperative to "populate or perish," a recurrent feature of Australia's political discourse since Federation, became a national priority during the interwar period in response to the rise of Japan. Earle Page, Leader of the Country Party in the Federal Parliament, captured these anxieties in 1921, explaining to the Parliament that:

> A difficulty will be in coming to some conclusion as to how Japanese aspirations may be satisfied in Asia, and not at our expense. If this cannot be done, the principal difficulty, however, in the way of a satisfactory arrangement may not be found in Asia or in the Pacific Islands; it may be found in the vast empty spaces of Australia, which are at once an invitation and an irritation to a crowded country like Japan if she is prevented from securing her natural outlet. . . . Ultimately, the only valid title to possession must be the effective occupation of Australia. If we simply mean to build five or six cities round the seashore, and allow the rest of Australia to be steadily depopulated by our methods of government, then our doom is as certain as that of Sodom and Gomorrah.[26]

Page would soon have the opportunity to alter the methods of government as he became the Treasurer in a new government led by Stanley Bruce in 1922. Bruce shared Page's preoccupation with populating Australia's "empty north," and the Northern Territory was singled out by both Bruce and Minister of

Home Affairs George Pearce as Australia's "Achilles' heel."[27] As Bruce put it in 1926:

> There is probably no more urgent problem for which we have to find a solu-
> tion than the development of the great and almost uninhabited territory
> to the north of the continent. . . . Such a great area, almost unconnected
> with the more populous parts of the continent, would be a focus of danger
> in the event of Australia being required to defend itself. The empty north
> is of immense strategic importance, and self-preservation demands that we
> devise means for introducing population into that vacant area.[28]

The Bruce government subsequently promoted innumerable schemes to encourage industry and labor to relocate to the Northern Territory in the 1920s. The government invested millions of pounds in experimental irriga-tion and sheep-grazing schemes around the capital city, Darwin. As in Papua, land and financial assistance was provided to white settlers. New mining projects were also heavily subsidized to compensate for higher transportation and labor costs.[29] Together, these programs amounted to tens of millions of pounds (McGregor, 2012) but achieved little success in attracting private labor or capital.

The advent of the Great Depression in 1929 forced the government to scale back its ambition and most of these initiatives were mothballed. The Administrator of the Territory, Robert Weddell, announced in 1932:

> Unsuccessful efforts have been made to induce the investment of capital
> in the Northern Territory, exemptions after exemptions being granted. It is
> proposed, in future, to grant exemptions only when absolutely necessary.[30]

Yet, the unceasing regional rise of Japan meant that the settlement of the Northern Territory remained a geopolitical imperative for Australia. The new Lyons government in 1932 radically shifted government policy in response. Rather than directly funding and subsidizing new projects in the Northern Territory, the Lyons government announced that the northern portion of the Northern Territory and Western Australia above the 20th parallel of latitude would be outsourced to a company under charter (Ling and the National Archives of Australia, 2011). The idea was that, much like the East India Com-pany or the British South Africa Company, the government would outsource the cost of colonization by allowing a private corporation to develop north-ern Australia. In exchange for constructing roads, railways, and ports, the company would be given a lengthy period of occupancy free from taxation.

Disappointingly for the government, there was only one response to the chartered company tender. In December 1933, pastoralists in the Northern Territory formed a cooperative whose aim was to develop the Barkly Table-land in the Territory. The cooperative planned to build a new sea port with a meatworks on the Gulf of Carpentaria, and a railway to ship the cattle from the Tableland. The project was estimated to cost £1 million (approximately $100 million today), of which one-ninth would be raised by the private sector and the remainder funded by a government loan. The cooperative would control the area for 100 years, pay no taxes or tariffs, and not be subject to the same labor market standards and immigration restrictions as the rest of Australia.

These terms were outrageously generous and, perhaps unsurprisingly, rejected by the government. As Minister James Hunter put it, in exchange for a one-ninth investment, the cooperative would have power "such as no company at present in existence in Australia has. In effect, this one-ninth would control and perform all the functions of a State government."[31] Given the massive financial risks entailed in investing in the Territory and high likelihood of failure, however, the investors were not willing to negotiate these terms. The government ultimately abandoned the search for a chartered company to develop the Northern Territory in 1935.

The abject failure to find a private partner was embarrassing and left the government without a plan for the defence of the Northern Territory. In response to political pressure, the Minister for the Northern Territory announced a new enquiry into the Territory in 1936. This enquiry, led by William Payne and John Fletcher, is historically valuable as it constitutes the most comprehensive external study of the failure of settlement in the Northern Territory over the interwar period. Its final report published in 1937 was scathing about the ineffectiveness of government policy. It begins by noting that:

> The Northern Territory as it exists to-day [sic] is a national problem. . . .
> Nearly all enterprises in the Territory—both Governmental and private—
> railways, pastoral and mining, are not making profits but are merely break-
> ing even or more frequently accumulating losses. Altogether, the Territory
> is a heavy liability to Australia.[32]

The authors calculated that since 1911, the Federal government had invested £15,000,000 into the Northern Territory with a white population increase measuring only slightly above 2,000 by 1937 (Payne and Fletcher, 1937, 8). They estimated therefore that every increase in the adult white population had cost the Federal government about £5,730 (Payne and Fletcher, 1937, 10), or approximately $500,000 today, an extraordinary sum of money given that Australia's GDP per capita was only $10,000 in 1929 (Bolt et al., 2018).

The report comprehensively documented the difficulties faced by firms in the Territory. Like Papua, the Northern Territory suffered from the mutually reinforcing problems of: (i) high transportation costs to markets in southern Australia, and (ii) high wages due to these increased transportation costs— the report notes that flour, for example, cost almost four times in the Territory what it cost in Brisbane. Consequently, Payne and Fletcher recommended ameliorating transportation costs by constructing new railways, eliminating the petrol excise, and lowering the cost of labor by abolishing income taxes in the Territory (Payne and Fletcher, 1937, ix).

Settling the Northern Territory, however, quickly took a backseat to direct expenditure on the military when Australia entered World War II in 1939. The worst fears of Australia's policymakers appeared to be realized following the bombing of Pearl Harbor in 1941. Soon after it conquered Singapore and expanded southward unchecked, Japan razed Darwin by aerial bombing on 19 February, 1942. Japan then launched an invasion force that was repelled only several hundreds of kilometers from Australia by American forces in May 1942.[33]

The Japanese invasion scare would become a frequently invoked justification for settling Australia's north after the war. As soon as it became apparent that the Allies would defeat Japan, the Chief of Australia's Military Forces, Thomas Blamey, declared:

> This war has demonstrated how vital are the Northern Territory and the northwest of Australia to the defence of the country as a whole. The long-term development of these areas is, in turn, intimately bound up with their defence.[34]

Blamey's call was echoed by Members of Parliament who continued to watch political developments in post-war Japan with anxiety. As Labor MP Charles Morgan put it in 1952:

> It is clear that Japan in its internal struggle can go either to the left or to the right under a totalitarian regime instead of being a democracy. . . . They will revive the old cry of *lebensraum* or living space. We must be watchful for such a contingency. . . . By a miracle, their invading army was turned

back, but the enemy may not repeat his mistakes again. That was only a testing period for the Japanese. . . . The longer we leave our empty North as empty as it is to-day [sic] the sooner will Australian youths have to fight the battle for Australia on Australian soil.[35]

Another round of schemes was launched after World War II, organized by the newly established Northern Australia Development Commission, to attract settlers through government investment projects, agricultural subsidies, and the abolition of taxes. As a result, Federal government expenditure on the Territory increased from £6.12 million in 1951–52 to almost £25 million in 1963–64 (Ling and the National Archives of Australia, 2011).

Once again, economic and migration outcomes proved disappointing. For example, one high-profile solution to the ongoing issue of transportation costs was to create an air transport facility in northern Australia that could rapidly transport processed beef from inland properties to meatworks on the coast (Ling, 2010, 161–163). Launched with much fanfare in 1949, this scheme eventually folded in 1965, by which point the federal government had spent over £100,000 on another white elephant. Similarly, a new company announced their intention in 1955 to create, with government support, one of the largest rice cultivation schemes in the world in the floodplains of the Adelaide river near Darwin. Poor yields and inadequate transportation infrastructure, however, forced Territory Rice Ltd. into liquidation in 1960 (Mollah et al., 1982).

Dismayed by this waste, the Federal government once more commissioned a report in 1959 to assess prospects for economic development in the Territory. This commission was headed by Professor H. C. Forster, Dean of Agriculture at the University of Melbourne. Forster's commission was clear-eyed about the impossibility of colonizing the Northern Territory. Its final report noted that "the history of development in the Territory is full of failures of one kind or another, which infuse a note of despair into any new plan to develop the north" (Australia and Forster, 1960, 10). Forster found that the Territory was trapped in a cycle of peripherality. Given mutually reinforcing economic forces drawing migration and investment to the cities in Australia's south, the report pointed out that there existed in the Northern Territory "the vicious cycle of there being no industry because there are no facilities, and there being no facilities because there are no industries" (Australia and Forster, 1960, 209). It correspondingly suggested that prospects for agricultural development in the Northern Territory were limited and that mass white settlement was not a realistic policy goal:

Under present day conditions, it is neither realistic not desirable to expect people to devote their lives, at a low living standard, to the development of land. There are too many opportunities elsewhere . . . for us to expect that these methods of the past have a role in the future. (p. 10)

In short, given high transportation costs and better economic opportunities available in Australia's southern cities, the era of frontier colonization in Australia was over.

Reflecting the gradual normalization of Australia-Japan relations and growing public awareness of financial waste in the Territory, the 1960s and 1970s witnessed substantial public and Parliamentary debate over the future of the Territory. Perhaps most notably, in 1965 Bruce Davidson published a widely read critique of Australia's efforts to develop the north. The *Northern Myth* pointed out that agriculture would always rely on massive government subsidies because any crop produced in the north could be produced in the south at a lower cost. Given the absence of any threat materializing from Japan, Davidson (1965) also questioned the security imperative of migration to the north. *Northern Myth* was highly influential in shifting the parameters of public and Parliamentary debate over the Territory in the 1960s.[36] By the 1970s, ecological preservation and long overdue attention to Australia's remote indigenous population had become the focus of the Federal government in the Territory. Unlike in Papua, however, the indigenous population in the Northern Territory was relatively small in number. So, despite being a burden on the public purse, the Northern Territory was not set on the path to independence.[37]

In sum, despite immense territorial insecurity, Australia's efforts to colonize the Northern Territory with white settlers in the mid-twentieth century spectacularly failed. Population growth in the Territory consistently lagged behind the rest of the country despite considerable government effort and public funds spent on settling the North. By 1961, there were fewer than 30,000 non-indigenous persons in the Northern Territory, constituting only 0.3% of Australia's non-indigenous population (Commonwealth Bureau of Census and Statistics, 1961).[38]

Assessing the Settler Colonial Transition

Recall my contention that states ultimately lose both the power and willingness to colonize peripheral regions as they develop economically. Contrasting Indonesia's "success" in colonizing West Papua with Australia's expensive, futile struggle to colonize its North over these past two chapters confirms this expectation. What has also become clear is that the causal mechanisms of rising living standards and transportation costs largely explain why Australia failed to colonize the Northern Territory and Papua New Guinea.

One way of understanding the challenge posed by transportation costs to colonization projects in a wealthy state is the distinction between individual and collective interests. If millions of settlers had moved collectively from the South to the North in the early twentieth century, there would have quickly emerged a flourishing market in Port Moresby and Darwin to economically sustain many agriculturalists in Papua and the Northern Territory. Two separate cores each with their respective peripheries would have emerged.[39] In the absence of any local urban market for their goods, agriculturalists and pastoralists in Australia's North necessarily had to sell their produce in the South. It was not, however, in the individual interest of any settler to move to the North and incur the crippling costs of shipping their produce back to the South.

Even in potentially very productive agricultural areas like Papua New Guinea, colonization requires a first generation of settlers to effectively engage in subsistence agriculture prior to the emergence of a rich, urban market for their produce. For the vast bulk of history, this has not been a constraint on policymakers as farmers have subsisted on very low incomes. For example, in 1992 the income of Indonesian transmigrants in West Papua ranged from $600 to $2,000 (Operations Evaluation Department, World Bank, 1994). Such an income was well above the average for Indonesians at the time, and so Indonesia's transmigration program was heavily oversubscribed. But offering farmers land in the periphery to subsist upon is not viable in a wealthy state like Australia. Developed states are saddled with empty frontiers. As one Australian Member of Parliament lamented in the 1950s:

> One of the sad and disappointing features of the rapid growth of our urban populations over the last few years has been the ever-decreasing number of people who are really interested in the effective occupation and development of our vast continent and in the discharge of our immense territorial responsibilities.[40]

But what of the greater resources at Australia's disposal? Certainly, the per capita cost of colonizing New Guinea was higher relative to Indonesia, but Australia also had more money at its disposal to fund colonization. Why did these two factors not cancel each other out?

Here, we must recall the importance of opportunity costs. States evaluate colonization relative to its policy *alternatives*. Indonesia settled 300,000 transmigrants to West Papua at an average cost per family of $5,000 (Van Der Wijst, 1985). Given the lack of outside options to Javanese farmers, all the state needed to do was fly families to the outer islands, provide seeds, and demarcate plots, and this proved a sufficient incentive for resettlement. For the same amount of money, Australia could have secured only 1,500 settlers in Papua New Guinea.[41] To obtain 300,000 Europeans in Papua New Guinea would have required the equivalent of today's $300 billion. The opportunity costs for spending this kind of money are simply too great, and would certainly have exceeded the value of any land or resources obtained. This, at least, was the conclusion of the watershed review conducted in 1953 by Belshaw, Swan, and Spate, who found that the prospective cost of settling Papua New Guinea was an "altogether unjustifiable toll on the Australian taxpayer" (p. 53).[42] Australia eventually settled for the far less costly alternative of simply abandoning Papua New Guinea altogether. Lower living standards and lower opportunity costs explain why Indonesia, not Australia, ended up colonizing New Guinea.

Conclusion

"Settler colonialism" is a concept largely developed by Australian scholars to make sense of Australian history. Because indigenous land was more valuable than indigenous labor in Australia, Patrick Wolfe and Lorenzo Veracini have argued, British colonialism there was governed by a distinctly eliminatory and genocidal logic.

But have we gotten the Australian case right? In a recent exchange, Rowse (2014) pointed out that it is difficult to see how the colonization of Australia followed a logic of elimination because indigenous peoples in the northern half of the continent were not actually eliminated by settlers. Seeking to defend settler colonial studies from Rowse's charge of inaccuracy, Veracini replied that different colonial formations existed in northern and southern Australia. Rationalizing history backwards, Veracini attributes the absence of indigenous elimination in northern Australia to the economic importance of indigenous pastoral and agricultural labor there. Britain's colonization of Northern Australia thus followed a logic more akin to the exploitation of Hong Kong or India than the colonization of southern Australia. Or, as he summarizes, "settler colonial studies thrives on the analytical distinction between colonial and settler colonial formations: it can easily concede that reliance on Aboriginal labor made the North different" (Veracini, 2014, 315).

This response by Veracini confuses cause and effect. As I have shown in this chapter, a kind of logic of elimination did operate in Australia's North, as the Australian state spent enormous sums of money trying to colonize its northern reaches with whites in the first half of the twentieth century. Yet, colonization failed. Only when faced with a stubborn absence of white settlers did the Australian state belatedly turn to employing indigenous labor. Attending to the sequencing of historical events reveals that an economic reliance on indigenous labor was actually the *effect*, not the cause, of the absence of settlers in northern Australia.

The central mistake in settler colonial studies at present is therefore neither the tendency, as Rowse (2014) argues, to see indigenous elimination as inexorable, nor the tendency, as Shoemaker (2015) argues, to ignore other forms of colonialism. Rather, the central error in the "logic of elimination" is the conflation of state and settler. The violent predation of indigenous land by settlers—as in southeast Australia in the nineteenth century—can occur in the absence of, or even contrary to, the intentions of policymakers. And even when states do operate with a "logic of elimination," the competing interests of settlers mean that—as in northern Australia in the twentieth century—state-sponsored colonization projects often fail. The history of settler colonialism in Australia is, in many ways, one of persistent metropolitan frustration. The interests and agency of settlers on the ground, not of distant elites, explain the opening and closing of the frontier in Australia.

Is the closure of the frontier with modernization just a story about the West or this a more general phenomenon? Over the next two chapters, I show that this phenomenon is generalizable by examining China's attempts to settle Han Chinese in its contested western periphery over the twentieth century. Communist states are particularly useful sites to understand the logic of state-led colonization because, given the absence of a market, migration flows there purely reflect state intentions. The next chapter, written with Anna Zhang, provides the first micro-analysis of settler colonialism in China using internal government statistics. We show that China was exceptionally effective at colonizing its non-natural, oil-rich, and ethnically Russian frontiers during conflict with the former USSR in the 1960s and 1970s. In the subsequent chapter, I then show that, as China marketized and its eastern cities became magnets for labor and capital since the 1980s, it has progressively lost the power to colonize its restive northwest. Like Australia, China failed to colonize its periphery not for lack of effort or a lack of fertile agricultural land. Rather, colonization in both China and Australia ceased when economic development in the core drained the state of willing settlers.

5

Best Friends Make the Worst Enemies: Demographic Engineering during the Sino-Soviet Split (with Anna Zhang)

BETWEEN 1952 and 1972, the share of the Chinese province of Xinjiang that was Han Chinese rose from 6% to almost 40%.[1] Rapid demographic change in Xinjiang was the intentional result of state policy. Over the second half of the twentieth century, China expelled the bulk of its ethnic Russian community and resettled some two million new Han migrants onto state-owned farms in Xinjiang.[2]

This massive change in Xinjiang's ethnic composition was far from inevitable and far from spread evenly across the province. In this chapter, we draw on an original panel of all Han settlement and minority expulsions in Xinjiang since the early 1950s to recover the logic of state-sponsored demographic change there. We find, consistent with the conventional scholarly wisdom, that China escalated the settlement of its border regions with the USSR, such as Xinjiang, in response to the geopolitical fallout of the Sino-Soviet split (1959–1982). But we also explain why only some areas of Xinjiang were settled by China over this time. We show that Han settlement during the Sino-Soviet split was particularly targeted at areas of Xinjiang populated by Russians, areas lacking a natural border with the USSR, and oil-rich areas. This chapter therefore provides new insight into how Xinjiang's ethnic geography was dramatically reshaped in the mid-twentieth century. Exactly mirroring the logic of Indonesia's colonization of West Papua in the 1980s (Chapter 3), geopolitical strategy explains why

Han today only predominate in resource-rich and low-lying border areas of Xinjiang.

China was far from alone in its settlement of Central Asia. Drawing on Soviet census statistics, we show that the Sino-Soviet split similarly led to the cleansing of ethnic Chinese and the settlement of Russians in sensitive border areas with China. Rising conflict between China and the USSR thus led to the coercive ethnic homogenization of their respective borderlands. As a result of the Sino-Soviet split, strategically important passages between China and the former USSR became homogenously Han Chinese and Russian respectively.

The Breakdown in Sino-Soviet Relations

What led to the dramatic decline in Sino-Soviet relations in the late 1950s, prompting China's rapid settlement of Xinjiang? China and the former USSR shared an extremely long land border and China long had a testy and competitive relationship with its northern neighbor. China's borders have almost all contracted since the late imperial era, and the only boundary between Russia and China that has remained constant since 1820 is a small portion of the northern border running along the Argun river. After a series of military defeats in the 1800s, China ceded a substantial amount of territory to Russia, and Russian troops facilitated outer Mongolia's independence in the early twentieth century.

At the time of Chinese Communist victory in 1949, the new Chinese government cast uncertainty on the legitimacy of these territorial losses given that they were the result of "unequal" treaties signed during a century of Chinese weakness. Frontiers defined by past treaties were all potentially renegotiable after 1949 and the subject of revanchist claims (An, 1973). Ultimately, in the 1960s, Chinese state media outlets would indeed begin to publicly press claims to large swaths of formerly Chinese territory in the USSR including the south-eastern area of Siberia, Vladivostok, and Central Asia.

Tensions largely unrelated to China's past territorial losses, however, began to rise between the USSR and China throughout the late 1950s, culminating in the Sino-Soviet split of 1959 (Jian, 2006; Chen, 2010). The origins of the split can be traced back to both ideology and geopolitics. Mao Zedong forcefully disagreed with Nikita Khrushchev's "Secret Speech" of 1956 that vehemently denounced Stalin's cult of personality and with Khrushchev's general policy of "peaceful co-existence" with the United States.

Beyond these more abstract ideological differences, USSR and Chinese geopolitical interests also began to diverge in the late 1950s. The USSR desperately wanted a warm water port on the Pacific where it could station its naval fleet year round. Khrushchev correspondingly proposed the construction of a joint submarine flotilla and long-wave radio transmitter on Chinese territory in 1958. This proposal was roundly rebuffed by Mao, who saw it as evidence of the return of Russian designs on Chinese territory and a form of "red imperialism." Mao also continued to seek Taiwanese reunification via military force whereas the USSR, fearing nuclear war with the United States, was reluctant to commit forces in support of this endeavor. These strategic differences ultimately manifested in the Quemoy incident of 1958 when, without informing the USSR in advance, China began to shell the Taiwanese islands of Quemoy and Matsu, taking the USSR and the United States to the brink of nuclear war.

Trust between the USSR and China finally broke down completely in 1959. The USSR viewed the Quemoy incident as evidence that China could not be trusted with nuclear weapons and stopped providing nuclear assistance to China in June 1959. The USSR also took a neutral stance on the Sino-Indian border clashes of August–October 1959, causing much consternation in Beijing. In a historic and vitriolic October meeting between Khrushchev and top Chinese leaders, well known as the turning point in the Sino-Soviet split (Chen, 2010), USSR neutrality over the recent Sino-Indian clashes proved a hotly contested sticking point. Whilst Western intelligence forces only became aware of the Sino-Soviet split in 1960 as the USSR publicly withdrew all her technical advisors from China, it is increasingly clear that 1959 represents the key year when Sino-Soviet relations broke down (Lüthi, 2010). As Jian puts it, "the Sino-Indian dispute, and the beginning of the Sino-Soviet split combine to mark the year 1959 as one of unusual significance, a year in which a new and very different chapter in the global Cold War began to unfold" (Jian, 2006, 101).

China's policies shifted over 1959 in response to heightened wariness of Soviet influence. These policies included banning the use of the Soviet Cyrillic alphabet and sealing the Xinjiang border with the USSR in 1959 (An, 1973, 72). The Soviets also later charged that the Chinese side began to initiate hostile border incidents and skirmishes that year (Robinson, 1972, 1177). Most importantly, the Chinese state began to strengthen its control over border regions by expelling ethnic Russians and settling Han along its northern frontiers in 1959.

Many Chinese residents along the Soviet border had been Soviet citizens in the 1930s when Beijing's authority was non-existent, and still retained ties with co-ethnics across the border. China's borderland also had a substantial number of White Russians who had fled the USSR after Communist victory in the 1920s. Mao feared that lasting Soviet influence over its ethnic minorities could be used to "detach" border regions from China (Mao, 1974, 190-191). To better consolidate its control over the borderland, pressure was placed on the significant cohort of Soviet citizens in China, numbering over 100,000 in Xinjiang alone, to leave Chinese territory. USSR citizens in Xinjiang saw their property and other legal rights progressively curtailed over 1959 and a large number were abruptly dismissed from work in state enterprises (Ginsburgs, 1978, 70). By the end of the year, more than 88 percent of registered USSR citizens in Xinjiang had been forcibly repatriated (Fravel, 2008, 104).[3]

At the same time, China began to escalate expulsions of Chinese nationals whom it viewed as allegiant to the USSR. No minority group was actively engaged in an insurgency against the Chinese state over the period of the Sino-Soviet split. But we reveal in this chapter that the Sino-Soviet split led to a significant reduction in Xinjiang's "fifth column" minority group—ethnic Russians. Archival evidence suggests that this reduction was most likely the result of expulsion of dual-nationals viewed as potentially allegiant to the USSR. According to the CCP Director of Foreign Affairs in Xinjiang, Deng Liqun, between 1954 and 1963, the total number of dual-national ethnic Russians forcibly "repatriated" to the Soviet Union ranged from 1,968 to 35,922, a range within which is our estimate of a total 8,000 decline in the ethnic Russian population due to the Sino-Soviet split. The USSR consulate in Xinjiang initially refused to take in its dual-nationals, which, according to Deng, only served to confirm China's suspicions that they were being used for espionage (Qi, 2002).

The mass resettlement of Han Chinese laborers and farmers to the USSR frontier simultaneously escalated in 1959. The strategy of diluting the dominance of non-Han individuals in border regions was colloquially called "mixing sand." Mass migration was achieved through a number of government campaigns that implored Han youth to go and support China's borderlands and that emphasized the ideological virtues of those "elected" to resettle. Most of these settlers both in Xinjiang and elsewhere in China were absorbed into state farms. These state farms, run by paramilitary organizations such as the Xinjiang Production and Construction Corps (XPCC or bingtuan), had their own schools, medical services, and government structures, and were almost entirely segregated from the local population. Approximately 80 percent of Han migrants to Xinjiang over the Mao era were assigned to different units of the XPCC (White, 1979). The XPCC was regarded as a loyal bastion of Han power in Xinjiang. For instance, internal intelligence documents from 1962 reveal that in the event of a Soviet invasion, XPCC settlers were expected to form militias to pacify anticipated unrest among autochthonous minorities (Xinjiang Provincial Government, 1998).

The focus of XPCC settlement was in northern, not southern Xinjiang. This is for two reasons. The first reason is that northern Xinjiang was richly endowed with oil. Geographic surveys dating back to the nineteenth century had identified oil in the Dzungar basin of northern Xinjiang. Because Beijing exercized little effective control over the area in the early twentieth century, it was the USSR that initiated the commercial production of oil of northern Xinjiang. In the 1930s, the USSR invested heavily in infrastructure designed to extract and transport Xinjiang's oil to the rest of the Soviet Union. By the early 1940s, northern Xinjiang had a number of rigs, pipelines, and roads connecting the Dushanzi oilfield to transport hubs on the Turkestan-Siberian rail line.

These oil deposits were critically important to the new People's Republic of China, which assumed effective control over Xinjiang in the early 1950s. As Wang Enmao, Xinjiang's Party Secretary in the 1950s, put it: "there is very little of anything above ground in Xinjiang—many areas are simply barren land—but buried below is a limitless supply of treasures" (Kinzley, 2018, 150). China's First Five Year Plan (1953–1957) emphasized the development of heavy industry, but China remained highly isolated from international oil markets. Accordingly, reducing Soviet control over oil production in Xinjiang became a national priority in the mid-1950s (Kinzley, 2018). In 1954, China nationalized the formerly joint Sino-Soviet Oil Company, constructed new pipelines and roads to transport Xinjiang's oil to China proper, and invested heavily in new oil wells. These efforts spectacularly paid off in late 1955 when workers discovered the Karamay oilfield just north of Dushanzi, which quickly became the most productive oilfield in the whole of China. By the early 1960s, a vast network of roads, rail, refineries, and heavy industry led by the XPCC and the China National Petroleum Corporation had formed in the oil-rich area between Karamay and Urumqi (Figure 5.1).

The second reason why northern Xinjiang became the focus of XPCC settlement is the nature of the border there with the USSR. Unlike the largely impassable Tian Shan mountains forming the southern border, the northern border, first defined in 1860 to connect existing Chinese sentry stations in low-lying pasture land, did not follow a natural boundary (Figure 5.1). Concerns about Soviet infiltration across the northern border in the late 1950s and

FIGURE 5.1. The province of Xinjiang, the Karamay oilfield, and Xinjiang's natural and non-natural borders with the former USSR.

early 1960s were widespread in official and academic sources in China (Dun and Zhang, 2014). Soviet authorities were reportedly very active at facilitating cross-border personnel and propaganda flows from Soviet Kazakhstan. This included fomenting dissent by broadcasting anti-Chinese radio messages from Alma-Ata and distributing material calling for the creation of an independent, pro-Soviet republic in Xinjiang. In response the Chinese government established a *cordon sanitaire* along the northern half of the Sino-Soviet border in Xinjiang in 1962 and allocated much of the borderland to the XPCC settlers. It specifically ordered the XPCC to form a "belt" of agriculture along the Xinjiang-Kazakhstan border in order to deter illicit cross-border flows of people and goods from the USSR.

Tensions between the USSR and China remained high throughout the 1960s and 1970s. But the early 1980s proved a watershed period for Sino-Soviet relations. The election of Ronald Reagan in the United States in November 1981 prompted a strategic rethink in Moscow and Beijing. Reagan's aggressive support of weapons sales to Taiwan, the mujahideen in Afghanistan, and the general reassertion of US military power abroad prompted China and the

USSR to take their first tentative steps toward reconciliation. Leonid Brezhnev offered a symbolic olive branch to China in Tashkent in March 1982 and negotiations between China and the USSR ensued over the rest of the year. These talks culminated in an agreement at the end of 1982 that reestablished cross-border trade and resumed Sino-Soviet diplomatic relations at the vice-ministerial level. An intensely conflictual period in Sino-Soviet relations was, at last, over.

Recovering the Logic of Demographic Change in Xinjiang

Recall that the *timing* of state-led colonization is generally shaped by the onset of conflict whilst the *location* of state-led colonization is shaped by the location of disloyal ethnic groups, natural resources, and non-natural borders (See Chapter 2).[4] In this context, the two ethnic groups of interest are the Han and Russians, both of whom constituted the majority and politically dominant ethnic groups in China and the former USSR respectively. The Sino-Soviet split (1959–1982) is the period of hostile relations. And within Xinjiang, the most strategically important targets for Han settlement are the Karamay-Dushanzi oilfield and the non-natural portions of the Sino-Soviet border in the northern half of Xinjiang (Figure 5.1).

To recover the logic of demographic engineering in Xinjiang, we compiled new panel datasets capturing demographic change in every county since 1952. We specifically draw on the 1952 Population Statistics of Minorities in China and the Xinjiang Uyghur Autonomous Region Statistical Yearbooks dating back to 1963.[5] Such data have not been compiled before and document politically sensitive changes in population in Xinjiang. The data in the yearbooks are based on official household registration information from the Xinjiang Ministry of Public Security. The only university library with these data worldwide and willing to share them with researchers is the library at the University of Washington.

For every county (based on 1952 boundaries) in Xinjiang in every year after 1952, we measured the (i) total county population, (ii) number of Han Chinese, (iii) number of Uyghurs, (iv) number of Kazakhs, (v) number of Hui, (vi) number of Kyrgyz, (vii) number of Russians, and (viii) number of XPCC (bingtuan) settlers. Some counties experienced border changes over time; however, this was almost always the result of a new county being created within an old county, so it was relatively straightforward to match post-1952 county data to 1952 county boundaries.[6] These data, whilst having

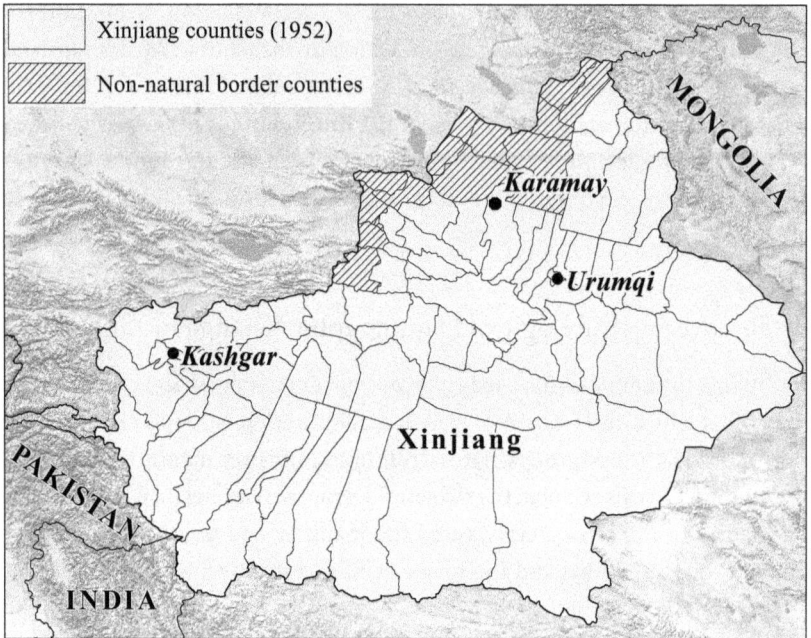

FIGURE 5.2. Xinjiang counties (1952), the Karamay oilfield, and the non-natural border counties with the former USSR.

their limitations,[7] represent the best historical source on population changes in Xinjiang.

Figure 5.2 illustrates where the non-natural border counties of Xinjiang are located.[8] Natural borders are those that were delimited to follow the Tian Shan mountain range and non-natural borders are those that were originally delimited to follow historic Chinese sentry stations in low-lying areas. And the Karamay-Dushanzi oilfield lies entirely within Shawan county.

To briefly recap, we expect that the Chinese state was focused on consolidating its control over areas of Xinjiang endowed with oil, and which were especially liable to incursions from the USSR. As such, we expect that Han settlement and expulsions of Russians during the Sino-Soviet split were both particularly extreme in Xinjiang's porous northern border counties and in Shawan county.

Settling Xinjiang

Figure 5.3 illustrates the change in the share of each county that was Han Chinese between 1952 and 1982.

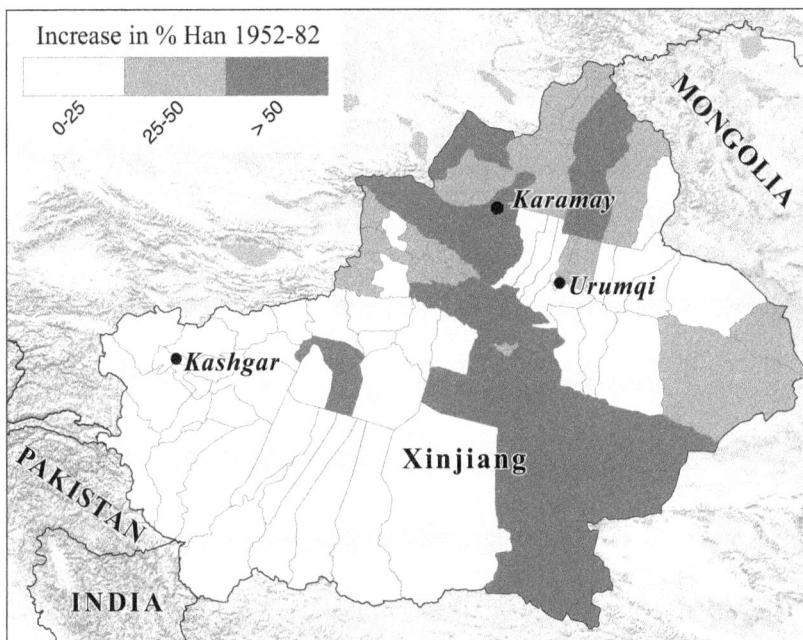

FIGURE 5.3. The change in Han percentage by county in Xinjiang (1952–1982).

This map reveals how China transformed the demography of strategically important areas of Xinjiang over the mid-twentieth century. The average increase in the percent of Han Chinese in northern Xinjiang over the Sino-Soviet split was approximately 40 percentage points, and up to 60 percentage points along Xinjiang's porous non-natural border—an extraordinary change in demographic composition in just thirty years. Han settlement in the southern border areas and Uyghur-populated areas of southern Xinjiang over the same period was markedly less extreme.

The statistical models corroborate the fact that the Han and bingtuan settlement was particularly extreme in the non-natural border counties during the Sino-Soviet split. The Sino-Soviet split led to a significant rise on average in both the number of bingtuan settlers and the proportion of Han Chinese across all counties in Xinjiang. However, this rise was particularly dramatic in counties adjacent to Xinjiang's non-natural northern border with the USSR (Appendix Table 5.1, columns 1 and 3).

Han settlement was also particularly extreme in oil-rich Shawan county (Appendix Table 5.1, columns 2 and 4). The total population in Shawan increased by over 2,000% in little over a decade, rising from 16,000 persons

TABLE 5.1. Each model is a difference-in-differences specification where the DV is the ethnic population of each Xinjiang county between 1952 and 1985. Standard errors are clustered at the county level using Arellano's covariance matrix.

	Average change in county population by ethnic group					
	Russian	Han	Hui	Kyrgyz	Kazakh	Uyghur
Sino-Soviet Split	−107.77***	9,899.93***	703.73***	−6.62	62.66	1,970.51
	(37.23)	(2,180.00)	(147.02)	(97.17)	(312.46)	(1,282.01)
First Differences	Yes	Yes	Yes	Yes	Yes	Yes
Counties	80	80	80	80	80	80
Observations	1896	1896	1896	1896	1896	1896

Note: $*p < 0.1$; $**p < 0.05$; $***p < 0.01$.

in 1952 to over 330,000 persons in 1963 of whom approximately 250,000 were XPCC members. Accordingly, Shawan was the county in Xinjiang with the single greatest change in demographic composition over the Sino-Soviet split; it went from just 13% Han in 1952 to almost 90% Han in 1982. As the government encouraged the bingtuan to establish munitions factories and industry in an area proximate to the Karamay-Dushanzi oilfields, a string of cities in Shawan—Karamay, Kuitun, and Shihezi—quickly became Xinjiang's major industrial hub. Shihezi experienced a particularly dramatic transformation from a small, rural village into the central bingtuan node within Xinjiang as a whole. As a result, Shihezi remains an anomalously industrial, Han Chinese outpost in northwest China to the current day.

Han dominance in Xinjiang over the Sino-Soviet split was augmented by the expulsion of ethnic Russians. The Sino-Soviet split is associated with an average expulsion of 108 Russians across every Xinjiang county, which constitutes an average 47% fall in the pre-split Russian population (Table 5.1). And only the ethnic Russian population significantly fell as a result of the Sino-Soviet split. The other minority groups in Xinjiang neither shared co-ethnicity with elites in the USSR nor were engaged in active rebellion, and so were not regarded as pressing threats.

The expulsion of Russians was particularly extreme in the counties of Xinjiang that shared a non-natural border with the USSR (Appendix Table 5.1 column 5). The Sino-Soviet split led to a fall of approximately 200 ethnic Russians in Xinjiang counties proximate to a non-natural border with the USSR, meaning approximately half the Russian population in each border county was expelled. The Sino-Soviet split is also associated with a disproportionate fall in the ethnic Russian population in Shawan county (Appendix Table 5.1,

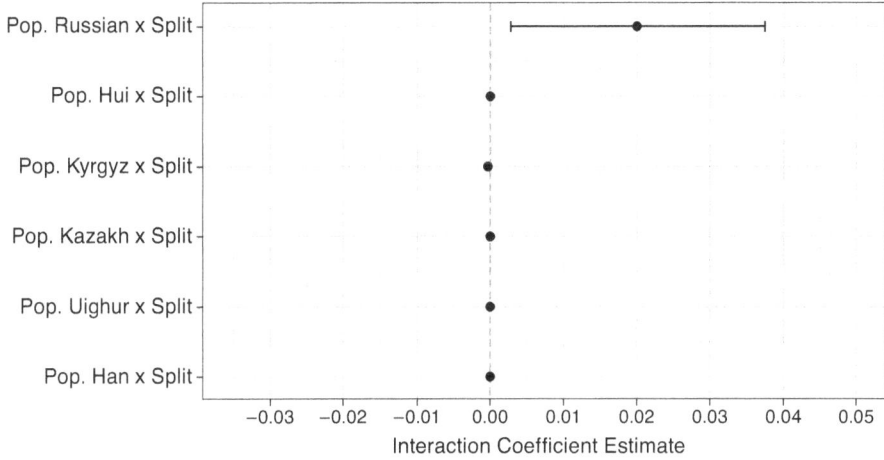

FIGURE 5.4. How *bingtuan* settlement in Xinjiang targeted particular ethnic minorities during the Sino-Soviet split, with 95% confidence intervals.

column 6). Only after relations between China and the USSR normalized in 1982 did the ethnic Russian population in Shawan begin to recover.[9]

Interestingly, Han settlement was also disproportionately targeted at those counties that had a significant ethnic Russian population (Figures 5.4 and 5.5). For example, a county that had 100 more Russians than an otherwise similar county is expected to have a 10% greater increase in Han during the Sino-Soviet split. Again, this effect is unique to the Russian minority; we do not obtain similar results when replacing the Russian population with the population of a county that is Hui, Han, Kazakh, Kyrgyz, or Uyghur (Figures 5.4 and 5.5).

These results therefore run contrary to past predictions that the Sino-Soviet split led to the cleansing or colonization of China's Kazakh and Uyghur minorities (Mylonas, 2012; Han and Mylonas, 2014). Although the Sino-Soviet split did lead to measures designed to cut off Kazakhs and Uyghurs from their cross-border kin, this did not take the form of ethnic cleansing. For example, during the 1962 Yili-Tacheng Incident approximately 75,000 ethnic Kazakhs and Uyghurs fled across the border to the USSR with their contraband and livestock (Zhang, 2014). Beijing was dismayed at the Kazakh exodus and sought to prevent any more Kazakhs and Uyghurs leaving for the USSR by sealing the border and retrieving information on those who left from Soviet officials. Given that the state sought to prevent their exodus, this suggests that non-Russian minorities were not viewed as pressing threats.

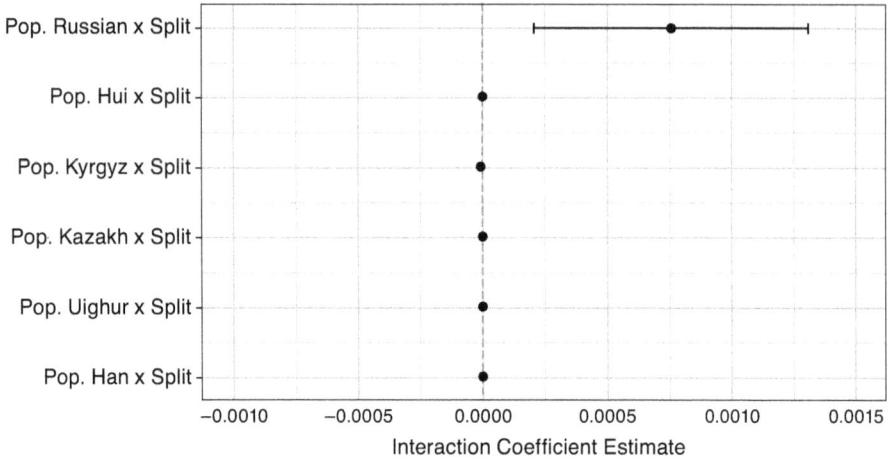

FIGURE 5.5. How Han settlement in Xinjiang targeted particular ethnic minorities during the Sino-Soviet split, with 95% confidence intervals.

Rather, in light of the politically central role that Russians played in the former USSR (Laitin, 1998), these results indicate that China's relatively small but politically influential fifth column minority was disproportionately forced to leave for the USSR as a result of the Sino-Soviet split. More broadly, the fact that ethnic Russians rather than Kazakhs or Uyghurs were targeted for displacement suggests that only having cross-border kin in a hostile foreign power is not enough to be regarded as a pressing threat—it is also essential that such kin be in a position of power. We have substantiated this interpretation through off-the-record discussions with a number of remaining ethnic Russians and interviews with bingtuan members in Yili Prefecture.[10] In essence, rapid demographic change in strategically important areas of Xinjiang was achieved through the tandem expulsion of ethnic Russians and an influx of Han settlers who took their place. Coercive migration was used by Beijing to consolidate control over oil-rich areas and permeable border zones vulnerable to illicit personnel, equipment, and propaganda flows.

Demographic Engineering in the Soviet Union

Did the Soviet Union also settle its frontier with China during this period? In this section, we show how patterns of demographic change in the former Soviet Union indeed indicate that the Sino-Soviet split similarly induced

(i) the mass resettlement of ethnic Russians and expulsion of Chinese on the Russian side of the Sino-Soviet border and (ii) the resettlement of Russians in Chinese-populated areas.

Czarist Russia had long licensed resettlement to the Far East and, under Stalin, the USSR had frequently used forced deportations to populate and develop Siberia. This resettlement policy experienced new life as a result of the downturn in Sino-Soviet relations. As An summarizes, "by the mid-1960s, the Soviet Union was displaying conspicuous haste in planning to develop the vast and thinly populated region of Siberia by pouring in substantial capital and people. This policy indicated the USSR's long-term goal to turn Siberia into a bastion against the Chinese, and had made feverish efforts to attract permanent settlers" (An, 1973, 87). The Sino-Soviet split also led to the expulsion of ethnic Chinese in Russia. The Russian Empire had long feared that China could use its large population and influence over the expatriate Chinese community to undermine the Empire's control over its newly acquired territories in the Far East. Following the decline in Sino-Soviet relations in 1959, the Soviet Union again deported a substantial component of the ethnic Chinese community that had migrated to the USSR to study and conduct shuttle trade in the Far East over the preceding decade (Lüthi, 2010).

This decline in the ethnic Chinese community and increase in the ethnic Russian community in the Russian Far East is corroborated by internal Soviet census data. Unfortunately, unlike in China, there do not exist publicly available yearly demographic data for the USSR. However, oblast-level demographic data exist for five censuses for the Russian Soviet Federative Socialist Republic between 1939 and 1989.[11] Whilst oblasts are quite large areas (equivalent to Chinese provinces), we can see whether the censuses during the Sino-Soviet split (1959–1982) report a disproportionate decline in the ethnically Chinese community and rise in the ethnically Russian community in the four Russian oblasts in the Far East bordering China (Figure 5.6).

This is indeed the case. The Sino-Soviet split led to an increase of approximately 157,000–240,000 ethnic Russians in each of the Far East Russian oblasts bordering China (Table 5.2 columns 1 and 2) and a total increase in population of 156,000–274,000 (columns 5 and 6). The approximately identical estimate of both total population and ethnic Russian change suggests that the increase in the Russian population is the product of internal migration rather than ethnic switching among USSR nationals. The results also suggest that ethnic Russian resettlement was targeted at areas populated by

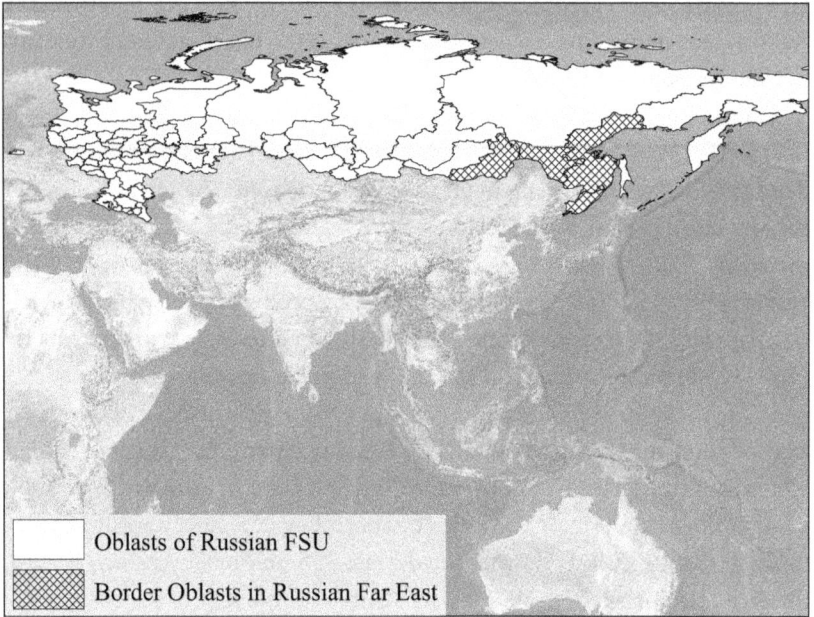

Oblasts of Russian FSU

Border Oblasts in Russian Far East

FIGURE 5.6. Oblasts of the Russian Soviet Federative Socialist Republic of the Former Soviet Union (FSU).

more Chinese during the Sino-Soviet split. While not always statistically significant, areas populated by more Chinese are estimated to have less Russian population growth outside the Sino-Soviet split relative to other areas and greater Russian population growth during the split (Appendix Table 5.2).

Finally, as in China, Russia consolidated control over its borderland through forced deportations. The Sino-Soviet split is also associated with a fall of approximately 1,000 in the total ethnic Chinese population in the four border oblasts but not elsewhere in Russia. This meant that, after the Sino-Soviet split, over one in three ethnic Chinese on Russia's frontier were expelled to China or elsewhere in the USSR.

Given the long time period in between each Russian census and the lack of oblast-level data from the other Soviet Republics, we acknowledge that our evidence that these demographic shifts are the result of geopolitics is weaker than in China. Nevertheless, patterns of demographic change either side of the border suggests that both China and the USSR responded in strikingly parallel ways to the Sino-Soviet split.

TABLE 5.2. Each model is a difference-in-differences specification where the unit of analysis is the Russian oblast in the former Soviet Union and the DV is demographic change as measured in five Soviet censuses (1939–1989). Standard errors are clustered at the county level using Arellano's covariance matrix.

	Russian pop.		Chinese pop.		Total pop.	
	(1)	(2)	(3)	(4)	(5)	(6)
Sino-Soviet Split	−114,953***	−190,907***	35	23	−141,101***	−248,855***
	(40,447)	(50,853)	(28)	(27)	(44,637)	(55,242)
Border China:						
Sino-Soviet Split	162,598***	243,112***	−950**	−967**	165,426**	274,457***
	(56,820)	(65,365)	(463)	(476)	(64,071)	(71,862)
First differences	Yes	No	Yes	No	Yes	No
Oblasts	77	77	77	77	77	77
Observations	356	356	298	298	356	356

Note: $*p < 0.1$; $**p < 0.05$; $***p < 0.01$.

Conclusion

A common saying in Xinjiang today is *beihan nanwei*. Translated literally, this means that the north of Xinjiang is populated by Han and the south by Uyghurs. This chapter uncovers how the strange patterning of Xinjiang's contemporary ethnic demography originated. Examining demographic change in China and the USSR during the Sino-Soviet split (1959–1982), we found that Han settlement during the Sino-Soviet split was particularly targeted at oil-rich areas, border areas with the USSR lacking a natural boundary, and areas populated by ethnic Russians. We also found that China's ethnic Russian minority were deported as a result of this conflict, particularly those who resided in oil-rich and non-natural border areas.

In sum, these results suggest that as China and the USSR fell out politically in the late 1950s and the USSR sought to undermine Chinese control over its frontier, China responded by expelling ethnic Russians and settling Han in strategically important areas. In turn, the USSR deported ethnic Chinese and settled Russians in its vulnerable Far East borderland with China. Together, these policies drastically altered the ethnic demography of Central Asia generally and northern Xinjiang specifically in a very short period of time.

Taking a much longer historical view, however, rapid change in the ethnic demography of China's frontiers is far from unusual. The resettlement of

Han Chinese has been central to how the nascent Chinese state consolidated control over Shandong in the second century BCE, Yunnan in the fifteenth century CE, Hainan in the seventeenth century CE, and Manchuria in the late nineteenth century CE. Yet, despite the importance of settler colonialism in Chinese history, Zhu and Blachford (2016, 30) note that it "remains an under-researched topic" due to scanty historical censuses and difficulties obtaining sensitive demographic data. A key contribution of this chapter is that it overcomes the censorship on academic studies on demographic engineering in the People's Republic of China by using a number of leaked official sources to compile a panel of state-sponsored demographic change. This chapter thus newly uncovers how demographic change in China has been historically shaped by China's strategic geography—specifically, the presence of non-natural borders, natural resources, and fifth columns.

Of course, both China and the former USSR in the mid-twentieth century were exceptional in the sense that both were Communist states. Neither China nor the USSR had to concern itself with making resettlement in the interest of settlers given that the state exercised complete almost control over individual occupation, housing, and consumption. Given the absence of outside options for settlers, both states proved exceptionally effective at using migration to shore up control over their respective borderlands over the mid-twentieth century. Yet, China ultimately marketized and began to rapidly develop over the late twentieth century. Marketization removed the constraints on individual migration across China, meaning that the state no longer had the power to force Han to remain in the periphery. And the next chapter shows that, as China's coastal cities have become magnets for labor and capital since the 1980s, Beijing has been increasingly unable to lure Han to its contested northwest despite the rise of an Islamist insurgency there. Rapid development in eastern China closed its western frontier.

6

Belt and Road to Nowhere: China's Ongoing Struggle to Colonize Xinjiang

XINJIANG IS in the midst of a crisis. Of the 10 million Muslims in Xinjiang today, approximately 1 million have been held in forced reeducation camps designed to reengineer them as secular members of the Chinese state. Individual autonomy is limited. Biometric scans are required to enter and leave any municipality. Public squares are deserted due to fear of listening devices and Muslims avoid mosques to avoid appearing religious. Even the private sphere is not safe from scrutiny. Minority families are forced to periodically host government officials who monitor signs of devotion to Islam such as abstention from pork and alcohol.[1]

The recent turn to mass incarceration in Xinjiang reflects not just Beijing's coercive strength but also its persistent weakness in the west. States are far from omnipotent—a fact the English King Canute reportedly demonstrated to his courtiers in the eleventh century by failing to reverse the ocean tides. In this chapter I explain why the Chinese state has consistently sought and *failed* to colonize Xinjiang since the early 1990s. The rise of a perceived Islamist insurgency in 1990 led to a reinvigoration of state efforts to settle Han Chinese in geopolitically sensitive areas of Xinjiang. Yet, Han settlers, much like Canute's ocean tides, have not responded to state schemes in ways that have cohered with official intentions. Rather, as China has developed and its coastal cities have become magnets for investment and migration, the state has been *less* able to effectively settle Han in its periphery and thereby consolidate control over Xinjiang.

Recall that middle- and high-income states may endeavor to settle threatened frontiers but their success in doing so will be limited. China is in the midst of this disequilibrium—it has sought to colonize Xinjiang with Han Chinese but the supply of Han colonizers has simply dried up. After 1990, Beijing substantially scaled up funding to the Xinjiang Production and Construction Corps (XPCC or bingtuan)[2] and encouraged it to expand its control over southern Xinjiang. But I show that these efforts have resulted in only marginal increases in Han predominance in southern Xinjiang since 1990. Drawing on fieldwork in Xinjiang and qualitative data, I trace this failure to the countervailing market forces drawing labor and capital to industrial centers elsewhere in China. China's economic rise has constrained colonization.

The exception to this general rule of failure is Xinjiang's oil-rich areas. Following the opening of a number of oilfields in the Tarim basin during the 1990s, China has had some success in drawing Han to oil-rich areas of southern Xinjiang. But the capital-intensive and specialized nature of petrochemical extraction has meant that the discovery of oil in southern Xinjiang has had relatively little impact on the demographic composition of the province as a whole. In stark contrast to its success in colonizing northern Xinjiang in the 1960s and 1970s (Chapter 5), China has spectacularly failed to attract Han to southern Xinjiang since the 1990s. As a result of its rapid economic modernization, China essentially lost the power to colonize its west—forcing its leaders to rely on ever more costly and coercive alternatives for pacifying its unsettled frontier.

The Rise of a Perceived Islamist Threat in China

Xinjiang was not always a site of political contention and religious repression. Following the ascension of Deng Xiaoping in 1978 and the end of the Sino-Soviet split in 1982, Xinjiang—along with the rest of China—experienced a period of pronounced liberalization. The government allowed the reconstruction of religious institutions that had been destroyed during the Cultural Revolution and approximately 24,000 mosques were built in Xinjiang over the 1980s (Shichor, 2005). With the opening of the border, Sunni Muslims in Xinjiang could move freely across Central Asia and consequently began to reestablish connections with Muslims in Pakistan, Afghanistan, Kyrgyzstan, and the broader Middle East. Hajj missions to Mecca resumed in October 1979 and pilgrims returned with fundamentalist religious literature reflecting the rise of Wahhabism in the Sunni world.

The regional rise of political Islamism would ultimately spill over into Xinjiang after the 1980s. The conflict in Afghanistan between the mujahideen and the Soviet Union proved a source of inspiration and military training for young Uyghurs. A large number joined the ranks of the mujahideen and were stationed in the north of Afghanistan at Mazur-Sharif by the late 1980s (Kerr and Swinton, 2008). After the Soviet Union withdrawal from Afghanistan in 1989, these militants returned to extend the jihad against the Chinese state. In April 1990, up to 200 Uyghur militants trained in Afghanistan attacked Chinese military forces in the border township of Baren near Kashgar. These fighters, led by the leader of the East Turkestan Islamic Movement, Zeydin Yusup, sought to establish an Islamist state in Xinjiang. Violence spread quickly across southern Xinjiang following the assault and up to 3,000 Uyghurs were reportedly killed in clashes (Hierman, 2007).

The Baren incident proved a political watershed in western China. As Becquelin (2000) summarizes, "the conjunction of organizational sophistication, radical Muslim ideology and the weaponry used by the insurgents was far beyond the expectations of the security apparatus, suggesting foreign support from beyond the borders" (p. 69). The Chinese state responded to the Baren incident by scaling up internal security and by cracking down on Islam. One month after the uprising, an additional 8,000 officials were dispatched to support local governments in southern Xinjiang. By July 1990, 7,900 individuals across Xinjiang had been arrested for separatist activities. New laws were passed later that year to ban foreign preachers, close down unregistered mosques (including 50 in Baren alone) and Muslim schools, and create exclusion zones around military installations (Hierman, 2007).

In its renewed fight against separatism in Xinjiang, the central government was specifically concerned about unfavorable demographic trends there. Given the prior focus of Han and bingtuan settlement in Xinjiang's north during the Sino-Soviet split (see Chapter 5), southern Xinjiang was overwhelmingly populated by Uyghur Muslims. The overall bingtuan numbers and the proportion of Han in Xinjiang had also declined over the 1980s as rusticated Han had begun to return to the fast growing eastern seaboard (Figure 6.1). Given much higher birthrates among the non-Han, official projections were that the proportion of Han in Xinjiang would continue to decline into the future, falling from approximately 40% in 1990 to 35% in 2000 and less than 25% by 2030.[3]

The central government responded to the perceived interlinked threat of Islamist terrorism, separatism, and religious extremism—what would come to

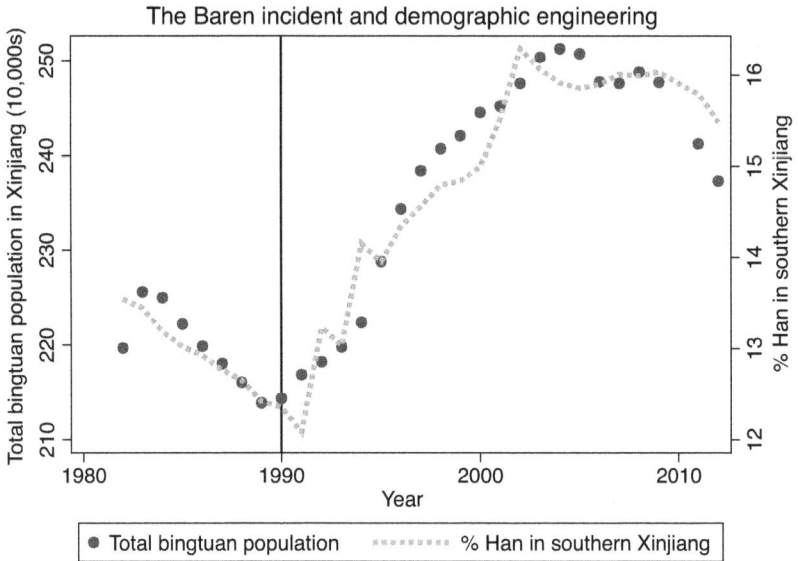

FIGURE 6.1. The percent of Han in southern Xinjiang and the total Xinjiang bingtuan population 1982–2014, with a line indicating the Baren incident of 1990.

be called the three evils (*sange shili*)—by encouraging Han to settle in Uyghur Muslim areas and border areas in southern Xinjiang. It did so in three main ways: (i) expanding the bingtuan, (ii) providing government benefits to Han settlers, and (iii) increasing government investment.

Taking each strategy in turn, after 1990 the central government scaled up funding to the bingtuan and encouraged the expansion of its territorial domain within southern Xinjiang. As a paramilitary unit directly under the State Council, the bingtuan usefully bypassed the Xinjiang provincial government and was exempt from *hukou* restrictions on work and migration. So, the bingtuan was viewed as the most effective organ for facilitating the rapid importation of Han settlers.[4] And a top secret Central Committee document leaked in the mid-1990s noted that the bingtuan's "duty of unifying labor with military affairs, opening of new lands and the developing of border regions should not change. . . . Our country should expand the bingtuan in southern Xinjiang" (Seymour and Anderson, 2015).[5] The bingtuan was specifically encouraged to expand cotton production in southern Xinjiang, which, despite its arid climate, was destined to become the "largest cotton-producing area in the country" according to Xinjiang's Party Secretary in 1996.[6] To make cotton production viable, water resources were redirected from northern to southern

Xinjiang,[7] the Taxkorgan river was dammed for irrigation, and new bingtuan units were established in a number of restive southern counties (Cliff, 2009). As a result, bingtuan cotton production rose 300% between 1991 and 1994 (Seymour, 2000) and its membership began to rise for the first time since the 1970s (Figure 6.1).

Secondly, local governments have created a number of Han-specific benefits designed to increase the percentage of Han in southern Xinjiang. In southern Xinjiang, any migrant can legally obtain an urban *hukou*—granting migrants valuable access to government schools, insurance, and healthcare.[8] Elsewhere in China, cities have long required advanced degrees, skills, or a job at a large company to obtain an urban *hukou*. In practice, however, local governments only issue urban *hukou* to Han who move to southern Xinjiang.[9] Local governments in southern Xinjiang have also offered reclaimed land on long-term lease to any new migrants. Again, in practice, these contracts are available only to Han who migrate from the east (Finley, 2013).

Thirdly, the central government began to scale up public sector investment in Xinjiang in the 1990s. After market reform, the government could no longer force Han to move to frontier areas as it did throughout the Mao era (Wallace, 2014). Most internal migration in the 1980s was rural-to-urban migration by laborers attracted by higher wages in coastal cities such as Shanghai and Shenzhen (Fan, 2007). And, seeking to contain inflation, Beijing had severely cut back government spending in its interior in the late 1980s—for instance, government fixed asset investment in Xinjiang dropped by a staggering 37.3% over 1988–1989 (Christoffersen, 1993, 145).

So, in order to settle Xinjiang with Han after 1990, Beijing had to provide lucrative new economic opportunities for new Han migrants. As a State Council study on Xinjiang from the mid-1990s titled "Channel the Migrants and Establish Agriculture in the Desert" summarized, "to attract migrants . . . *the main point is to allow people to accumulate riches*" (Wang and Chen 1996, p. 439). The government launched the Open Up the Northwest campaign in 1992, which aimed to double government investment in Xinjiang in three years. As a result, the province's GDP ballooned from 7.5 billion yuan to 15.5 billion between 1991 and 1994. This sustained increase in government investment meant that Xinjiang was one of the fastest growing provinces over the 1990s, consistently topping 10% GDP growth every year.[10]

Complementing increased cotton production, government investment in Xinjiang in the 1990s focused on increasing oil production in strategy colloquially called "black and white" (*yihei yibai*). In the late 1980s, the China

National Petroleum Corporation (CNPC) had discovered rich oil deposits in the Taklamakan desert—the heart of the Tarim basin that makes up southern Xinjiang. Speculation abounded that the basin could hold upwards of 300 million tons of oil.

The central question was whether oil and gas extraction in the Tarim basin could ever be economic. Given difficulties of access, CNPC's efforts to develop a petroleum industry in the remote Taklamakan desert required heavy government subventions. As Yan Dunshi, chief geologist of CNPC for over thirty years, explained in 1999 to a fellow industry insider:

> The cost of drilling a super-deep well, one that is more than 5,000 m deep, in the middle of the desert in Tarim, is extremely high. Just to make a big rig substructure in the desert would cost around 15 million yuan, almost a hundred times more than it would cost in the oilfields of the east (Mao, 2019, 284).

In order to overcome these costs and make petroleum production in Tarim viable, Beijing subsidized the CNPC through generous loans from the Bank of China and investment in associated infrastructure. For instance, in 1993 CNPC requested the construction of a 4,200 kilometer west-east oil and gas pipeline from Tarim to Shanghai. Beijing initially baulked at the price tag of several billion US dollars, with observers warning that the pipeline could never be economically viable given cheaper alternatives on the global market (Chang, 2001; Downs, 2004). But the pipeline eventually became the flagship project in President Jiang Zemin's "Open Up The West" program, with construction work beginning in 2000.[11] A flurry of other projects was also launched to create a viable petroleum industry in Tarim. Perhaps most dramatically, in 1995 a 522 kilometer-long desert highway was built to the newly discovered Tazhong oilfield through the heart of the Taklamakan Desert. Rows of irrigated trees had to be planted on either side of the road, in one of the most inhospitable environments on the planet, in order to stop the shifting sands from swallowing the asphalt.

These investments succeeded at increasing petroleum production in Xinjiang, even if initial estimates of Tarim's oil reserves proved somewhat optimistic. After the completion of the oil pipeline from Lunnan to Korla in 1992, oil production at Lunnan increased 500% over the next four years (Wang, 1999, 101). Large-scale commercial production also began at the Tazhong oilfield in the heart of the Taklamakan desert in 1996 following the completion of a pipeline to Lunnan (ibid.). As a result, oil production in Xinjiang doubled in the 1990s[12] and the Tarim basin went from producing almost no oil to producing some 4 million tons a year in 1998 (Mao, 2019, 273). By the mid-2000s, petroleum extraction provided tens of thousands of well-paying jobs for the Han who made up approximately 95% of the industry's workforce (Zhu and Blachford, 2012).

Extremely high levels of government investment in Xinjiang have remained in place since the 2000s. Most recently, Xi Jinping's "Belt and Road" initiative, launched in 2012, has taken government investment in southern Xinjiang to new heights, with its flagship policy the creation of a Special Economic Zone in Kashgar. By 2015, fixed asset investment had reached an extraordinary 104% of Xinjiang's GDP,[13] reflecting the fact that every dollar of government investment has returned far less than a dollar in economic output. As Keynes famously warned, two railways are not twice as good as one. Beijing's largesse has resulted not in productive infrastructure but in a number of white elephants and roads to nowhere. For instance, an extraordinarily expensive road opened in southern Xinjiang in 2019 to connect a small town of 10,000 people to an even smaller hamlet of 3,000 people, and a number of its 600 hairpin turns are featured in Figure 6.2.

Together, these policies have stemmed the decline in the Han share of the population in Xinjiang, which has plateaued at approximately 40% since 1990. Yet, China's hold over Xinjiang remains contested. A series of attacks by Uyghur militants since 2009—culminating in a gruesome knife attack by eight militants in a train station in south-east China in 2014 that killed 31 civilians and injured 140 others—have hardened the Chinese government and the broader populace against the Uyghur population, whom they regard as aiding and abetting political Islamists (Zenz and Leibold, 2019).[14] Immediately after these attacks, President Xi Jinping emphasized to officials that "The methods that our comrades have at hand are too primitive. None of these weapons is any answer for their big machete blades, axe heads and cold steel weapons. . . . We must be as harsh as them and show absolutely no mercy."[15] The paranoiac eradication of all Islamist influence in Xinjiang through mass reeducation and sterilization reflects a shift to an even more extreme and costly level of coercion to defeat a perceived secessionist threat.

Recovering the Logic of Demographic Change in Xinjiang

Beijing may well have sought to resettle Han to southern Xinjiang since 1990, but where has the state actually been successful at "sinifying" Xinjiang over

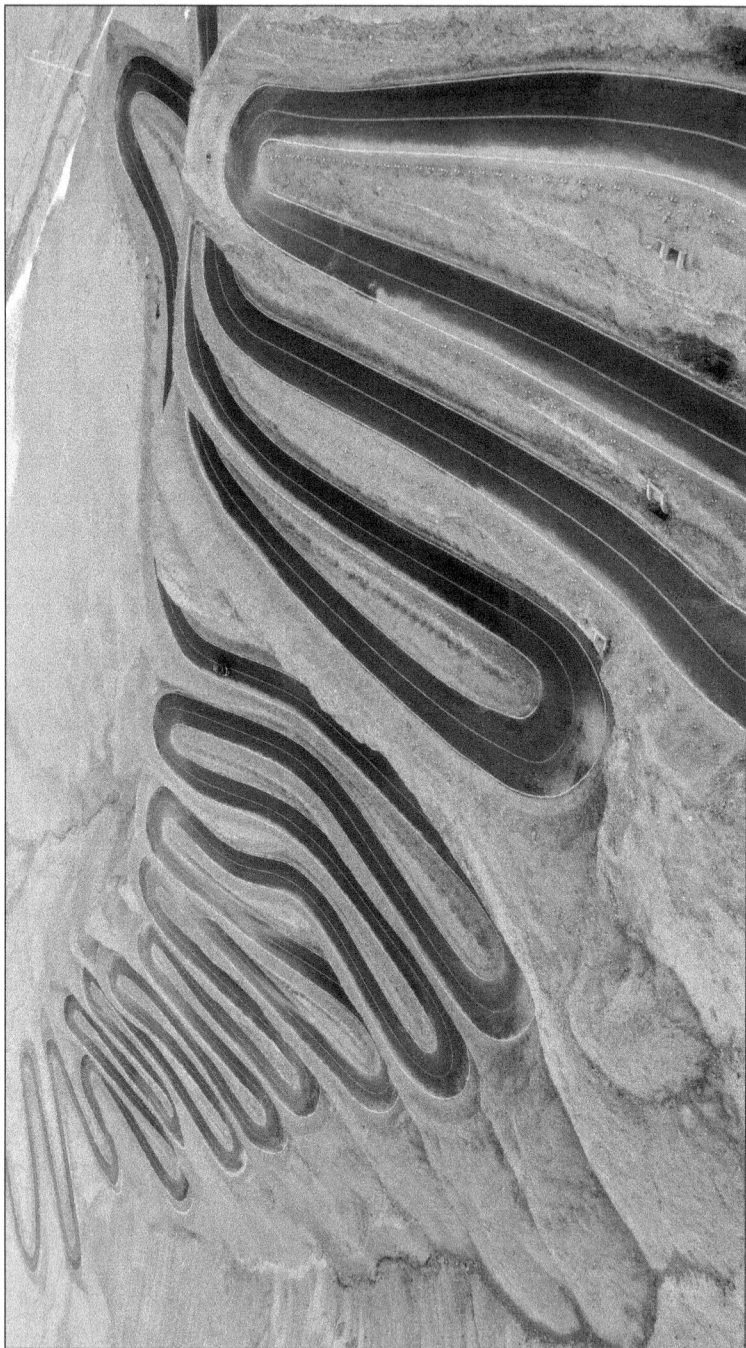

FIGURE 6.2. The Panlong or Plateau Sky Road connecting Waqia to
Tashkurgan in southern Xinjiang. Photo courtesy of Xinhua / Alamy Stock Photo.

this period? Recall that in the theory chapter, I argued that the *timing* of state-led colonization is shaped by the onset of conflict whilst the *location* of state-led colonization is shaped by the location of disloyal minority groups, natural resources, and proximity to porous borders. The core ethnic groups of interest are the Han and Muslims, who constituted the stereotypically loyal and disloyal ethnic groups respectively. As in previous chapters, I examine how demographic patterns in Xinjiang changed after the rise of a perceived threat in 1990.

I use the same Xinjiang county-year panel discussed in the previous chapter, which draws on confidential internal statistical yearbooks that I collected in partnership with Anna Zhang. This dataset represents the best historical source on demographic changes in Xinjiang but it does have its limitations. One limitation is that it does not capture flows of military personnel or temporary migrants. However, the exclusion of soldiers and temporary migrants means that we are actually more accurately measuring permanent migration, which is the central outcome of interest.

Unlike the threat posed to northern Xinjiang by the USSR during the Sino-Soviet split, the perceived threat posed by Islamists after 1990 was focused on southern Xinjiang. To see whether Han settlement was disproportionately targeted at southern border areas where insurgents tended to smuggle weapons from Afghanistan (Raczka, 1998, 388), I created a binary measure of whether a county is a southern border county (see Figure 6.3).[16] To the extent that Han settlement was targeted at these counties, we can be assured that the Chinese state was particularly focused on consolidating its control over areas of Xinjiang proximate to regional Islamist bases.[17]

In order to see whether Han settlement generally shifted to Muslim-majority areas after 1990, I also measured the number of Muslims in each county. China does not collect yearly data on its religious minorities. However, we can use its yearly ethnic data and aggregate the total county-level population of each of the Muslim-majority ethnic groups in Xinjiang (the Uyghurs, the Kyrgyz, the Hui, and the Kazakhs) as a proxy for the total Muslim population.[18] China did not begin to deport Muslims *en masse* from southern Xinjiang until 2016, and so I do not report results for ethnic cleansing.[19]

Finally, to see whether Han settlement in Xinjiang has been shaped by the location of valuable natural resources, I leverage two "natural experiments" of history—the opening of the Lunnan and Tazhong oil fields during the 1990s. I first examine whether Han predominance disproportionately increased in the county of Luntai after the start of commercial production at the Lunnan

FIGURE 6.3. Southern Xinjiang, its oil fields, and the southern border counties.

oilfield in May 1992. I then secondly examine whether Han predominance also increased in Qiemo county after the start of production at the Tazhong oilfield in 1996. The location of these counties and oilfields can be seen in Figure 6.3.

The Failed Colonization of Southern Xinjiang

Figure 6.4 illustrates the change in the share of each county that was Han Chinese between 1989 and 2014.

This map reveals that, although the overall Han percent of the population of Xinjiang has stagnated at approximately 40% since the early 1980s, there is significant spatial variation in demographic change. Most of northern Xinjiang, with the exception of the urban center of Urumqi and the oil-rich counties of Hami and Shanshan, has actually experienced a fall in Han demographic predominance since the 1990s. However, this is not true of southern Xinjiang, where most counties have experienced a small increase in Han predominance since 1990.

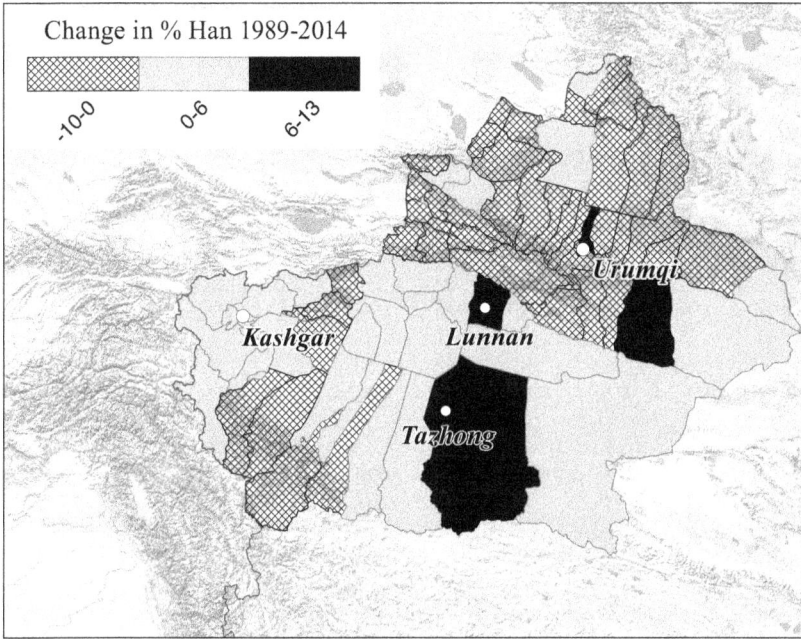

FIGURE 6.4. The change in the share of an area that is Han Chinese
by county in Xinjiang (1989–2014).

The statistical models indicate that Han settlement indeed shifted to the
southern border counties after 1990 (Appendix Table 6.1). The Baren incident is associated with a statistically significant increase in the Han percentage of the southern border counties and in areas with substantial Muslim
populations. The increase in Han demographic presence has been generally
concentrated in southern Xinjiang and progressively declines as you move further from the Afghanistan/Pakistan border. So, aside from oil-rich areas, the
only areas of Xinjiang that have generally experienced an increase in Han predominance after 1990 are counties proximate to external havens for Islamist
insurgents or with substantial Muslim populations.

Consistent with the mitigating effects of economic development, however,
the magnitude of these demographic changes is quite small. In southern Xinjiang, the Baren incident, and the post-1990 era generally, is only associated
with a 1–2 percentage point increase in the proportion of the population that
is Han. To consider the size of this change, recall that over the Sino-Soviet split
(1959–1982) the average increase in Han Chinese predominance in northern
Xinjiang was approximately 40 percentage points. So, these data also indicate

Han settlement in Luntai after oil production

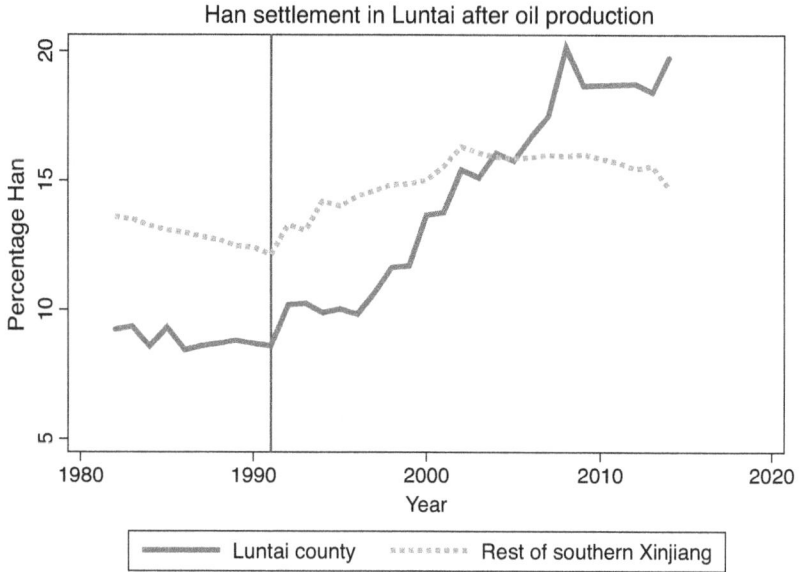

FIGURE 6.5. The effect of Lunnan oilfield production (1992–present) on Han predominance in Luntai county relative to the rest of southern Xinjiang.

that Beijing has generally struggled to achieve meaningfully large increases in the percentage of Han in contested areas during the post-Mao period.

Also in contrast to the Mao era, the bingtuan has failed to significantly redirect settlement to southern Xinjiang after the Baren incident. Bingtuan settlement after 1990 tended to be focused on existing bingtuan industrial centers such as Aksu and Shihezi. The models bear out the absence of bingtuan settlement in Muslim majority and southern border areas—a result that is unchanged no matter how one models proximity to southern Xinjiang (Appendix Table 6.2). Despite paying lip service to the need to defend Xinjiang from new threats emanating from the south, the bulk of the increase in the bingtuan population illustrated in Figure 6.1 has been in northern, not southern, Xinjiang. In stark contrast to its success in colonizing northern Xinjiang during the Sino-Soviet split, the bingtuan has proven relatively ineffective at colonizing southern Xinjiang.

The only areas of southern Xinjiang where the state has achieved large increases in Han predominance since 1990 are oil-rich areas (Figure 6.4, Appendix Table 6.3). After the start of Lunnan oilfield production in 1992, Han settlement to the surrounding Luntai county increased dramatically

Han settlement in Qiemo after oil production

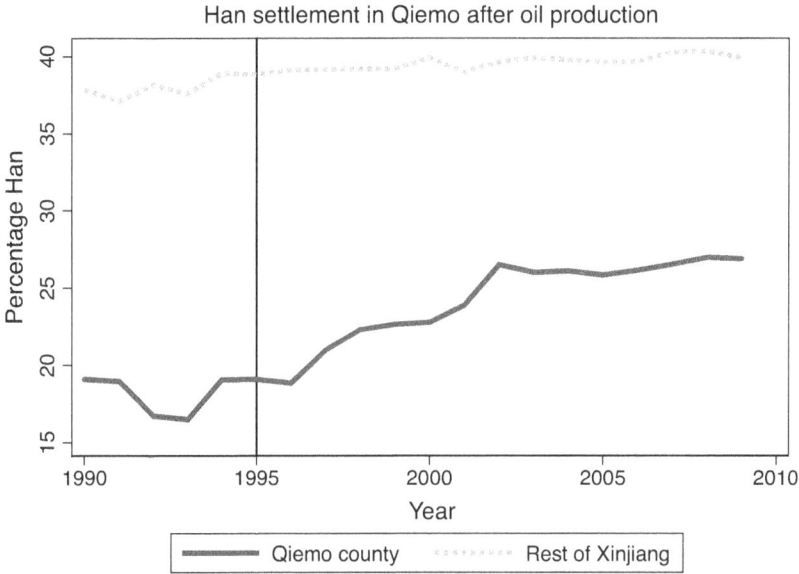

FIGURE 6.6. The effect of Tazhong oilfield production (1996–present) on the percent of Han in Qiemo county relative to the rest of Xinjiang.

(Figure 6.6). Lunnan town was literally "born from oil"[20] (*yinyou ersheng*) as thousands of oil workers quickly emigrated to the area in the early 1990s, drawn by high wages paying up to 2,000 yuan a month.[21] CNPC's preference for Mandarin-speaking, university-educated engineers, however, meant that the Uyghurs were locked out of this resource boom; in 1996, not a single worker at the Lunnan oilfield was Uyghur (Finley, 2013, 67).[22] As a result of this sustained influx of technical workers from eastern China, the proportion of Han in Luntai increased approximately 20 percentage points between 1992 and 2012, whereas the rest of southern Xinjiang only had a small increase in Han predominance over the same time period. Similarly, after commercial production at the Tazhong oil field started in 1996, Han migration to the surrounding Qiemo county increased dramatically (Figure 6.6). The share of Han in Qiemo increased from 19% to 26% between 1996 and 2006, whilst the share of Han in the rest of Xinjiang stagnated at 40% over the same time period.

However, the capital intensive and highly specialized nature of petrochemical extraction has meant that even these oil rushes have had little impact on the demographic composition of Xinjiang as a whole. For instance, the approximately 15,000 increase in the permanent Han population of Luntai since 1992 has had a very noticeable impact on the demographic composition of Lunnan county. Likewise for the approximately 10,000 Han who have settled in Qiemo county since 1996. But these increases are but a drop in the ocean of Xinjiang as a whole, making up approximately 0.1% of the province's population in 2010.

The reader may object that many Han from eastern China would have been drawn to oil-rich areas of Xinjiang even absent the Baren incident. After all, Han Chinese made up the vast bulk of engineering graduates in China in the 1990s and so would likely have always made up the bulk of oil workers in Xinjiang. Can we really conclude that the settlement of oil-rich regions of southern Xinjiang by Han Chinese since the early 1990s is politically motivated? Put differently, is such migration settler-led or state-led?[23]

The evidence indicates that Han migration to oil-rich areas of southern Xinjiang should be considered a case of state-led colonization. Recall that petroleum production in the Tarim basin requires substantial government subsidy. To say nothing of the idiosyncratic geological challenges posed by the Taklamakan desert, sheer remoteness makes oil and gas production there uncompetitive. For instance, in the late 1990s the cost of shipping crude from Tarim to Shanghai was $6 per barrel, over double the cost of shipping from the Gulf (Wang, 1999, 100). These transportation costs are reinforced by the higher cost of providing goods and services to workers. The cost of providing one *jin* (half a kilogram) of tofu to workers on the CNPC oilfields in Tarim, for instance, was 40 yuan in 1990s (Mao, 2019, 284)—an order of magnitude higher than in the east. Accordingly, the cost of onshore oil and gas extraction for Chinese firms relative to western firms was 25% and 30% greater per barrel respectively in 1999 (Chang, 2001, 226). Chinese producers and consumers all implicitly subsidized CNPC and Sinopec in the 1990s in the form of artificially high domestic gas and oil prices.

Government investment in pipelines and roads in Xinjiang have ameliorated these otherwise crippling transportation challenges but at the price of appalling capital waste. For instance, the landmark West-East pipeline has proven to be a white elephant. Upon its completion in 2003, projected annual gas output was slashed from 12 billion cubic meters to just 4 billion cubic meters (Chang, 2001, 223), as industry saw no reason to switch from cheaper coal sources (Downes, 2008b, 131). CNPC ultimately sold half of its share in the Central Asian pipelines in 2015 for a small fraction of the construction cost.[24] CNPC's investment in Tarim has, crucially, taken away money from its otherwise much more competitive eastern oilfields. As Yan Dunshi, former chief geologist of CNPC, complained:

> Appropriating the East's limited funds and redirecting it to the West, going all out in Tarim, resulted in the cancellation of many projects in the eastern oil and gas fields. The production of the eastern oilfields dropped dramatically, and 'stabilizing the East' became just empty talk (Mao, 2019, 279).

Perhaps most egregiously, the Taklamakan desert highway built to open up the Tazhong oilfield has proven to be a poor investment. A toll station had been initially been built in 1995 to help subsidize the road's construction, but was subsequently abandoned. So few cars traversed the road that the money from tolls could not even cover the wages of the collectors (Mao, 2019, 287). And the long-term viability of this highway still remains in doubt given the ever shifting desert sands and salinity of the borehole water used to irrigate the fringing trees.

Queried about the extent of this capital waste, one manager in the CNPC campaign headquarters emphasized that "In spending money hand over fist like this in Tarim, the key point is that it isn't [CNPC's] own money. It's public money, so why not spend it? No one cares" (Mao, 2019, 303). In light of the manifold subsidies provided by the central government without which there would have been no migration at all, the colonization of oil-rich areas of southern Xinjiang since 1990 by Han is best understood as state-led.

Why, aside from oil-rich areas, has Beijing had so little success in colonizing southern Xinjiang? In essence, market reform and rapid economic development in eastern China have crippled the state's capacity to effectively manipulate the direction of internal migration. Although China has remained a nominally Communist country since 1949, much has changed internally since the 1970s. Market reform removed the state's power to coercively relocate migrants across the country (Wallace, 2014), whereas rapid economic growth in eastern China has limited the state's power to entice Han westward.

With respect to the bingtuan, the better economic options for Han in eastern China has proven a persistent challenge for recruitment. As a report from the mid-1990s warned, "the living standard of the million wasteland-reclaiming soldiers of the Corps is well below that of the workers in China proper (*neidi*)"[25] To raise the living standards of its members in southern

Xinjiang, the bingtuan has established new cities there—most notably, Alaer and Tumshker (Bao, 2018). But these cities have become ghost towns. Due to high transportation costs and distance from pools of skilled labor, Alaer and Tumshker are empty of people for much of the year.[26] Moreover, in order to ensure its agricultural and cotton production arms in southern Xinjiang remain profitable, agricultural members of the bingtuan have been provided with little subsidized support. Bingtuan farmers are still told what they must grow and at what price they must sell their crop to other bingtuan enterprises, and have been expected to invest their own capital. Accordingly, the agricultural sector of the bingtuan has struggled to attract new members. So, although overall bingtuan numbers have increased slightly since the 1990s, new bingtuan members have primarily joined its better-paid industrial enterprises in northern Xinjiang.

Marketization also created a perverse incentive on the part of the bingtuan to scale up its more profitable industrial enterprises in northern Xinjiang. The bingtuan corporatized throughout the 1990s and transitioned into an umbrella State Owned Enterprise with a substantial collection of individual companies. Bingtuan enterprise managers have been evaluated since the 1990s on their capacity to become self-sufficient and make a profit. Responding to this pressure, the bingtuan as a whole has increasingly shed its unprofitable agricultural arms and redirected investment to its higher-value industrial and service enterprises based in Shihezi in northern Xinjiang (Cliff, 2009). Of course, this outcome contradicts the center's broader objective of scaling up the bingtuan's presence in southern Xinjiang.

Efforts by local governments to draw Han to southern Xinjiang by providing free land on long-term lease and an urban *hukou* have proven more effective but at significant social cost. Prior to the most recent crackdown, Uyghurs in southern Xinjiang bitterly noted the difficulties they had in accessing land and government benefits relative to the Han. The allocation of irrigated land to the Han put significant pressure on scarce water resources and catalyzed communal conflicts between Uyghur and Han farmers in a number of rural southern counties (Finley, 2013).

The subsequent chill in interethnic relations was noted by long-term residents of Xinjiang.[27] Between 2009 and 2014, there were frequent rumors of syringe and knife attacks on Han civilians across Xinjiang. As a result, few Han ventured alone into Uyghur-dominated areas in southern towns such as Yarkand or Hotan and those that did were under the close watch of armed police. Given this febrile security environment, Han Chinese began to leave

Xinjiang after 2009 (Figure 6.1) as terrorist attacks and repressive security measures provoked much fear among the settler population.

Finally, government investment in Xinjiang managed to attract seasonal Han laborers and construction workers but this has had relatively little impact on permanent migrant numbers. Xinjiang was one of the top provincial destinations for labor migration during the 1990s and by the 2000 census there were 790,000 individuals in Xinjiang registered as "floating" (*liudong renkou*). The floating population, though visibly increasing Han presence on the streets, has limited political utility from the perspective of the central government. Floating migrants, rather than creating a permanent Han presence in China's west, have little attachment to Xinjiang as they view the province as a place to temporarily earn money before returning home.[28] Seasonal migrants usually remain in constant contact with their families back in the east through WeChat, return to their hometowns during the winter, and often live and associate only with fellow migrants from their hometowns within Xinjiang (*laoxiang*).

When in Xinjiang, one hears a great deal of derision directed toward these "internal expats" by Uyghurs and long-standing Han residents alike (*lao Xinjiang ren*) for their avarice and self-segregation.[29] The government press also periodically criticizes the seasonal migrant population for undermining social stability and the *hukou* system, and lauds seasonal workers who make the "right" decision to permanently settle in Xinjiang (Zhang, 2010, 278–81). But even seasonal laborers who have worked in Xinjiang since the early 1990s resist relocating their *hukou* to Xinjiang because this would end the prospect of eventually returning home. As the government cannot force seasonal migrants to transfer their *hukou* to Xinjiang, permanent Han migration has been insufficient to overcome the higher rates of natural increase of minority populations since the 1980s. Hence, the Han share of the permanent population in Xinjiang largely stagnated at 40% and began to precipitously fall after the attacks of 2009.

Moreover, seasonal migrants, rather than being attracted to the relatively poor and remote Uyghur heartland in southern Xinjiang, tend to live and work in already Han-predominated cities of northern Xinjiiang (Tong, 1994). This can be seen in the 2000 census, which, unlike the yearly Xinjiang Statistical Yearbooks, enumerated the entire physically present population of Xinjiang. Whereas seasonal migrants without registration constituted a sizeable 20% of the population of major northern cities like Urumqi or Shihezi at the turn of the millennium, they were less than 3% of southern border areas (Figure 6.7, see Appendix). Seasonal migrants, just like permanent Han migrants, have generally been attracted to Xinjiang's northern industrial centers, *not* the Muslim heartland in the south. In any case, given their absence of ownership of any property in or legal attachment to Xinjiang, migrant workers have led the exodus of Han from Xinjiang over the past decade.[30]

In sum, Beijing's efforts to encourage the Han to settle in southern Xinjiang since the rise of an Islamist insurgency in 1990 have proven quite ineffective. Market reform has meant that in order to direct Han migration to strategically important areas, the state has had to make migration sufficiently lucrative for Han migrants. Yet, with rapid economic development elsewhere in China, few Han have found the prospect of becoming an agricultural bingtuan member appealing, and seasonal workers have felt no need to permanently transfer their residency. The only areas of southern Xinjiang that have experienced meaningful increases in permanent Han predominance over the past thirty years have been the few counties there endowed with oil, and even oil production has required enormous subsidy. As China has developed and marketized, its capacity to effectively alter the demography of Xinjiang through migration has declined. The era of frontier colonization in China is over.

Of course, this does not mean that China will soon lose control over Xinjiang. Beijing can always substitute for even more coercive and risky tools to retain control over its western frontier. In this sense, the Orwellian era of mass surveillance, forced sterilization, and minority "re-education" in Xinjiang may have only just begun. But given the extreme cost of mass incarceration and the likelihood that forced assimilation measures will backfire, the long-term viability of China's sovereignty over southern Xinjiang remains in doubt. China remains vulnerable to a breakdown in its coercive apparatus, after which it is likely that Xinjiang will—as in 2009—once again descend into widespread ethnic violence given the accumulated resentments of the Uyghurs. As one long-time Han resident of Xinjiang recently fretted: "I don't know what will happen if we ever let the Uighurs out."[31]

Conclusion

Few subjects are as contested in the study of Chinese politics as demographic change in western China. Existing studies generally fall into two main camps. In the first camp, it is commonly asserted that Beijing has recently encouraged Han Chinese to migrate to Xinjiang and Tibet with the objective of turning these areas into Han colonies. Han migration has been labelled "Sinification," "cultural genocide," "internal colonialism," and "colonization with Chinese characteristics."[32] For instance, Becquelin (2000, 89) prominently asserted at the turn of the millennium that "The Han population is expanding, settling further away in towns, and has started to spread out steadily in southern Xinjiang."[33] The second camp dominated by Chinese scholars, on the other hand, downplay the hand of the state. Internal migration since the 1980s has been driven by autonomous market forces, they argue, and aggregate demographic change in both Tibet and Xinjiang over the last forty years has been, in any case, quite limited.[34]

Both schools of thought miss the mark. Western scholars who argue that Xinjiang is being "internally colonized" invariably cite the fact that the Han percent of the population in Xinjiang has climbed from just 4% in the 1940s to 40% today and the various government projects encouraging Han migration to southern Xinjiang.[35] But the past two chapters have demonstrated this demographic shift occurred entirely prior to the 1980s and there has been little demographic change in southern Xinjiang over the past thirty years. The Uyghur heartland of southern Xinjiang has largely not been colonized by Han settlers. Even those counties endowed with oil have experienced an *exodus* of Han over the past decade as settlers have fled Xinjiang's repressive security environment.[36]

Equally, however, scholars in the second camp are wrong to suggest that the limited demographic change in Xinjiang since the 1990s has been purely apolitical. Recall that the percentage of Han and the overall bingtuan population were falling in Xinjiang over the 1980s. Stabilizing these politically unfavorable demographic trends required government intervention. Scaling up petroleum production in southern Xinjiang in the 1990s would have been impossible without the construction of economically unviable piplines and the maintenance of artificially high domestic gas and oil prices. Likewise for bingtuan cotton production; by the late 1990s, the amount of money spent on cotton subsidies alone was equivalent to all provincial government revenue.[37] Keeping Han in China's western periphery required, and still requires, extraordinary amounts of government money.[38]

My findings in this chapter instead lend credence to scholars of China like Fan (2007), Wallace (2014), and Sorace and Hurst (2016), who have emphasized the qualified power of the state to shape contemporary migration flows.[39] Beijing reinvigorated efforts to populate Muslim-majority areas of Xinjiang and southern border areas with Han Chinese after the Baren uprising. Yet, with the exception of a few oil-rich areas, development schemes totalling in tens of billions of dollars have resulted in strikingly small increases in Han predominance. Given relatively high wages in coastal cities, few Han have found the prospect of becoming a bingtuan laborer appealing. And Han laborers who have moved to Xinjiang for temporary contract work have seen no need to permanently emigrate there. Beijing's efforts to colonize southern Xinjiang since 1990 resulted in a large seasonal migrant population prior to 2009, but failed at anchoring a Han settler population permanently in the periphery. As one Chinese academic lamented immediately prior to the mass incarceration of Muslims: "The real dilemma is . . . the exodus of Han from Xinjiang, especially in the four prefectures of southern Xinjiang, and how the Han population cannot be developed" (Liao, 2016). China consistently tried and consistently *failed* to colonize southern Xinjiang in the 1990s and 2000s.

In this sense, Australia's Northern Territory in the mid-twentieth century (see Chapter 4) and southern Xinjiang today share many structural similarities. Both are largely rural and remote frontiers that would, given patterns of investment and job creation in modernized economies, ordinarily be sources of out-migration. Yet, anxieties about their proximity to potential threats has meant that both southern Xinjiang and the Northern Territory have been the sites of substantial government investment in infrastructure and irrigation schemes designed to rapidly increase their population and change their demographic composition. In both cases, these schemes have resulted in a number of white elephants and roads to nowhere. But both Australia and China failed to achieve their desired demographic outcomes.

Colonization is outmoded by modernization. In middle- and high-income countries, efforts to reverse the flow of migrants toward cities in the core are akin to King Canute's efforts to reverse the flow of the ocean tide: spasmodic, fleetingly successful, and ultimately futile.

7

Settler Colonialism around the World in the Late Twentieth Century

IN MY experience, when people are asked to think of settler colonial projects around the world today, they do not tend to nominate West Papua or Xinjiang. The plight of the Tibetans in China, the Rohingya of Myanmar, the Kashmiris of India, and the Darfuris of Sudan have occupied more space in the popular consciousness. Of course, even these cases are dwarfed by the attention paid to Israeli settler colonialism in the Palestinian territories. Israel remains the only country whose settlements have been condemned by the UN Security Council. Indeed, Israel has been subject to more condemnations by the United Nations Human Rights Council than the rest of the world combined.

Comparison prompts us to ask necessary, if somewhat fraught, questions. Firstly, how prevalent is settler colonialism around the world? Is the vocal condemnation of Israel by certain countries somewhat hypocritical? Secondly, can the argument of this book travel to other contexts? If I had examined the history of Sudan, Israel, India, and Myanmar rather than of Indonesia, Australia, the former USSR, and China, I may well have found a very different underlying logic to colonization. So, paraphrasing Geddes (1990), have the cases that I've chosen affected the answers that I've gotten?

Cross-national comparisons are also a fraught activity for methodological reasons. There are a number of challenges when trying to compare any phenomenon across countries. First, there is often no agreed definition for nebulous concepts like colonization. Second, even if we accept a particular definition such as "the coercive displacement of indigenous peoples by settlers," there is no necessary agreement about the criteria that need to be satisfied to fit this definition. For example, what counts as "coercive"? Or, what amount of migration qualifies? And even when we have a common definition and standard for measuring a concept like colonization across different countries, there is no necessary agreement on whether a particular case fits the criteria. The historical record can be ambiguous.

Yet, without looking at the universe of cases, there remains that lingering concern: have I chosen to look just at the cases that fit my theory? In this chapter, I address that concern by looking at patterns of settler colonialism and ethnic cleansing from around the world in the late twentieth century. There has been no prior study of settler colonialism and ethnic cleansing using systematically compiled data from around the globe. If my theory has value beyond the four countries that I've examined in detail, then we should expect that economic development, territorial conflict, ethnic minority loyalties, and natural resources systematically explain the incidence of colonization and ethnic cleansing across all the countries of the world. So, the goal of this chapter is to characterize the correlates of state-sponsored migration around the world. Correlation may not be causality but correlation is custom; correlations allow us to understand how customary, or exceptional, particular cases of settler colonialism are.

In this chapter, I show that my cases are far from exceptional. Colonization and ethnic cleansing tend to occur in less developed and territorially insecure states. Such states tend to colonize and cleanse disloyal minorities, oil-rich minorities, or minorities proximate to contested border zones. I also find little support for the importance of democratization or international norms. In short, patterns of forced migration around the world corroborate the existence of a settler colonial transition; Israel, not Indonesia, is the exception that proves the rule.

Who are the Colonizers Today?

To measure ethnic cleansing and settler colonialism around the world, I draw on data from the Minorities at Risk Project (2009). MAR is a research group of political scientists who track the situation of 284 "at risk" ethnic minorities whose populations exceed 100,000.[1] MAR specifically tracked which minorities around the world were subject to expulsion and land dispossession between 1980 and 2003, which I use as proxies for ethnic cleansing and colonization respectively. For further details on these and other data that I draw on in this chapter, see the Appendix. For the interested reader, I also address issues of measurement error and selection bias in the MAR data in the Appendix.

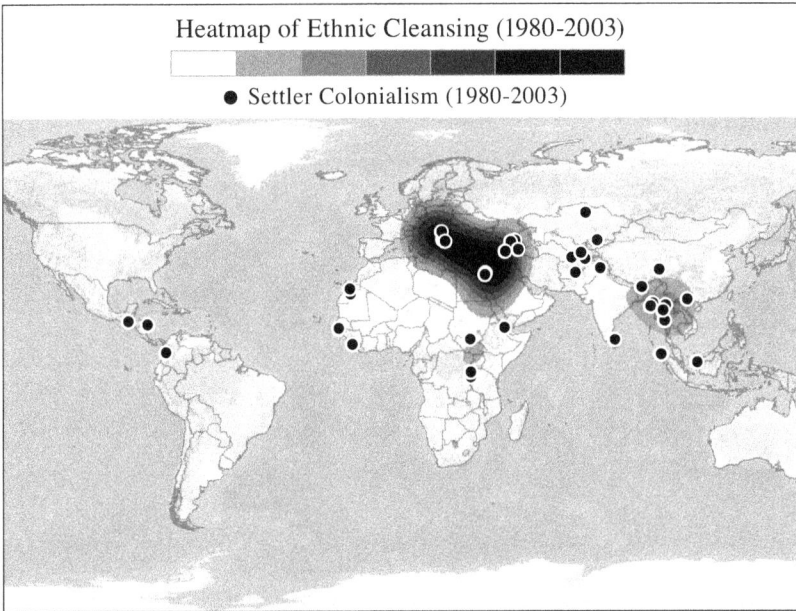

FIGURE 7.1. Heatmap of ethnic cleansing and a dot density of settler colonialism around the world in the late twentieth century. See Appendix for sources and data description.

These data reveal that colonization and ethnic cleansing are quite common phenomena. Between 1980 and 2003, over 25% of countries had at least one ethnic minority that was subject to colonization or ethnic cleansing. Figure 7.1 illustrates that ethnic cleansing and settler colonialism tended to cluster in the countries of Eastern Europe, the Middle East, and East Asia in the late twentieth century. Despite being ethnically heterogeneous and underdeveloped, countries in sub-Saharan Africa and Latin America were notably characterized by a relative absence of ethnic cleansing over this same time period.

What accounts for these large regional differences in coercive migration? Colonization and ethnic cleansing clustered in the borderlands of South Asia, the Middle East, and the Balkans over this period because these were the areas of greatest territorial conflict. If we proxy territorial conflict through the presence of military clashes over territory or a MID,[2] it is immediately evident that Eastern Europe, the Middle East, and East Asia had the most intense levels of territorial conflict over this period (Figure 7.2).[3] On the other hand, border conflicts were largely absent in sub-Saharan Africa and Latin America during the late twentieth century and so states faced relatively little need to engage in coercive territorial consolidation (Herbst, 1990; Darden and

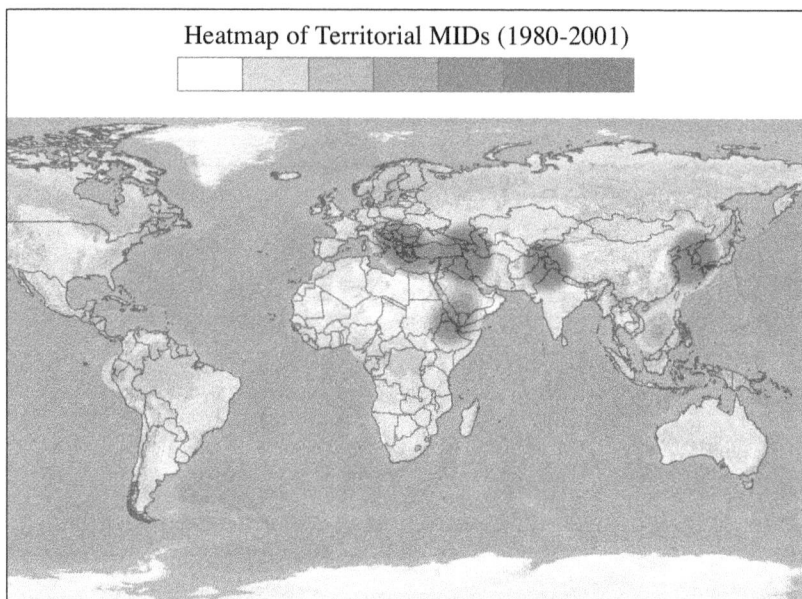

FIGURE 7.2. A heatmap of territorial conflict as measured by interstate territorial MIDs in the late twentieth century. See Appendix for sources and data description.

Mylonas, 2016; Bulutgil, 2016).[4] Competitive state building is therefore central to understanding the logic of settler colonialism and ethnic cleansing in the modern world.

Consistent with the existence of a settler colonial transition, settler colonialism and ethnic cleansing are also phenomena largely limited to the Global South. After countries reach a middle-income GDP per capita of approximately $6,000, minority groups are almost never subject to ethnic cleansing or colonization (Figures 7.3 and 7.4). This level of development would have been Czechoslovakia over this period, or China today. The exception to this rule is Israel. Israel was the only country with an average GDP per capita over $6000 in the late twentieth century that consistently colonized and cleansed an ethnic minority.

Why might $6,000 be an important threshold for the end of settler colonialism? Once a country has attained a GDP of $6,000, it is an unambiguously middle-income country. It is then no longer viable to resettle small-scale farmers to peripheral areas. For example, in 1992, the income of transmigrants in Indonesia ranged from $600 to $2,000 USD depending on their proximity to markets and when they were relocated (Operations Evaluation Department,

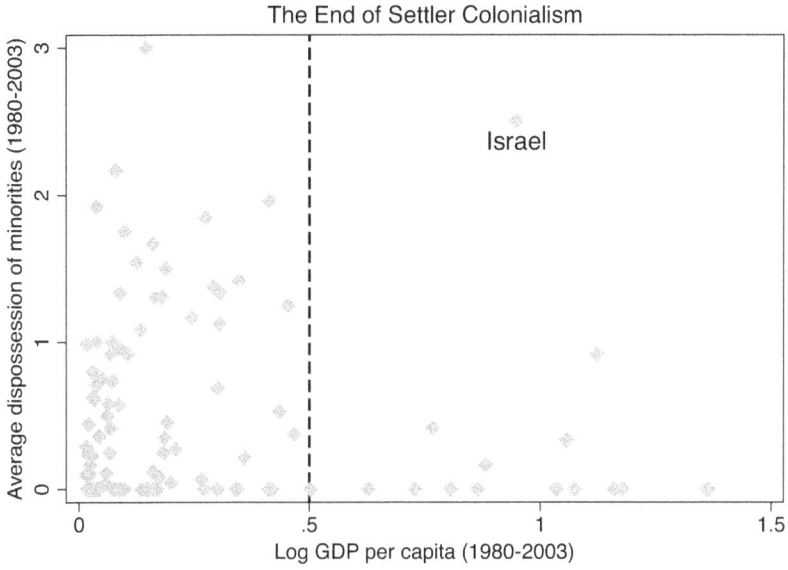

The End of Settler Colonialism

FIGURE 7.3. The relationship between economic development and settler colonialism at the country level (1980–2003) with a dashed line at approximately $6,000 GDP per capita.

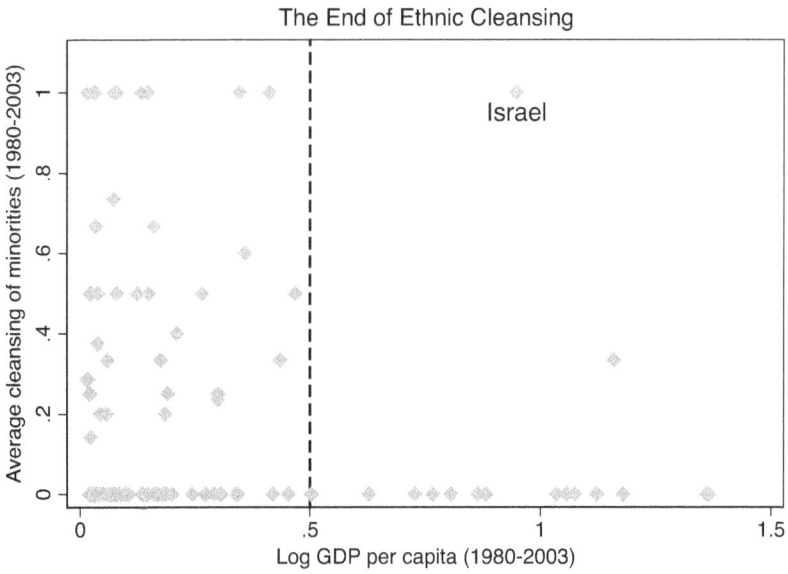

The End of Ethnic Cleansing

FIGURE 7.4. The relationship between economic development and ethnic cleansing at the country level (1980–2003) with a dashed line at approximately $6,000 GDP per capita.

World Bank, 1994). So it is no surprise that Indonesia had a waitlist for transmigration; the income for transmigrants was generally well above that of the country as a whole.[5] But the colonization of West Papua would have been impossible if Indonesia had an average income of $6,000 USD in the 1980s and 1990s, as there simply would have been no settlers willing to take up Papuan land. More developed states have to use indirect tools, such as infrastructure investment and tax breaks, to encourage settlers to migrate to contested frontiers. But given countervailing market forces drawing labor and capital to urban centers, such efforts—as has been demonstrated in China and Australia—are usually ineffectual.

Why is Israel so different, then? Israel's policymakers are concerned with territorial expansion given Israel's foundational Zionist ideology and its need for a territorial buffer in a hostile neighborhood (Butt, 2017; Lustick, 2019). But developed states often try to settle peripheral areas to no avail. As discussed in Chapter 2, what is most idiosyncratic about Israel is that its settlers are *willing* to colonize the Palestinian West Bank for two reasons. First, much of Palestine, like East Jerusalem, is actually located extremely close to Israel's urban core.[6] As such, settlers have been keen to take up subsidized mortgages in East Jerusalem given that they can still easily access jobs and services in Israel proper (Allegra, 2013). Second, for those settlements far from Jerusalem, there are a number of ideologically motivated Zionists—most of whom are actually American—willing to incur a substantial drop in quality of life to live in their Promised Land.[7] As peripheries are usually (i) too far to commute to the urban core and (ii) not religiously important to settlers, all other developed states are obliged to settle for less land.

Democratic and autocratic political institutions, on the other hand, do not explain the incidence of violence against minorities. Figures 7.5 and 7.6 plot the relationship between regime type, settler colonialism, and ethnic cleansing, drawing on data from the Polity IV project (Marshall and Jaggers, 2007), which scores every country on a scale ranging from −10 (full autocracy) to 10 (full democracy). These data reveal that liberal democracies are no less likely to cleanse or colonize ethnic minorities. Indeed, democratic institutions are weakly associated with an *increase* in the dispossession of ethnic minorities.

This finding should not, however, be completely surprising. Democracies like Israel do not appear to respect human rights in wartime more than autocracies (Downes, 2007). And even the darlings of humanitarian institutions often prove extremely coercive toward minority groups whose political loyalties are suspect. Facing insurgent attacks, elected leaders may be even *more*

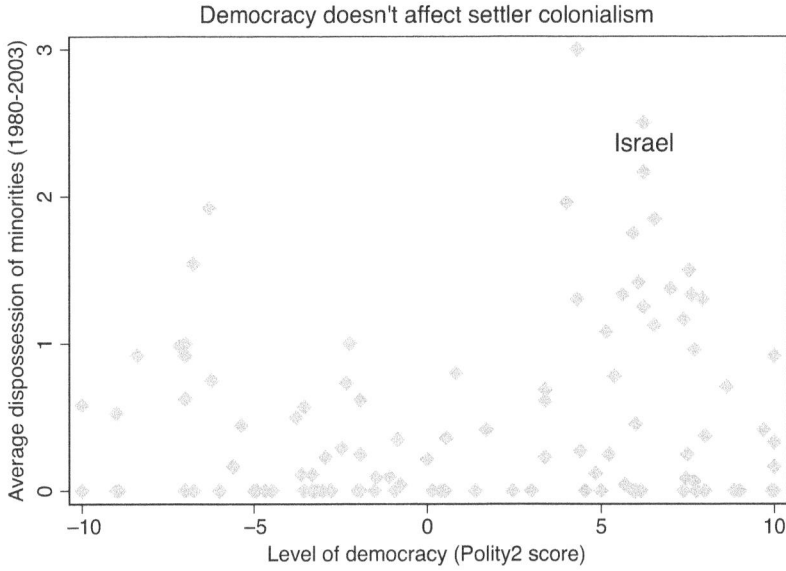

Democracy doesn't affect settler colonialism

FIGURE 7.5. The relationship between economic development and regime type, as measured by the Polity2 score from the Polity IV project (Marshall and Jaggers, 2007), which ranges from −10 (full autocracy) to 10 (full democracy).

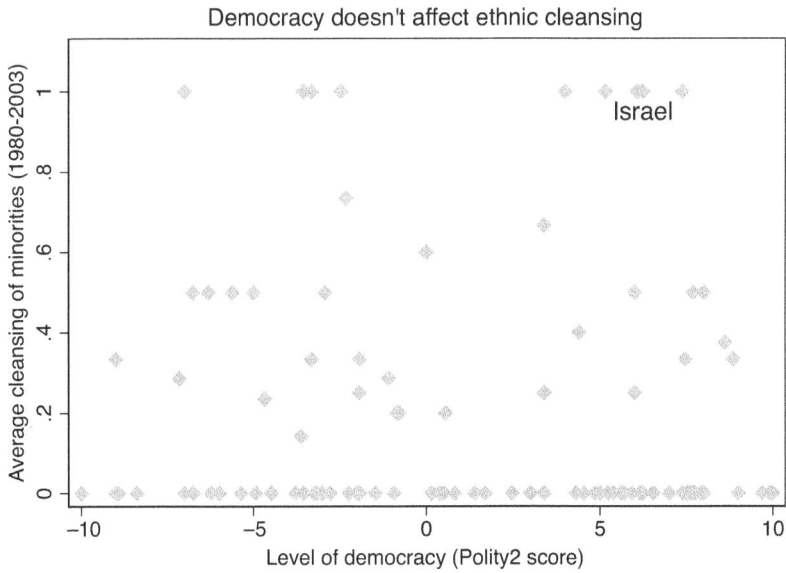

Democracy doesn't affect ethnic cleansing

FIGURE 7.6. The relationship between ethnic cleansing and regime type, as measured by the Polity2 score from the Polity IV project (Marshall and Jaggers, 2007), which ranges from −10 (full autocracy) to 10 (full democracy).

susceptible to public pressure to quickly defeat minority insurgents by any means necessary.[8]

Consider the fact that two of the most recent campaigns of ethnic cleansing in the world were presided over by Nobel Peace Prize winners. In late August 2017, the Myanmar military systematically razed Rohingya villages along the border with Bangladesh, driving almost three quarters of a million Muslim Rohingya across the border. UN High Commissioner for Human Rights Zeid Ra'ad al-Hussein called the campaign a "textbook example of ethnic cleansing."[9] This campaign was shortly followed by an announcement that burnt villages would become repopulated by Buddhists. As a spokesman of the Ministry of Border Affairs quite plainly put it: "We need a human fence."[10]

Rather than distance herself from this campaign of ethnic cleansing and settler colonialism, Aung San Suu Kyi—a democratic icon and de facto head of government of Myanmar at the time—gave a speech at the Hague in 2019 defending the military's actions. Suu Kyi emphasized how the displacement of the Rohingya was a tactical decision to quickly defeat a secessionist insurgency. As she put it:

> In the Myanmar language, 'nae myay shin lin yeh'—literally 'clearing of locality'—simply means to clear an area of insurgents or terrorists. . . . May I go back to the situation in Rakhine on the morning of August 25, 2017. More than thirty police stations and villages, and one military base, had been attacked before sunrise in a highly coordinated fashion, by an organised armed group operating along a densely forested hill-range that provides ample opportunity to hide. *Many of the [Arakan Rohingya Salvation Army] fighters had been recruited from local villages in the weeks and months preceding the attack.*[11]

This speech echoes Governor Macquarie's justification for cleansing the Gandangara in colonial New South Wales (see Introduction). In both cases, leaders—facing heavy criticism for their "weakness" in the face of ongoing insurgent attacks and unable to distinguish between indigenous combatants and non-combatants—regarded ethnic cleansing as the most expedient tool for defeating a nascent insurgency. Susceptibility to public pressure paved the way to human rights abuses.

Lest this point not be emphasized enough, consider the case of Ethiopian Prime Minister Abiy Ahmed, who received the Nobel Peace Prize in 2019 for resolving Ethiopia's conflict with Eritrea. Ahmed also received acclaim for

propagating a new national narrative in Ethiopia—*medemer*—that emphasized the strength in its ethnic diversity. But just a few months after receiving the Nobel Prize, Ahmed launched a major offensive in the northern
region of Tigray to eliminate the ruling militia there. Harrowing reports of
ethnic cleansing and mass rape suffered by Tigrayan people soon followed.[12]
As for Suu Kyi, abstract ideological commitments to humanitarianism and
ethnic equality proved somewhat shallow for Ahmed. War places immense
pressure on elected leaders to to quickly defeat insurgencies by displacing
entire ethnic groups, resulting in similar levels of forced migration across
democracies and autocracies. Development, not democracy, ends ethnic
cleansing.

Who are the Colonized Today?

Having established that land dispossession and ethnic cleansing tend to occur
in countries in the Global South characterized by territorial conflict, we
can now uncover the types of minorities that are targeted for displacement.
Consistent with the importance of war, colonized ethnic groups tend to be
rebellious minority groups, fifth column minorities, and minorities inhabiting
resource-rich areas. Indeed, if a minority's homeland is endowed with gas or
oil, there is on average almost a 50% increase in the likelihood of colonization.

For example, the Kurds of Iraq have been consistently subject to some of
the most extreme levels of colonization in the world according to the MAR
data. The Kurdish homeland of northern Iraq has long been coveted by various actors due to its rich deposits of petroleum. Quickly following the 1973 oil
shock, the Iraqi state forcibly displaced Kurds and Assyrians from the oil-rich
area around Kirkuk and Khanaqin and repopulated the area with Arabs from
southern Iraq in a policy of "Arabization" (*ta'rib*). By the late 1980s, the Iraqi
government had expelled over a quarter of a million Kurdish men, women,
and children and repopulated a long stretch of its border from Khanaqin
near Iran to Sinjar near Syria with Arabs. Unfortunately, as detailed by Mufti
(2004), this was only the first of many waves of displacement. During the 1991
Gulf War, the Kurds rose up and expelled many of the Arab settlers, but over
100,000 Arabs were again sent to Kurdistan over the 1990s as the government
sought to regain control over its restive north. By 1998, nearly one million of
the three million people living in northern Iraq had been displaced at one time
or another. As for the West Papuans, natural resources have proven a curse for
the Kurds of Kirkuk.

Stereotypically disloyal minorities are also disproportionately subject to displacement. Whilst fifth columns make up approximately 4% of all minorities at risk, they constitute over 40% of all minorities subject to ethnic cleansing in the MAR data. For instance, reflecting the extreme nature of territorial competition between the newly independent Balkan states, fifth column groups—Croats in Serbia, Serbians in Croatia, and Croats and Serbians in Bosnia—were all were subject to ethnic cleansing in the 1990s. Much like the cleansing of ethnic Russians and Chinese during the Sino-Soviet split (see Chapter 5), the cleansing of these groups was motivated by the suspicion based on shared ethnicity that they were allegiant to a hostile neighbor.

Less consistent with my theory is the fact that minorities engaged in rebellion are not disproportionately subject to ethnic cleansing. Rather, rebellious minorities and minorities closer to contested territory are only more likely to be subject to colonization. For example, in the MAR data the Saharwis of Morocco and the Tripurans and Assamese of India are all recorded as subject to land dispossession but not ethnic cleansing. These groups have either been engaged in civil wars or are located in highly contested border zones—the Saharwis are located in Morocco's contested Western Sahara and the Tripurans and Assamese in the contested borderland between India, Bangladesh, and China. Each of these minority groups has been subject to an influx of settlers, progressively transforming them into minorities in their own homelands.

This suggests that the logic of ethnic cleansing and that of colonization differ slightly. States tend to cleanse their territory of fifth columns whilst internally colonizing, not expelling, rebellious minorities. The most obvious explanation for this relationship is that fifth columns, unlike rebellious minorities, have a "homeland" that they can be expelled to. Purely internal ethnic cleansing—forcibly displacing minorities not across an international border but internally to another part of the state—is self-defeating by comparison because the state cannot stop displaced people from simply returning home.

This rather subtle insight is best illustrated through an example. Consider Ethiopia's failure to secure control over the northern region of Tigray during the mid-1980s through internal ethnic cleansing. Over the late 1970s and early 1980s, the ruling party in Ethiopia, the Derg, was engaged in a number of conflicts with minority militias like the Tigray People's Liberation Front (TPLF) that sought political autonomy. Unable to distinguish between TPLF combatants and Tigrayan non-combatants, the Derg systematically destroyed

Tigrayan livestock, farms, and food stores in a scorched earth policy designed to deny secessionist insurgents in Tigray any food.[13] The Derg also announced plans in late 1984 to relocate approximately 500,000 families, or about 2 million persons, from northern Ethiopia into "not densely settled and agriculturally suitable" parts of south and southwest Ethiopia (Rahmato, 2003, 32). Opposition groups alleged that the real aim of this policy was to depopulate Tigray, allowing the Derg to more easily defeat the TPLF.

The trouble for the Derg, however, was that it had no power to force resettled Tigrayans to remain in the south. Ethiopian officials initially expressed much optimism that Tigrayans, once provided with free land in the south, would be filled with gratitude toward the central government and would want to remain there indefinitely (Rahmato, 2003, 29). But the coercive nature of resettlement—in which hundreds of thousands of famine victims were forcibly deported from the north—combined with the malarial and marginal nature of land in southern Ethiopia, led to widespread deaths and desertions. As explained later by the head of the resettlement program: "Resettlement programs became our Siberia. As a result, in the minds of the people they were equated with concentration camps" (Keller, 1992, 619). Desertion rates were extremely high, ranging up to 60–70% in some settlements (Rahmato, 2003, 58), and Tigrayan deserters began to stream back into the north, providing new recruits for the resurgent TPLF. Ethnic cleansing is generally effective at producing lasting demographic change only when paired with international borders or the introduction of settlers, both of which effectively prevent displaced peoples from returning home.

For this reason, ethnic cleansing tends to be most prevalent in interstate conflicts such as the wars between Greece and Turkey, Serbia and Croatia, and China and the former USSR, as fifth columns can be permanently expelled to their "home" state. When a rebellious minority are unambiguously not "foreigners" such as the Tripurans in India, the Baluchis of Pakistan, and the Achenese in Indonesia, states tend to respond to secessionist mobilization by settling minority lands. For instance, in the wake of ongoing secessionist mobilization in its northeast over the 1970s and 1980s, India refrained from expelling minorities there to neighboring states. Instead, it provided land in the northeast to resettled Hindus along important strategic passages to Bangladesh and China in order to forestall cross-border minority insurgencies (Hussain, 2008, 60).

This pattern is also consistent with my findings in Xinjiang over the past two chapters. China expelled "fifth column" ethnic Russians to the former

USSR and colonized their lands during the Sino-Soviet split (Chapter 5). But after the rise of a perceived Islamist insurgency in 1990, China subjected Muslims in Xinjiang to colonization but has not expelled them to a neighboring state (Chapter 6). As Uyghurs are unambiguously Chinese citizens (unlike ethnic Russians), China has attempted to prevent the formation of a "Uyghurstan" by flooding their lands of Uyghurs with Han Chinese.

Only since 2016 and in the wake of the failure of Han colonization has China begun to internally deport Uyghurs to factories in eastern China. Internal documents reveal how mass Uyghur relocation is designed "not only [to] reduce Uyghur population density in Xinjiang, but also is an important method to influence, fuse and assimilate Uyghur minorities."[14] But again, as Ethiopia found during the 1980s, there is good reason to doubt the long-term viability of internal ethnic cleansing as a strategy for securing control over Xinjiang. All accounts indicate that resettled Uyghurs are under heavy surveillance in eastern China and face the threat of incarceration if they attempt to return home. China therefore remains highly vulnerable to any breakdown in its coercive apparatus, after which coercively resettled (and likely newly radicalized) Uyghurs will return to Xinjiang. In the absence of Han settlers or a "home" state to expel Uyghurs to, China's hold over southern Xinjiang remains fragile.

Multivariate Analysis

Although the patterns of ethnic cleansing and settler colonialism described above are suggestive of a number of causal relationships, it is unclear whether these relationships still hold when examining all factors together. Multivariate regression can allow us to understand the effect of a particular factor, such as economic development, whilst holding constant other factors, such as a country's level of democracy. As the results largely confirm the descriptive patterns, any reader unfamiliar with such methods is welcome to skip to the conclusion of this chapter.

Table 7.1 reports the results of the baseline OLS model. The results largely corroborate the descriptive patterns as log GDP per capita and territorial insecurity—as proxied by the relative size of a country's armed forces[15]—both predict whether a country engages in ethnic cleansing and settler colonialism, even when controlling for other factors such as regime type. Settler colonialism and ethnic cleansing are most likely to occur in less developed and territorially insecure states.

TABLE 7.1. OLS regression of settler colonialism and ethnic cleansing across the world 1980–2003. Unit of analysis is the ethnic group-country-year. Robust standard errors included. Higher values indicate more demographic engineering.

	Correlates of demographic engineering around the world			
	Settler colonialism (0–3)		Ethnic cleansing (0/1)	
	(1)	(2)	(3)	(4)
Cross-national predictors				
Log GDP per capita	−0.19**	−0.25***	−0.08**	−0.10***
	(0.084)	(0.083)	(0.032)	(0.033)
Military as % of labor force	3.22***	3.10***	1.97***	1.71***
	(1.225)	(1.148)	(0.643)	(0.645)
Democracy	0.09*	0.11**	−0.07***	−0.05**
	(0.051)	(0.052)	(0.024)	(0.024)
Year	−0.02***	−0.02***	0.00	0.00
	(0.006)	(0.006)	(0.002)	(0.002)
Cross-group predictors				
Proximity to Territorial MID	1.46***	1.18***	0.34***	0.27**
	(0.281)	(0.282)	(0.121)	(0.120)
Rebellion	0.54***	0.47***	0.04	0.02
	(0.083)	(0.084)	(0.033)	(0.034)
Fifth column	0.14	0.12	0.14**	0.12**
	(0.135)	(0.133)	(0.055)	(0.058)
Petroleum	0.27***	0.19***	0.05**	0.03
	(0.046)	(0.049)	(0.020)	(0.022)
Relative pop. density	−0.33***	−0.33***	0.32***	0.31***
	(0.126)	(0.121)	(0.050)	(0.048)
Observations	1,930	1,930	2,005	2,005
Spatial controls	Yes	Yes	Yes	Yes
Political status FE	No	Yes	No	Yes

Note: ***$p < 0.01$, **$p < 0.05$, *$p < 0.1$.

Domestic political institutions still have a weak or mixed relationship with settler colonialism and ethnic cleansing. Using Magaloni, Chu, and Min (2013)'s binary measure of whether a country is a democracy or an autocracy, democracies are on average slightly less likely to engage in ethnic cleansing but are more likely to engage in settler colonialism. When using other measures of democracy, including Boix, Miller, and Rosato (2013), the Polity2 score from the Polity IV project (Marshall and Jaggers, 2007), and the V-Dem Electoral Democracy/Polyarchy index (Lindberg et al., 2014), there is also generally no significant relationship between democratization and settler colonialism and ethnic cleansing. This suggests, contrary to McGarry (1998) and Rummel (1995), that there is quite little evidence that democracies are less likely to engage in demographic engineering than autocracies.[16]

Across different minorities, proximity to contested territory and resource-rich areas both prove significant predictors of whether a minority is subject to ethnic cleansing or dispossession. Active rebellion and fifth column status are also important predictors of which minorities are subject to dispossession even when controlling for other potentially important factors. In sum, these data indicate that settler colonialism in the contemporary world is largely driven by the location of valuable natural resources and territorial conflict in the Global South.

Interestingly, there is support for the long-standing idea that minorities inhabiting relatively sparsely populated areas are disproportionately subject to dispossession (e.g., Lee 1966; Zelinsky 1971; Fearon and Laitin 2011). Consistent with the ongoing importance of population pressure in shaping cases of settler-led colonization, minorities inhabiting sparsely populated areas within densely populated nations—such as the highlanders of Vietnam, the Moro of Mindanao in the Philippines, the Amazonians of Brazil, and the Adivasis of Jharkand in India—have been particularly vulnerable to dispossession of their lands.

Finally, there are inconsistent patterns with respect to global trends in coercive demographic change over time: ethnic minorities around the world are less likely to be dispossessed of their land over time, but no less likely to be subject to ethnic cleansing. So, contrary to the expectations of the existing scholarship (e.g., Preece 1998; Walling 2000; Gurr 2000; Power 2002; Bannon 2005; Ther 2014), the evidence is not consistent with a secular decline in violence against minorities over the late twentieth century.[17] Admittedly over a quite limited time period of only slightly over two decades, there is nonetheless no evidence of a declining trend in ethnic cleansing in the raw data and in the multivariate regressions. Any regional declines in ethnic cleansing in the late twentieth century can be more directly traced to rising levels of economic development and the resolution of interstate territorial disputes.

In sum, global patterns of colonization and ethnic cleansing over the late twentieth century generally support my finer-grained evidence from China, Australia, the former USSR, and Indonesia. Across both different countries and different ethnic groups, conflict, the value of territory, and perceived ethnic group loyalties are central to explaining the incidence of coercive demographic change. To understand why states colonize and cleanse ethnic minorities, we should therefore reorient ourselves away from institutional

SETTLER COLONIALISM AROUND THE WORLD   149

or normative explanations and refocus our attention on the dynamics of competitive state building and economic modernization.

Conclusion

In Northern Ireland today, you can tell whether you are in a Protestant or a Catholic neighborhood by whether you see Israeli or Palestinian flags. Northern Ireland was colonized by British Protestants in the early 1600s as Britain sought to provide a line of defence against Catholic Spain. Catholics were subjugated by Protestant settlers over the following centuries. By flying the Palestinian flag today, Irish Catholics express their support for colonized peoples all around the world. Their murals call for "Solidarity with Palestine!" and condemn all forms of indigenous dispossession. On the other hand, Protestant murals laud Benjamin Netanyahu and his hardline security policies. By flying the Israeli flag, Protestants express their solidarity with Israelis against "terrorists"—Catholic and Palestinian alike.

Comparison is a fraught business. Comparison can erase historical specificity. Comparison can also descend into "what-aboutism," in which forms of political subjugation are unhelpfully ranked against one another. Yet, comparison is fundamentally how we make sense of our lived experience. The conflict in Northern Ireland today is, in many ways, unique. But it is telling that Protestants and Catholics alike find meaning in articulating their identities through the lens of the Israeli/Palestinian conflict. Comparison allows us to understand recurrent patterns and situate our experiences in a wider historical context.

Just as comparing Northern Ireland and Israel/Palestine reveals a number of underlying similarities, comparing all cases of state violence around the world reveals that settler colonialism has an oft-recurrent logic. This chapter is the first analysis of settler colonialism and ethnic cleansing using systematically compiled data from around the world. I find that settler colonialism and ethnic cleansing tend to occur in territorially insecure and less developed states. Such states tend to colonize disloyal minorities, minorities inhabiting contested border zones, and minorities endowed with valuable natural resources. On the other hand, the data undercut theories that emphasize the importance of democratic institutions or international norms. The absence of support for these alternative explanations stands as a critique but also as an invitation for work that can further refine these theories and substantiate their explanatory value against globally representative data.

Perhaps the greatest value in comparing all instances of settler colonialism around the world at once is that this can reveal how representative, or exceptional, particular cases are. Descriptively, this chapter has revealed that settler colonialism and ethnic cleansing are phenomena that have occurred in a range of states around the world. This generalizable quality highlights an imbalance in the almost singular attention paid by the United Nations to the case of Israel/Palestine. Other cases of settler colonialism over the late twentieth century, such as the Moroccan settlement of the Western Sahara, the Sri Lankan settlement of its Tamil areas, the Indonesian settlement of West Papua, the Thai settlement of its southern Malay provinces, the Indian settlement of its northeast, the Iraqi settlement of Kurdish areas, the Rwandan settlement of its formerly Tutsi-dominated east, the Bangladeshi settlement of the Chittagong Hills, and China's settlement of Xinjiang, among others, are notably absent from discussion by comparison.

What accounts for this inattention? Mundy and Zunes (2015, 69) have pointedly and, I believe, quite accurately suggested that this absence of attention in part reflects the salience of race and the consequently "invisible" nature of ethnic inequality in non-Western societies:

> It is this "brown-on-brown" quality—visible in East Timor, Sri Lanka, and Iraq as well—that also helps to account for the invisibility of the settler. . . . The kinds of strong international condemnation that Israel receives for violating the Geneva Convention's prohibition of settlement in occupied territories have never really been voiced in relation to the Western Sahara, though the same prohibition applies.

I do not seek to minimize the brutality or importance of Israel's ongoing efforts to colonize Palestine today. Rather, I seek to highlight an analytical inconsistency. Israel is exceptional *not* because it has cleansed and colonized a contested periphery. Israel is exceptional because it is the only Western state that continues to actively settle the lands of indigenous peoples today. The violence in the West Bank thus provides a singular opportunity for politicians in the Global South to relitigate past struggles against Western colonizers. National leaders in states like Iraq, Morocco, Bangladesh, China, and Indonesia have quite cynically used the cause of the Palestinians at the United Nations to burnish their anti-colonial credentials whilst displacing and colonizing their own minorities in much the same way.

What is instead most striking is that, with the notable exception of Israel, almost no middle or high-income country engaged in settler colonialism and ethnic cleansing over the late twentieth century. This is not because the leaders of these states were any less ethno-nationalist or self-interested than their counterparts in the Global South. As past chapters have revealed, officials in middle- and high-income states do sometimes seek to cleanse peripheral minorities and colonize their lands. Yet, colonization is impossible without a large class of settlers willing to repopulate a periphery. Economic modernization therefore bears a distinct silver lining for indigenous peoples. For, as states modernize, they lose the power to colonize.

8

Conclusion: Decolonization, the Highest Stage of Capitalism

The Indonesian government is deliberately trying to keep our population low [and] flood the country with Indonesians. This is not what we Papuans need and it is not what we are asking for. My people are only asking for the Indonesian government to give us a chance to choose whether we want to remain part of Indonesia or become independent. We are asking for our fundamental human right to self-determination; not that our country become "Indonesianized."

—BENNY WENDA, EXILED WEST PAPUAN LEADER

China said they would give Xinjiang autonomy, but instead, it has been suppressed and they moved millions of Han Chinese to Xinjiang. The autonomous rule was never implemented. . . . If they allow self-determination and a dialogue, then [the conflict] will be resolved peacefully. The Chinese authorities should comply with the United Nations convention on self-determination in Xinjiang.

—REBIYA KADEER, EXILED UYGHUR LEADER

The quotes that begin this chapter reflect the plight of marginalized indigenous peoples around the world today. Benny Wenda and Rebiya Kadeer both identify a paradox. Colonization and decolonization are alternative pathways available to states to resolve conflicts over sovereignty. And Indonesia and China were among the most vocal supporters of indigenous self-determination during the global struggle against European imperialism over the mid-twentieth century. Yet soon afterwards, both countries repressed independence movements in Xinjiang and West Papua and colonized these lands with settlers. Strident anti-colonial rhetoric in Indonesia and China has coincided with deeply colonial practices along their contested frontiers. If not for ideological consistency, then, when and why do states become colonizers?

The conventional wisdom, drawing on Marx, explains colonization as a teleological process driven by the spread of capitalism into productive agricultural areas.[1] Where indigenous land is more valuable than indigenous labor, the argument goes, states are driven by a genocidal impulse to displace indigenes and reallocate their lands to commercial agriculturalists. Assuming that settlers always do the bidding of states, scholars have retrospectively explained colonization projects with reference to the ideas or economic interests of a handful of elites in the metropole. We have forgotten that the metropole can have little control over the actions of settlers. And we have forgotten the great many colonization schemes that failed not for lack of trying on the part of states but for lack of settlers.

This book has instead departed from two different theoretical building blocks. First, states and settlers have different interests. States seek to maintain control over territory at minimal cost whereas settlers migrate to wherever is most profitable. Second, states have a number of options for securing control over contested territory. When viewed alongside its policy alternatives, it becomes clear that displacing indigenes and settling their lands is actually a process that entails great financial cost and political risk to states, even as indigenous dispossession may enrich individual settlers.

Together, these moves allowed me to distinguish between the dynamics of different colonization projects depending on the configuration of state and settler interests. In agrarian settings characterized by population pressure in the core, settlers may illegally displace indigenes from their land. States, facing political disorder in the periphery, will then find it expedient to passively license frontier colonization in order to avoid conflict with settlers. In general, states only actively colonize indigenous peoples in contexts of geopolitical insecurity. Policymakers can resolve territorial conflicts at great cost by cleansing and repopulating strategically important areas with stereotypically loyal ethnic groups. And this strategy proves effective so long as settlers remain interested in frontier land. But economic development, by making cities magnets for migration, decisively undermines the colonizing power of the state.

Drawing on these theoretical insights, this book has retold the global story of colonization in a more historically faithful way. Paying close attention to historical contingency and the intentions of policymakers, I have underscored how, even in canonical cases of European settler colonialism like the United States and Australia, frontier colonization was licensed at critical junctures not because of elite genocidal impulses but because settler expansionism and fear of independent settler republics forced the hands of policymakers. Then, drawing on micro-data on settlement patterns in China and Indonesia, I have uncovered the contingent circumstances under which policymakers *do* actively colonize indigenous peoples. Violent uprisings have historically combined with the location of valuable resources and porous borderlands to dynamically shape patterns of colonization and ethnic cleansing at a local level. Finally, I have uncovered when and why states cease colonizing indigenous peoples. Drawing on cases of failed colonization in China and Australia, I have shown how economic development and urbanization prevents states from settling contested frontiers. Settler colonialism is therefore far from "impervious to regime change" (Wolfe, 2006, 402) or the teleological end point of capitalism (Scott, 2009, 4–12). Quite the opposite. Economic development breaks the political alliance between states and settlers, shielding indigenous peoples from colonization.

Two general implications from these findings follow. The first implication is that social scientists ought to refocus attention on the dynamics of political modernization. The notion that economic change drives political change has a long intellectual heritage. Karl Marx, Émile Durkheim, Max Weber, and Eric Williams all emphasized, in different ways, the contrast between "traditional" and "modern" political institutions. But there are few ideas as unfashionable today as modernization theory, conventionally understood as a theory of democratization. A cluster of American scholars writing in the mid-twentieth century—Walt Whitman Rostow, Clifford Geertz, Edward Shils, Daniel Lerner, Gabriel Almond, David Apter, Lucian Pye, and Seymour Martin Lipset—argued that economic development, by disrupting the psychological and social bedrock of patrimonialism, lays the foundation for liberal democracy.[2]

Today, this strand of modernization theory is mainly cited as an example of a "bad" idea. It is easy to understand why. The theory of regime change rests on vague, contestable assumptions like the notion that people have a "hierarchy of needs," with a desire for political voice reserved for the materially satiated. It smacks of social scientists falsely universalizing the North Atlantic experience.[3] And, in any case, the evidence in favor of modernization theory is mixed. Although wealthy countries today tend to be democratic, it is unclear whether countries do actually tend to democratize as they grow wealthier.[4]

Yet, it remains difficult to shake the notion that the world's unprecedented rise in living standards over the past two centuries has probably changed *some* aspects of political life. The basic premises of modernization theory remain, in fact, pretty widely shared. A series of bipolar distinctions—rural and urban; illiterate and literate; agricultural and industrial; feudal and egalitarian—are still what social scientists understand as "development," implicitly understood as a generic set of social changes associated with rising living standards. This, combined with the widespread derogation of modernization theory, has created a situation of intellectual dissonance. As Francis Fukuyama (1997, 146) points out:

> [It] is difficult to find a single social scientist who will any longer admit to being a "modernization theorist." I find this odd because most observers of political development actually do believe in some version of modernization theory.

In other words, the linear, universal concept of "modernization" has a zombie-like character in the academy today; its predictions about democratization are repeatedly pronounced dead but its basic premises walk among us all still.

The exception to this state of affairs is in the field of demography, where the concept of modernization continues to flourish in the form of transition theory. The idea that all countries go through a "demographic transition" characterized by falling maternal fertility and infant mortality was first derived from the experience of West in the early twentieth century and has since been observed in all other regions of the world (Notestein, 1945; Chesnais, 1993). Demographers have also noted the powerful association between rising living standards and other social changes such as urbanization and the direction of internal migration. These shifts have been variously termed the "urban transition" (Friedmann and Wulff, 1975), the "mobility transition" (Zelinsky, 1971), or the "agricultural transition" (Lobao and Meyer, 2001). And these transitions appear be universal processes: no wealthy country is primarily rural, has net rural migration, or has high maternal fertility. Drawing upon this intellectual tradition, I proposed that all countries undergo a *settler colonial transition* in which, with economic development, they lose both the power and the will to colonize indigenous peoples.

Social scientists would do well to focus on demography when attending to the effects of modernization on other aspects of political life. Unlike the hand-wavey micro-foundations of conventional modernization theory, the relationship between rising living standards, the fertility and migration decisions of individual families, and aggregate demographic shifts are well established and universal. Given the generic nature of falling family sizes and rising urbanization with development, there are no doubt a number of other "political transitions" waiting to be discovered.

Such discoveries will help revitalize the field of political demography, which is devoted to examining how the size, distribution, and composition of population is shaped by and in turn shapes politics. Political demography is largely moribund within the academy (Teitelbaum, 2015), a fact lamented by periodic edited volumes (Weiner and Teitelbaum, 2001; Goldstone, Kaufmann, and Toft, 2012; Côté, Mitchell and Toft, 2018).[5] This is especially stark in the study of internal migration. Despite the fact that the vast majority of migration is internal, political scientists and sociologists almost exclusively focus on international migration (King and Skeldon, 2010).[6] But population scholars pay little attention to the political determinants of internal migration, too. Theories of migration in demography explain settler colonialism as the mechanical outcome of economic factors like relative land availability or population density (e.g., Lee 1966; Zelinsky 1971; Chesnais 1993). Demographers tend to ignore politics because, as Teitelbaum (2015, 88) highlights:

> Many (though not all) demographers seemed sceptical that actions by states could have much impact upon demographic trends, driven as they were thought to be by social and economic forces too powerful to be affected by mere governments.

This skepticism is unfounded. I have shown in this book how, when settlers are willing to relocate, governments can quickly and dramatically alter the demography of frontiers like Xinjiang and West Papua. Patterns of internal migration and demographic change in these areas were shaped not just by autonomous economic or social factors but by fundamentally political factors like the timing of rebellions or the location of non-natural borders. Just as political scientists would benefit from paying greater attention to demography, demographers would benefit from paying greater attention to politics.

The second general implication of my findings is that economic change—and not ideological change—has been the most powerful global force for decolonization. This statement may seem oxymoronic as the term "decolonization" is increasingly synonymous with ideological change. Since the publication of Kikuyu writer Ngũgĩ wa Thiong'o's book *Decolonising the Mind* in 1984, decolonization in the humanities has come to refer to any form of cultural production that "decenters" the European canon and elevates the perspectives and languages of non-European peoples.[7] Contemporary movements to "decolonize" university curricula only make sense in a context where decolonization has become unmoored from any reference to territorial sovereignty.

We should resist inflating the concept of decolonization to the point that it just becomes a metonym for diversity. As Tuck and Yang (2012) point out, for indigenous peoples who continue to suffer displacement and political marginalization, decolonization is not an abstract metaphor or rhetorical device but a tangible political demand. Decolonization is the antonym of colonization—it is the process through which indigenous peoples (re)assume sovereignty, control over land, and political self-determination. This principle was well recognized by the delegates at the General Assembly of the United Nations on 14 December 1960 when they reproduced the Bandung communiqué, declaring that "the subjection of peoples to an alien subjugation, domination and exploitation constitutes a fundamental denial of human rights. . . . All peoples have the right to self-determination."[8] Decolonization is the process through which indigenous peoples achieve self-determination and self-rule. It is the outcome of a fundamental shift in the political power of indigenous peoples vis-à-vis states and settlers.

Understood in this more concrete way, how do indigenous peoples achieve decolonization? Certainly *not* through the efforts of the United Nations Special Committee on Decolonization, which anachronistically equates the end of "alien subjugation" with the end of overseas European rule. Since 1990, the United Nations General Assembly has designated three successive "international decades for the eradication of colonialism." On the UN's list of "non-self-governing territories" slated for decolonization, however, one does not find territories whose peoples are plainly not self-governing, like the West Papuans, the Uyghurs, the Kashmiris, and the Kurds. Rather, one exclusively finds overseas European territories like Bermuda, Tokelau, and the Falkland Islands—island territories that typically lack any popular independence movement. This baffling state of affairs is what allowed China's deputy permanent representative to the UN to give a speech in June 2021 condemning British colonialism in the Falklands, a territory whose people voted 99.7% in favor of remaining a British overseas territory in 2013. The irony that Beijing could use the criteria for "non-self-governing territory" at the United Nations to attack Britain for allegedly denying the Falklands self-determination at the precise time that China was rounding up independence activists in Hong Kong and Xinjiang should be self-evident.

The assumption that decolonization is a process that only applies to European empires is also lamentably implicit in academic works on the topic (e.g., Strang 1990; Shipway 2007; Jansen and Osterhammel 2017). Scholars of decolonization tend to bracket the process through which indigenes achieved independence from France, Britain, Portugal, and the Netherlands on an ad hoc basis.[9] But Thomas (2014) shows how decolonization in France and Britain essentially boiled down to a single decision made by the metropole about each colony: "fight or flight." This decision—and its attendant calculus about the availability of financial resources, settlers, and likelihood that coercion will be successful—is exactly what confronts all multiethnic states facing secessionist threats, whether China in Xinjiang, Pakistan in Balochistan, or Indonesia in West Papua (Butt, 2017). And once we broaden theories of "fight or flight" to include non-Western states, conventional explanations for Europe's decision to flee from empire in the mid-twentieth century—which often emphasize new global norms of self-determination—begin to fall down. For, as even a cursory comparison of Australia and Indonesia in New Guinea illustrates, global norms and abstract ideological commitments do a poor job at explaining why some multiethnic states respond to the prospect of territorial dissolution by "fighting" rather than "flighting."

The violent denial of minority self-determination in the Global South has been a source of surprise and lament for anti-colonial activists. For instance, following the publication of his seminal book *The Colonizer and the Colonized* in 1957, Albert Memmi became a leading figure in the struggle against European colonialism. However, Memmi's follow-up work in 2005, *Decolonization and the Decolonized*, decries the persistence of violence against ethnic minorities in Asia and sub-Saharan Africa. Memmi (2006, 148) reserves particular scorn for ostensibly radical anti-colonial intellectuals who ignore or even justify violence against indigenous peoples in the Global South in the name of modernization and national development, excoriating them for taking "refuge in outdated theories instead of daring to confront a novel situation."[10] As he puts it:

> National and ethnic liberation movements were legitimate and urgently needed. . . . But while we must continue to work so that all nations, young and old, all minorities finally stand as equals among equals, it is no less necessary, for that very reason, to examine why those pitched battles did not always produce the anticipated results. (Memmi, 2006, x)

Decolonization, understood as indigenous self-determination, remains an unfulfilled promise in much of the world. Indonesian rule over West Papuans,

Benny Wenda highlights, has been synonymous with land dispossession, cultural loss, and an influx of politically privileged settlers from the core—a post-colonial condition shared by the Rohingya of Myanmar, the Kashmiris of India, the Moro of the Philippines, the Uyghurs of China, the Kurds of Iraq, and the Balochis of Pakistan, among others. Across the Global South, independence from European rule did not lead to indigenous self-determination but reconstituted a new set of repressive neo-colonial relationships. In other words, the settler-state-indigene triad in countries like Indonesia and China may have changed after 1949 but the existence of this triad remains unchanged.

How, then, do we break the settler colonial triad? In a recent book *Neither Settler nor Native*, Mahmood Mamdani attributes the violence of the post-colonial period in the Global South to the principle of nationalism itself. Nation-states are legitimate insofar as they govern on behalf of a majority ethnic group. But the existence of a privileged ethnic majority (e.g., Han Chinese) entails the existence of an underprivileged minority (e.g., Uyghurs, Tibetans) who are then violently excluded from the nation. The formation of new nation-states and new ethnic majorities thus produces a relentless cycle in which colonized becomes colonizer, and natives become settlers. As Mamdani (2020, 4) puts it, "Because the nation-state seeks to homogenize its territory, it is well served by ejecting those who would introduce pluralism." In other words, the nation-state is an inherently violent organization wedded to ethnic homogenization. Only by challenging ethnocentric nationalism, he concludes, can we achieve decolonization and break the political cycle that produces settlers and natives.

Mamdani deserves credit for, in Memmi's words, confronting "a new situation" and the puzzle of neo-colonialism in the Global South. But his attribution of ethnic cleansing to ethnocentric ideologies is an instance of "ahistorical history." Recall that Indonesian nationalists like Sukarno were among the world's most vocal proponents of racial and ethnic equality. Chinese nationalists like Sun Yat-sen were similarly committed to equality between Han and non-Han, an ideological principle prominently enshrined in the current Constitution of the People's Republic of China. If one is looking for an ingrained impulse to eliminate ethnic minorities, one will not consistently find it in the writings of Chinese or Indonesian nationalists. Instead, by examining historical processes as they unfolded over time, I have shown how Indonesia and China cleansed and colonized specific minorities at specific historical junctures in order to increase their control over contested frontiers. The cleansing and colonization of minorities like the Uyghurs and West Papuans were contingent events, not teleological outcomes.

What are the implications for decolonization if violence against indigenous peoples is primarily driven by the use of ethnicity as an heuristic for political loyalty? The informational importance of ethnicity long predates the era of nationalism. For instance, it is striking how policymakers continue to follow the counsel of Florentine political philosopher, Niccolò Machiavelli, who in the early sixteenth century identified the geopolitical logic of colonization. In restive and ethnically diverse areas, Machiavalli argues, it is prudent for states to displace indigenes and allocate their lands to settlers.[11] When policymakers cannot identify friend or foe in diverse peripheries, visible ethnic identities become proxies for political allegiances and statecraft becomes a violent game of demographic chess. Consistent with Machiavellian calculations, when faced with indigenous uprisings in their peripheries, policymakers in twentieth century China and Indonesia subordinated abstract anti-colonial commitments to harder-nosed geopolitics. Schemes to cleanse and repopulate West Papua and Xinjiang were less ideological than pragmatic; less the necessary product of exclusionary ethno-nationalism than of ruthless expediency.

In light of the yawning gap between the anti-colonial rhetoric and colonial practices of states like Indonesia or China, it is an error to regard normative change—as Mamdani does—as the key to empowering marginalized indigenes. Machiavellian elites in the metropole will always be tempted to resolve conflicts over sovereignty through the most cost-effective means, even if colonizing and cleansing indigenous peoples invites accusations of hypocrisy or neo-colonialism. Eric Williams (1944) famously found that humanitarian arguments against slavery only gained influence in the British Empire *after* the economic interests of slave-holders began to oppose those of industrialists in the metropole. Similarly, we should expect that humanitarian arguments in favor of indigenous self-determination only gain influence *after* coercive strategies for locking in the gains of imperialism like colonization prove ineffective or unprofitable to the metropole.

Thankfully, there is good reason to believe that humanitarian and self-interested motives for granting indigenes self-rule will be increasingly in alignment. Colonization is a Sisyphean task in developed countries. Modernization ends the partnership between states and settlers by transforming cities from squalorous demographic sinks into the most productive and desirable places to live on the planet. Accordingly, even states wedded to racism and imperialism like Australia, the United States, and Portugal were ultimately forced to divorce themselves from distant colonies like Papua New Guinea, the Philippines, and Angola over the twentieth century due to the constraining effects of economic development. Faced with the abject failure of white settlement schemes and metropolitan resistance to granting citizenship to large numbers of poor non-whites, Western policymakers settled for less and fled from empire.

Precisely the same dynamic characterized Israel's more recent withdrawal of its claim to Gaza. Following its failure to attract more than 10,000 settlers to the Gaza Strip after 1969, even the most vocal supporter of Israel's settlements—Prime Minister Ariel Sharon—was forced to abandon the cherished idea of *Eretz Yisrael* (Greater Israel). With little prospect that Jews would ever outnumber Arabs in Gaza, Sharon was obliged to settle for less in 2005. As he lamented publicly: "It is no secret that I, like many others, believed and hoped that we could forever hold on . . . [but] Gaza cannot be held onto forever. Over one million Palestinians live there and they double their numbers with every generation."[12]

Israel's "disengagement" from Gaza in 2005 was an acknowledgement of demographic reality. As Shimon Peres, Sharon's deputy, quite baldly put it: "We are disengaging from Gaza because of demography."[13] Gaza was simply too distant from Israel's wealthy urban core and subject to too many rocket attacks to ever successfully colonize with Jewish settlers. But this is not true of East Jerusalem and the West Bank given that these areas are so close to Israel's urban core. As long as gradually colonizing the Palestinian West Bank remains feasible, Israel's leaders will resist settling for anything less.

By eliminating settlers as a political force, economic development therefore breaks the settler colonial triad. East Jerusalem and the West Bank are best understood as the exceptions that prove the rule. By constraining colonization in all but the commuter zones of major cities, economic development provides the demographic foundation for indigenes to achieve self-rule—whether in Papua New Guinea, Gaza, or Angola. Decolonization is the highest stage of capitalism.

Two caveats to this conclusion are worth noting here. First, decolonization in the form of national independence is no guarantee that the lives of most indigenous peoples will materially improve. Papua New Guinea, the Philippines, and Angola, after all, remain three of the world's most unequal and underdeveloped nations today as measured by life expectancy, education, and income per capita.

To understand why decolonization left the global distribution of wealth largely intact, it is worth returning to Fanon (1963, 6)'s warning that the colonial world will only be destroyed "when the colonized swarm into the forbidden cities" of the colonizer.[14] Fearing mass migration to the metropole by its colonial subjects, Australia in the 1960s and 1970s pushed for the independence of Papua New Guinea, whose population was deemed to be too large to incorporate on an equal basis without a substantial loss of metropolitan wealth. France in the 1950s similarly only granted equality to indigenes from smaller colonies (like Polynesia or Martinique) whilst denying equality to indigenes from larger colonies (like Algeria and Vietnam) who could demographically swamp the metropole (Lawrence, 2013). As French Radical Party leader Edouard Herriot famously warned, France "risked becoming the colony of its former colonies" if it extended political equality to its colonial subjects (Thomas, 2014, 89). National independence, by preventing the "swarming" of the metropole by the colonized, effectively prevented the equalization of living standards between the core and the periphery. Economically at least, decolonization in the form of national liberation largely preserved—rather than destroyed—the colonial world.[15]

And the second obvious caveat is that economic development is no guarantee that indigenous peoples will be able to secure even the dignity gains of national independence in the short term. Middle- and high-income states can always rely on sheer coercive power to forestall making major political concessions to indigenous peoples. This is precisely the outcome that we see in Xinjiang today, where China has constructed an ever more elaborate system of roadblocks, checkpoints, surveillance, and mass incarceration in response to ongoing Uyghur unrest and the abject failure of Han colonization.

But economic development remains a powerful force for decolonization, as coercive power is no panacea for resolving sovereignty conflicts in the long run. Colonization and militarization may both pacify diverse peripheries but, as Machiavelli (1950, 9) notes, the effectiveness of these two strategies as tools of state building diverges as time goes on. Whereas colonization creates a financially self-sufficient and permanent demographic presence in a periphery aligned to the metropole, military garrisons lead to crippling ongoing expenses that fuel the perception (and reality) of foreign occupation. Repression also produces brittleness by leaving states vulnerable to a breakdown in the coercive apparatus, as encapsulated by the rapid dissolution of the USSR by long marginalized minorities who rejoiced in throwing off the "yoke" of Russian dominance—a geopolitical lesson that continues to haunt China's leaders today (Zhao, 2016; Leibold, 2019). Finally, repression is demograph-ically self-defeating as the creation of a police state in contested peripheries deters settlers, as evinced by the recent exodus of Han from Xinjiang.

The alternatives to colonization for permanently altering the ethnic com-position of contested frontiers are moreover quite limited. Forced assimila-tion, like militarization, tends to rebound in the medium term by fostering indigenous resentment (Hechter, 1975; Fouka, 2016; Abdelgadir and Fouka, 2020), and schemes to boost extremely low birth rates among the Han in Xin-jiang have so far proven ineffectual due to China's demographic transition. China also cannot cleanse Uyghurs from Xinjiang because, unlike with the ethnic Russians during the 1960s, there is no "home" state to expel Uyghurs to, leaving mass incarceration and sterilization as the remaining options for reshaping Xinjiang's ethnic composition. The recent turn to genocide in Xin-jiang should therefore be seen for what it is: a last-ditch attempt by Beijing to permanently alter southern Xinjiang's ethnic composition in light of the persistent failure of Han colonization schemes there since the 1990s.[16]

Drained of the power to settle Han in Xinjiang, the only long-run options available to China's leaders short of indefinite repression remain the same as those available to Portuguese, American, and Australian policymakers in the mid-twentieth century, and to Israel in 2005. China can either decol-onize Xinjiang by winning the loyalty of indigenes through autonomy (a "one state solution") or decolonize Xinjiang by granting indigenes indepen-dence in areas where they make up a demographic majority (a "two state solution"). Despite the ongoing horrors inflicted on indigenous peoples in Xinjiang, West Papua, and elsewhere, I therefore remain cautiously optimistic that states will continue—however imperfectly—to accede to the demands for self-determination expressed by indigenous activists like Benny Wenda and Rebiya Kadeer. Demography is decolonial destiny. For, without settlers, unsettled frontiers can only be permanently settled in partnership with indige-nous peoples.

Appendixes

APPENDIX TO CHAPTER 5

TABLE 5.1. Each model is a county-level difference-in-differences specification modelling the change in demography within Xinjiang as a result of the Sino-Soviet split by county contiguity with a non-natural border and the presence of oil (Shawan county). Standard errors are clustered at the county level using Arellano's covariance matrix.

	Log % Han		Log Bingtuan pop.		Russian pop.	
	(1)	(2)	(3)	(4)	(5)	(6)
Sino-Soviet split	0.07***	0.08***	3.15***	3.38***	−65.82*	−73.22***
	(0.01)	(0.01)	(0.30)	(0.27)	(37.65)	(25.55)
Border USSR:Sino-Soviet	0.07***		1.54***		−253.34**	
split	(0.02)		(0.50)		(109.05)	
Shawan: Sino-Soviet split		0.17***		2.47***		−44.88*
		(0.01)		(0.27)		(25.55)
First Differences	Yes	Yes	Yes	Yes	Yes	Yes
Counties	80	80	80	80	80	80
Observations	1896	1896	1175	1175	1896	1896

Note: $^*p < .1$; $^{**}p < .05$; $^{***}p < .01$.

TABLE 5.2. Each model is a difference-in-differences specification where the unit of analysis is the Russian oblast in the former Soviet Union and the DV is demographic change as measured in five Soviet censuses (1939–1989). Standard errors are clustered at the county level using Arellano's covariance matrix.

	Pop. Russian		Total Pop.	
	(1)	(2)	(3)	(4)
Pop. Chinese	−89.074	−124.581	−87.321	−168.993
	(65.630)	(95.403)	(72.151)	(103.637)
Sino-Soviet Split	−83,686.400*	−247,387.700***	−92,541.810*	−304,289.700***
	(43,419.210)	(51,584.180)	(48,041.130)	(56,547.010)
Pop. Chinese:	37.131	707.274***	35.669	788.590***
Sino-Soviet Split	(56.818)	(149.566)	(66.121)	(173.788)
First differences	Yes	No	Yes	No
Oblasts	77	77	77	77
Observations	298	298	298	298

Note: $^*p < 0.1$; $^{**}p < 0.05$; $^{***}p < 0.01$.

APPENDIX TO CHAPTER 6

TABLE 6.1. Each model is a first-difference difference-in-differences specification where the DV is the log percentage of registered residents in a county who are Han. Islamist threat is coded as starting with the Baren incident of 1990 and lasting to the current day. Standard errors are clustered at the county level using Arellano's covariance matrix.

	Log % Han in Xinjiang counties			
	(1)	(2)	(3)	(4)
Islamist Threat	−0.01**	0.001	0.02***	−0.002
	(0.003)	(0.003)	(0.004)	(0.003)
Southern Xinjiang:				
Islamist Threat	0.02***			
	(0.004)			
Southern Border:				
Islamist Threat		0.01**		
		(0.004)		
Distance to Afghanistan/Pakistan:				
Islamist Threat			−0.17***	
			(0.05)	
Muslims (100,000s):				
Islamist Threat				0.002**
				(0.001)
Counties	80	80	80	80
Observations	2468	2468	2468	2468

Note: *$p < 0.1$; **$p < 0.05$; ***$p < 0.01$.

TABLE 6.2. Each model is a first-difference difference-in-differences specification where the DV is the log *bingtuan* population in a county. Islamist threat is coded as starting with the Baren incident of 1990 and lasting to the current day. Standard errors are clustered at the county level using Arellano's covariance matrix.

	Log XPCC population in Xinjiang counties			
	(1)	(2)	(3)	(4)
Islamist Threat	0.44	0.34*	0.16	0.42
	(0.30)	(0.19)	(0.11)	(0.27)
Southern Xinjiang: Islamist Threat	−0.29			
	(0.31)			
Southern Border: Islamist Threat		−0.23		
		(0.20)		
Distance to Afghanistan/Pakistan: Islamist Threat			1.90	
			(2.88)	
Muslims (100,000s): Islamist Threat				−0.03
				(0.09)
Counties	80	80	80	80
Observations	2468	2468	2468	2468

Note: $^*p < 0.1$; $^{**}p < 0.05$; $^{***}p < 0.01$.

TABLE 6.3. Each model is a first-difference difference-in-differences specification where the DV is the log % Han or log bingtuan population in a county. Standard errors are clustered at the county level using Arellano's covariance matrix.

	Log % Han		Log XPCC pop.	
	(1)	(2)	(3)	(4)
Lunnan oil production (1992–)	0.01***		0.004	
	(0.001)		(0.004)	
Lunnan oil production (1992–): Luntai county	0.01***		−0.004	
	(0.001)		(0.004)	
Tazhong oil production (1996–)		0.001		0.03**
		(0.001)		(0.01)
Tazhong oil production (1996–): Qiemo county		0.02***		−0.17
		(0.001)		(0.01)
Counties	80	80	80	80
Observations	2468	2468	2468	2468

Note: $^*p < 0.1$; $^{**}p < 0.05$; $^{***}p < 0.01$.

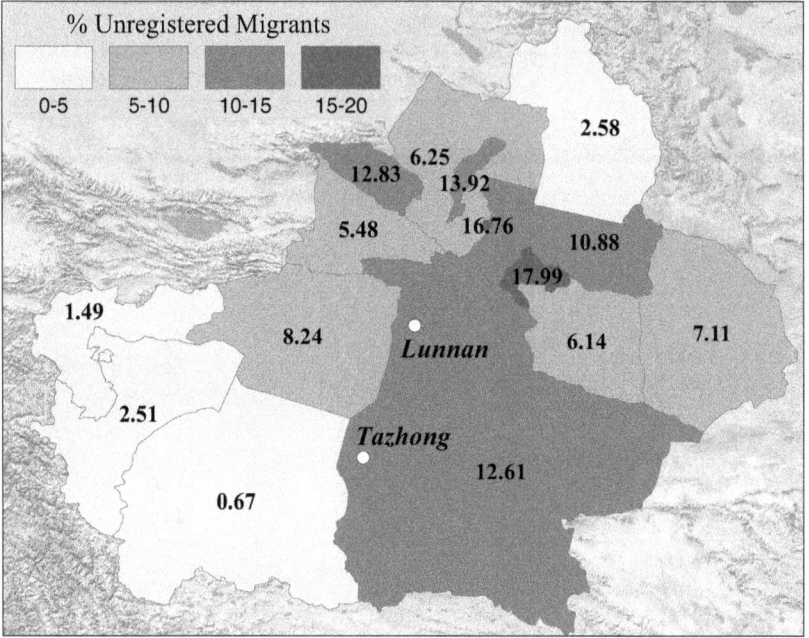

FIGURE 6.7. The share of people by prefecture in Xinjiang who were "floating" (*liudong renkou*), i.e., unregistered migrants, in 2000. Source: Toops (2004, 23)

Data Description

In this section, I describe how I construct the dataset that I used in this chapter. To construct measures of ethnic cleansing and settler colonialism, I draw on data from the MAR project. I specifically use the MARGene data release, which has proxies for ethnic cleansing and settler colonialism between 1980 and 2003. Yearly coverage in these data are limited to 1980, 1985, 1990, 1992, 1994, and then every year between 1996 and 2003.[1] I proxy ethnic cleansing by whether a minority has been subject to "hardship migration either by compulsion of the state, or threat of attack" in a particular year (1 if present, 0 if not). Second, I proxy the incidence of settler colonialism by whether a minority has been subject to dispossession from their land, which is coded by MAR on a 0–3 scale by severity.

MAR has been criticized for not tracking the outcomes of politically advantaged and majority groups, and so the data is poorly suited to studying group competition over control of the central government (Wimmer, Cederman, and Min, 2009a; Hug, 2013). For political violence, however, excluding politically advantaged and majority groups from the sample is reasonable because such groups are not a potential target of colonization.[2] Drawing on existing data has the disadvantage that I cannot specify the criteria used to measure settler colonialism and ethnic cleansing. The proxy for settler colonialism, in particular, is imperfect because it conflates settler-led and state-led colonization. Minorities such as the indigenous peoples of Brazil as well as the West Papuans and Palestinians are all recorded as being subject to high levels of land dispossession in the data. Some predictors, such as fifth column status and proximity to contested territory, only apply to state-led colonization. At the risk of attenuating the importance of these factors, I keep this measure as is rather than go through each of these cases to determine whether dispossession was driven by state or private actors. Using existing, peer reviewed data has the advantage that it has been compiled by an external team of researchers in a transparent way. As such, my findings are easily replicable and it is clear that I did not pick and choose the criteria to measure settler colonialism in a way that best suits my theory.

A second shortcoming of the MAR data is that it does not have information on the location of ethnic groups, which is necessary to test predictors like proximity to contested territory and valuable resources. To overcome this, I manually match each MAR minority to their counterpart in GeoEPR. GeoEPR provides digital polygons capturing the approximate location of all politically relevant ethnic groups since 1946 (Wucherpfennig et al., 2011).

Using these data, I construct four key predictors of colonization. First, the distance of every minority in each year to conflict over territory between states.[3] I proxy conflict over territory by the presence of a Militarized Interstate Dispute (MID) over territory. A conflict between states is coded by COW as a MID if it involves less than 1,000 battle deaths. MIDs are commonly used by scholars in international relations to measure hostility between states and I limit my analysis to MIDs that are coded as being over territorial claims.

I then use the geocoded MID data from Braithwaite (2010) to measure the distance from each minority group to a territorial MID in the previous decade. I use the previous decade both because MIDs are infrequent events and a decade is a reasonable time frame for military clashes to retain political relevance. For ease of interpretation, I invert the distance measure such that higher levels indicate closer proximity of a minority to interstate territorial conflict over the prior decade.

Second, to capture proximity to valuable resources, I create a binary measure of whether a minority's homeland is endowed with petroleum. These data come from Lujala, Ketil Rod, and Thieme (2007) and capture the location of all known oil and gas fields throughout the world.

Third, I measure minority rebellion through a yearly measure of whether that minority group is engaged in a civil war against the state, as coded by EPR.

Fourth, I code a minority group as a fifth column minority if it satisfies two conditions. First, the minority must have a kindred group that dominates state power (an existing variable in the MAR data). Second, that foreign state must be a rival state. Here, I use Thompson (2001, 560)'s measure of "strategic rivals," or states that view each other as (1) competitors, (2) a source of military threat, and (3) an enemy.[4] Subjective rivalry, focused upon the perceptions of policymakers, best captures suspicion toward ethnic minorities with political ties to a competitor.[5] This criterion for fifth columns, whilst restrictive, captures the minority groups that are canonical fifth columns in the late twentieth century, such as Arabs in Iran, Turks in Greece, Somalis in Kenya, and Croats in Serbia.

At the country level, the main predictors of settler colonialism are levels of development and territorial insecurity. I measure economic development through a country's log GDP per capita (World Bank, 2012). I proxy territorial insecurity by the yearly proportion of the country's labor force that is in the army, which also comes from the World Bank. Intuitively, and as demonstrated formally by Fearon (2018), the equilibrium size of a country's military increases with the threat posed to its territorial integrity, i.e., this captures the extent to which a country is devoting scarce labor to the preservation of the state. The results are similar when proxying territorial insecurity through yearly military expenditure as a proportion of a country's GDP.

Cases of settler-led colonization tend to occur in states characterized by a major imbalance in population density. To capture this, I measure the population density of each ethnic minority homeland relative to the state as a whole.[6]

I also compile a number of other group-level covariates from the EPR data. Two confounding explanations for whether a minority is colonized are (i) location and (ii) political power. There is substantial spatial heterogeneity (e.g., proximity to international borders, climate, and distance from the national capitals) that may affect which minorities suffer displacement. To control for this, I include both linear and quadratic terms for latitude and longitude of the geographic center of each minority group. I also control for the yearly access to political power of each minority group (on a ten-point scale from EPR). Only minorities that lack the power to influence public policy would generally be subject to colonization. So I include "political power fixed effects," meaning that we are only comparing the effects of variables of interest between minority groups with exactly the same influence over policymaking.

The leading alternative theoretical explanations for settler colonialism are (i) regime type and (ii) international norms. To measure regime type I use the binary measure of whether a country is a democracy or an autocracy from Magaloni, Chu, and Min (2013). The advantage of this dataset is that it does not contain any hybrid democracy-autocracy regimes and has little missing data. There are, of course, many measures of democracy and the results are similar when using other measures.

As shown by Bulutgil (2016) in Europe, countries where ethnicity is particularly salient may be disproportionately characterized by ethnic cleansing. To control for this, I also include specifications with Bulutgil (2016)'s two proxies for the salience of ethnicity as a political cleavage. These proxies generally have mixed relationships with settler colonialism and ethnic cleansing in this sample.[7]

Finally, to see whether there has been a decline in ethnic cleansing over time, consistent with the progressive consolidation of an international norm against state violence, I also include the year as a predictor. Summary statistics for all these variables are available in Appendix Table 7.1.

Addressing Biases in the MAR Data

The MAR data used in this chapter are not perfect. There are two major concerns. The first is that the proxies for ethnic cleansing and settler colonialism—hardship migration driven by threats from the state and land displacement—may be the result of factors other than state policy. To see whether this concern is valid, I conducted a "placebo" analysis in which I tested whether the determinants of colonization and ethnic cleansing also predict other forms of migration not driven by the state. If this is the case, then the reported relationships may indeed be spurious.

However, this is not the case. When replacing the proxies for ethnic cleansing and settler colonialism with other measures of migration in MAR—whether a minority group has voluntarily migrated to another area, has been subject to economic hardship migration, or has migrated to another area for economic reasons—there is no relationship with proximity to contested territory, fifth column status, rebellion, and territorial insecurity (Appendix Table 7.2 columns 1–3). The coefficient signs are generally flipped. Together, this suggests that the proxies for settler colonialism and ethnic cleansing are primarily capturing political migration processes.

Second, an issue with the MAR data is that it limits the analysis to those minorities around the world that are "potentially at risk." As minorities actually subject to violence are disproportionately likely to end up in the sample, MAR data, when used to analyze the correlates of settler colonialism, partially selects on the dependent variable, which can lead to invalid inferences (Wimmer, Cederman, and Min, 2009a; Hug, 2013; Birnir et al., 2018).

To address this, I run my analyses on all ethnic groups in the Geo-EPR dataset, which is a representative sample of all politically relevant ethnic groups around the world with an identifiable location. I make the assumption that all groups not in the MAR dataset were *not* subject to violence (i.e., they score o on ethnic cleansing and displacement). This may seem a strong assumption but MAR actually misses very few cases where minorities are subject to state-sponsored violence, as this is precisely what these data were designed to capture. So, it is not unreasonable to assume that groups not in MAR were not subject to state-sponsored violence over the late twentieth century. Making this assumption significantly increases the sample size and overcomes sample biases by making the dataset more representative of all ethnic groups.

When replicating the main Table 7.1 with this new sample, the coefficients on all the variables tend to be exactly the same in sign and statistical significance, though the effect sizes are much reduced (Table 7.3 models 1–2, 4–5).[8] This suggests that sample bias is not an issue as we obtain almost exactly the same results when using the truncated MAR sample and the more globally representative EPR sample.

Summary Statistics

TABLE 7.1. Summary statistics for cross-country regression variables.

Variable	Mean	St. Dev	Min	Max
Ethnic Cleansing	0.22	0.41	0	1
Settler Colonialism	0.52	0.96	0	3
Proximity to Territorial MID (per 10,000 km)	−0.08	0.09	−0.78	0
Rebellion	0.03	0.18	0	1
Fifth column group	0.04	0.19	0	1
Military as % of labor force	0.02	0.02	0.001	0.35
Military as % of GDP	0.02	0.03	0	0.33
Log GDP per capita (per $1000 USD)	0.24	0.34	0.01	1.6
Year	1995	6.59	1980	2003
Petroleum	0.46	0.49	0	1
Pop. density per 1000 km^2 (group)	0.09	0.15	0.0001	1.64
Pop. density per 1000 km^2 (country)	0.11	0.36	0.001	6.19
Democracy (Magaloni, Chu, Min)	0.37	0.48	0	1
Democracy (Boix-Miller-Rosato)	0.39	0.49	0	1
Democracy (Polity2)	1.45	6.57	−10	10
Democracy (VDem)	0.43	0.25	0.02	0.90
Domestic competition	27.12	25.18	0	70
Family farms	43.26	22.70	0	98
Political status	6.23	1.94	1	10
Longitude	24.84	58.33	−152.71	177.97
Latitude	16.59	21.10	−39.05	66.94
Voluntary migration	0.12	0.31	0	1
Hardship migration	0.04	0.21	0	1
Economic migration	0.16	0.37	0	1

TABLE 7.2. OLS regression of settler colonialism and ethnic cleansing across the world 1980–2003. Unit of analysis is the ethnic group-country-year. Robust standard errors included. Higher values indicate more migration/land competition.

	Placebo test: Other forms of migration		
	Voluntary migration	Economic hardship migration	General economic migration
	(1)	(2)	(3)
Cross-national predictors			
GDP per capita	0.39 $*$ $**$	−0.06 $*$ $**$	0.33 $*$ $**$
	(0.035)	(0.011)	(0.036)
Military as % of labor force	−0.27	−0.08	−0.35
	(0.307)	(0.135)	(0.335)
Democracy	0.01	−0.00	0.01
	(0.014)	(0.014)	(0.019)
Year	−0.00	−0.00	−0.00
	(0.002)	(0.001)	(0.002)
Cross-group predictors			
Proximity to Territorial MID	−0.11	−0.04	−0.14
	(0.067)	(0.069)	(0.094)
Rebellion	−0.05 $*$ $**$	−0.03 $**$	−0.08 $*$ $**$
	(0.011)	(0.012)	(0.016)
Fifth column	−0.15 $*$ $**$	−0.04 $*$ $**$	−0.19 $*$ $**$
	(0.024)	(0.008)	(0.023)
Petroleum	−0.04 $*$ $**$	0.02 $**$	−0.02
	(0.012)	(0.010)	(0.015)
Relative pop. density	−0.09 $*$ $**$	−0.11 $*$ $**$	−0.20 $*$ $**$
	(0.026)	(0.027)	(0.042)
Observations	2,005	2,005	2,005
Spatial controls	Yes	Yes	Yes
Political status FE	Yes	Yes	Yes

Note: $***p < 0.01$, $**p < 0.05$, $*p < 0.1$.

TABLE 7.3. Replication of main Table 7.1, accounting for selection bias in the MAR data. OLS regression of settler colonialism and ethnic cleansing across the world 1980–2003. Unit of analysis is the ethnic group-country-year. Robust standard errors included. Higher values indicate more demographic engineering. Models 1–4 are replications of Table 7.1 including all ethnic groups in Geo-EPR.

| | Correlates of demographic engineering accounting for selection bias | | | |
| | Settler colonialism (0–3) | | Ethnic cleansing (0/1) | |
	(1)	(2)	(3)	(4)
Cross-national predictors				
Log GDP per capita	−0.08***	−0.08***	−0.03***	−0.04***
	(0.025)	(0.025)	(0.010)	(0.010)
Military as % of labor force	1.91***	1.70***	1.34***	0.99***
	(0.511)	(0.497)	(0.248)	(0.236)
Democracy	0.02	0.07***	−0.04***	−0.02**
	(0.021)	(0.021)	(0.010)	(0.009)
Year	−0.01***	−0.01***	0.00	0.00
	(0.002)	(0.002)	(0.001)	(0.001)
Cross-group predictors				
Proximity to Territorial MID	0.44***	0.44***	0.14***	0.16***
	(0.133)	(0.127)	(0.051)	(0.051)
Rebellion	0.53***	0.43***	0.13***	0.09***
	(0.060)	(0.059)	(0.023)	(0.023)
Petroleum	0.14***	0.17***	0.02**	0.03***
	(0.019)	(0.020)	(0.008)	(0.009)
Relative pop. density	−0.01***	−0.01***	0.01*	0.01***
	(0.000)	(0.000)	(0.000)	(0.000)
Observations	5,613	5,613	5,613	5,613
Spatial controls	Yes	Yes	Yes	Yes
Political status FE	No	Yes	No	Yes

Note: ***$p < 0.01$, **$p < 0.05$, *$p < 0.1$.

NOTES

Chapter 1. Introduction

1. Asian-African Conference (1955, 23).

2. As Malcolm X put it: "It was at Bandung where Black and Brown communities discovered who the real enemy was—blonde hair, blue eyed and white skinned Europeans" (Swan, 2018, 59).

3. For the most famous public statement of Sukarno's position, see Sukarno (1961).

4. On the entanglement of West Papua and Bandung, see Swan (2018).

5. Estimates of the total number of civilians killed varies substantially. See Anderson (2015); Amnesty International (2018).

6. This figure stems from original data collection. On the logic of transmigration in West Papua, see Chapter 3.

7. "Statement with regard to the Sixtieth Anniversary of the Bandung Conference," United Liberation Movement for West Papua, 18 April 2015, available at https://bandung60.files .wordpress.com/2015/04/ulmwp-bandung-conference-statement-in-english.pdf, accessed 29 July 2021.

8. *The Age*, 14 August 1914, Library of Australia. For early elite debates over Australia's expansion to the South Seas, see McGrath (2000).

9. Statements by Prime Minister Barton on 12 November 1901 and Prime Minister Hughes on 14 September 1920, Commonwealth of Australia Parliamentary Debates, House of Representatives. See also Chapter 4.

10. "Freedom for Australia too," *The Australian*, September 16th 1975.

11. For this reason, the word "settler" in Romance languages like French (*colon*) shares a root with colonization. See also Osterhammel (1997, 4).

12. I follow Sen and Wasow (2016) by defining race and ethnicity as a composite category or "bundle of sticks" based on individual language, phenotype, ancestry, and cultural traits, and I treat race as a subcategory of ethnicity. See Winant (2015); Wimmer (2015) for a recent conceptual debate.

13. This difference has long been noted by scholars. Australia and Canada have been called "colonies proper" by Friedrich Engels, "real colonies" by Karl Marx, "Neo-Europes" by Acemoglu, Johnson, and Robinson (2001), "settlement colonies" by Osterhammel (1997), and, increasingly often, just settler colonies.

14. Extract Letter from Marquis Cornwallis to Mr. Dundas, dated London 7 November 1794. Available in Thacker (1854, 15). Emphasis added.

15. Not all migration resulting in demographic change is colonization. For instance, gentrification does not typically entail expropriation so it is non-coercive, and should be analytically distinguished from colonization.

16. On the phenomenon of refugee settlers, see Espiritu (2018).

17. The terms "transmigration" and "resettlement" may be more commonly used in nation-states, but if land redistribution is ethnically discriminatory then it is inconsistent not to use the term "colonization." West Papuans in areas designated for transmigration by Indonesia were only allowed to remain at a ratio of one Papuan family to nine non-Papuan families, making the transmigration program highly discriminatory in practice. The term "internal colonialism" is also often used to describe colonization projects within nation-states, and to distinguish this from Europe's "external" colonization of the New World (e.g., Hechter 1975; Mylonas 2012). The trouble with this concept is that it begs the question of what constitutes an "external" and an "internal" colonizer; on what basis can we consider Australia but not Indonesia an external power in New Guinea? The Territory of Papua was long considered an inalienable part of Australia. The "external" nature of Australian rule in New Guinea only becomes clear in hindsight, much like would be the case if West Papua ever secedes from Indonesia. Settler colonialism is essentially one way that "external" colonies become "internal."

18. "Anger over India's diplomat calling for 'Israel model' in Kashmir," Al Jazeera, 28 November 2019.

19. As Glenn (2015, 61) recently contended: "settler colonialism has been driven by the impulse to gain sovereignty over land, bodies, and labor by turning them into private property that can be bought, exploited, and sold." On settler colonialism as primitive accumulation, often articulated with reference to the concept of "accumulation by dispossession" (Harvey, 2005), see Veracini (2010); Brown (2014); Coulthard (2014); Hirano (2015); Lloyd and Wolfe (2016).

20. As Wolfe (2006, 395) puts it, European commercial agriculture "progressively eats into Indigenous territory, a primitive accumulation that turns native flora and fauna into a dwindling resource and curtails the reproduction of Indigenous modes of production."

21. Italics added for emphasis.

22. See Elkins and Pedersen (2005); Pateman (2007); Fujikane and Okamura (2008); Veracini (2010); Lloyd (2012); Cavanagh and Veracini (2016); Lu (2019).

23. Lange, Mahoney, and Vom Hau (2006, 1427) are more nuanced, arguing that only liberal (British) colonizers always prefer to settle frontier areas, but similarly conclude that "The British pursued [settler colonialism] only in sparsely populated regions that featured a favorable disease climate."

24. Report of the Parliamentary Select Committee on Aboriginal Tribes (British settlements), Great Britain House of Commons, 20 February 1837, p. 31

25. Report of the Parliamentary Select Committee on Aboriginal Tribes (British settlements), Great Britain House of Commons, 20 February 1837, p. 75

26. Governor Bourke's Proclamation August 26 1835. Available at https://www.founding docs.gov.au/item-did-42.html, accessed 20 April 2020.

27. Despatch from Governor Bourke to Lord Glenelg 10th October 1835. Reprinted in Braim (1846, 104).

28. See Boyce (2011, 211) for an excellent discussion about the internal discussions within the Colonial Office about this change in policy.

29. Despatch from Lord Glenelg, Secretary of State for the Colonies to Governor Bourke, 13 April 1836, as recorded in Bonwick (1883, 349).

30. In one case, for instance, a settler in the remote Western District killed seventeen Aborigines by "gifting" them food laced with arsenic. The Chief Protector of the Aborigines was dispatched from Melbourne to arrest the culprit, who promptly fled (Ryan, 2010). Settler punishment for violence against Aborigines was extremely rare due in large part to jury acquittals. Nonetheless, by failing to deter settler violence and dispossession, the British colonial state bears primary responsibility for the killings. For the debate over whether indigenous massacres in colonial Australia warrant the term genocide, see Reynolds (1976); Moses (2000); Windschuttle (2000); Barta (2008); Madley (2008); Macintyre and Clark (2013).

31. Even in New South Wales, the elimination of much of the Aboriginal population was not premeditated by British leaders when they first established a penal colony there in the late 1700s (Langton, 2010; Edmonds and Carey, 2016; Clendinnen, 2017). Rather, the first Governor of New South Wales, Arthur Phillip, had been explicitly directed by King George III in 1788 that settlers in his penal colony were to "endeavour by every possible means to open an Intercourse with the Savages Natives and to conciliate their affections, enjoining all Our Subjects to live in amity and kindness with them" and if any Aborigines were "wantonly destroy[ed]" then the offenders were to be punished. Draught Instructions for Governor Phillip, 25 April 1787, British Public Records Office, London, United Kingdom.

32. Journals of the Continental Congress 1783, 602.

33. Washington to Lee, 1784, reprinted in Matteson (1933, 529).

34. For an excellent study of the haphazard, unplanned nature of early American expansion and settler-federal conflicts over the predation of native land, see Ablavsky (2021). Indeed, conflict between the metropole and settlers over native land also predated the American state. On how British restrictions on settlement over the Appalachians in the 1760s helped foster the American Revolution, see Gipson (1950, 103). There are, of course, exceptions where indigenous dispossession was organized and led by federal officials. But the principle that American federal authority generally followed settler volition would define America's westward expansion and its geographic limits over the nineteenth century (Frymer, 2017).

35. See the Moffat treaty of 1888, the text of which is reprinted in Hole (2016).

36. See the Charter of the British South Africa Company, as published in the *London Gazette*, 20 December 1889.

37. For instance, a motion censuring "the impolicy [*sic*] of permitting the Chartered Company of South Africa to establish any claim or contract any engagements with regard to the territory or government of Matabeleland, or to continue its warlike operations in that territory" garnered substantial but not majority support in the British House of Commons in November 1893. House of Commons Debates, 9 November 1893, vol 18 543–627.

38. More broadly, organizational theorists have long emphasized the importance of "decoupling," organizational behavior that deviates from formal rules or leader intentions. Consistent with decoupling, Ben Kiernan (2007, 252) notes that "the British rarely pursued extermination, but frequently foresaw it." On violence during civil war as an outcome of decoupling, see Weinstein (2006); Kalyvas (2006); Wood (2018).

39. This does not mean that the recent turn to the politics of recognition in countries such as Canada and Australia have not reproduced certain inequities and problematic standards of indigenous "authenticity," as compellingly detailed by Povinelli (2002) and Coulthard (2014). And nor does it mean that the politics of recognition have not failed to actually empower minority indigenous communities with real political autonomy or self-determination, as is clearly the case. Rather, the point is that it seems to require an undue amount of conceptual stretching to claim that the recent turn to symbolic incorporation and affirmative action have been designed to "eliminate" indigenous peoples, as past state attempts to displace or forcibly assimilate indigenous peoples were certainly designed to do.

40. As Cooper (2005), Appiah (1993), and many others have emphasized, the history of colonialism is littered with the failures of the metropole to penetrate and impose its rule over the periphery. Only attending to positive cases, as in Belich (2009)'s otherwise excellent study of European settler colonialism over the nineteenth century, is known as "selecting on the dependent variable" in the social sciences. For more on case selection bias and the distortions it produces in comparative historical research, see Geddes (1990).

41. The Portuguese New State (Estado Novo, 1926–74) incorporated Angola as an "overseas province" within an imagined multi-continental nation during the early twentieth century. Determined to make these overseas provinces pay their own way, however, little money from the metropole was spent on their administration or on funding Portuguese settlement (Bender, 1978, 102). Portugal had made fitful efforts to encourage Portuguese settlement to Angola before 1961 but, unlike its efforts during the 1960s, these were usually poorly funded and organized. See Pitcher (1991); Bastos (2008).

42. For more on the JPP, see Bender (1972); Ekaney (1976); Cain (2013); Penvenne (2005).

43. This means that the government spent approximately today's $250,000 per settler and more money on the JPP program, as Bender (1978) notes, than it spent on Angola as a whole in the early 1950s.

44. On the additive model of settler colonial studies, see the edited volumes of Elkins and Pedersen (2005); Mar and Edmonds (2010); Bateman and Pilkington (2011); Cavanagh and Veracini (2016); Adhikari (2020a); Lloyd, Metzer and Sutch (2013); Laidlaw and Lester (2015). As Youé (2018, 83) aptly lamented with reference to Cavanagh and Veracini (2016), "even when the case is made for comparative, transnational history or *histoire croisée* . . . we are more often than not restricted to a narrowly focused, temporally limited sequence of empirical case studies. That too is the manner of compilation in the *Routledge Handbook of the History of Settler Colonialism.*" Frymer (2017) is the notable exception, though he does not look beyond the United States.

45. Report of the Parliamentary Select Committee on Aboriginal Tribes (British settlements), Great Britain House of Commons, 20 February 1837, p. 104

46. As states are trying to extract maximal resources at minimal administrative cost, security interests explain other costly policies that nonetheless improve state capacity. For instance, De Juan, Krautwald, and Pierskalla (2017) finds that German policing in colonial Namibia was shaped by the twin goals of resource extraction and indigenous pacification, and Lawrence (2016) suggests that variation in French direct rule in Algeria was shaped above all by security interests and local patterns of (dis)order.

47. On ethnicity as an heuristic during conflict, see Mylonas (2012); Zhukov (2015); Bulutgil (2016); Balcells and Steele (2016); Hägerdal (2019); Blaydes (2017). On ethnicity as an heuristic during elections, see Posner (2005); Ferree (2006); Chandra (2007); and on collective targeting generally see Valentino, Huth, and Balch-Lindsay (2004); Downes (2008a).

48. On the Appin Massacre, see Connor (2002); Langton (2010); Karskens (2015). A similar pattern characterized the elimination of the Bidjigal in early 1791 and the elimination of much of the Wiradjuri peoples from Bathurst country in 1824. On Indigenous massacres and resistance in Australia, see Reynolds (2006) and the project "Colonial Frontier Massacres in Australia, 1788–1930" headed by historian Lyndall Ryan.

49. Proclamation of Governor Lachlan Macquarie, 4 May 1816, *Historical Records of Australia*, Library Committee of the Commonwealth Parliament, Sydney, 1917, series I, vol. IX: 144.

50. The Governor's Diary & Memorandum Book Commencing on and from Wednesday the 10th Day of April 1816. Lachlan and Elizabeth Macquarie Archive. Emphasis added by the author.

51. *San Francisco Bulletin*, 1 September 1856, as cited in Madley (2004, 179).

52. "Japan population declines at fastest pace yet, with only Tokyo seeing significant growth," *The Japan Times*, 12 June 2018.

53. See Huntington (1968); Hechter (1975); Bates (1974); Horowitz (1985) for early and important critiques of modernization theory. More recently, modernization theory has been criticized for ignoring the possibility of states in the Global South to forge "alternative modernities"; see Chakrabarty (2000).

54. On the Enlightenment and rationality as partial causes for declining violence, see Pinker (2012). On the inability of Marxism to account for the ongoing relevance of ethno-national identities, see Anderson (1983).

55. For a compelling case that inclusive national ideologies have helped prevent state violence in sub-Saharan Africa, see Straus (2015). My point is that exclusionary ideologies (like a commitment to a White Australia or Zionism) still leaves open the possibility of either genocide or decolonization, as evinced by Australia's willingness to decolonize Papua New Guinea or Israel's "disengagement" from the Gaza Strip. While racism does make it less likely that a state will extend full citizenship to members of an "undesirable" ethnic group or engage in assimilation, something beyond racism must still account for why states elect to remove "undesirable" populations from the nation-state through either violence or decolonization.

56. Racial ideologies are best understood as a consequence of colonization as settlers rationalize their political and economic privileges. Europeans invented the concept of race after their initial colonization of the Americas in order to rationalize a legal hierarchy between different types of colonial labor (Allen, 1994). Colonization preceded and produced racism. See McNamee (2020) for more on how different postcolonial racial ideologies across the Americas were shaped by the extent of European colonization, which structured the extent to which whites could maintain a monopoly on power.

57. "Xi Jinping: China's ethnic groups should closely embrace one another like pomegranate seeds," 28 September 2015, *China Communist Party News*. Available at https://archive.ph/OUb8R, accessed 29 September 2021.

58. Hoey (2003, 112).

59. "PM Modi addresses the nation," August 08 2019. Full text available at https://www
.narendramodi.in/prime-minister-narendra-modi-s-address-to-the-nation-on-8th-august-2019
-545901, accessed 29 September 2021.

60. On the importance of controlled comparisons for understanding variation in comparative politics, see Tarrow (2010); Slater and Ziblatt (2013). On the comparative historical method generally, see Fredrickson (1980); Lange (2012); Mahoney and Thelen (2015); Falleti and Mahoney (2015). By using primary demographic data to reconstruct the history of different colonization schemes, I also avoid the tendency when doing comparative history of relying too heavily on secondary sources (Lustick, 1996).

61. This may seem a very compressed time period but China's development has been unusually fast. China in 1989 was at the same development level as Great Britain in 1850 ($2,000). But by 2008, China was at the same development level as the UK in 1950 ($7,000). So, China has experienced much of the West's development over the past forty years.

Chapter 2. A Theory of Settler Colonialism

1. I would like to thank Harris Mylonas for directing me to this case.

2. Voutira (2003, 538).

3. "Russia offers free land to stop Arctic depopulation," *BBC News* 16 July 2020.

4. "On Russia's Vast Frontier, Lots of Free Land and Few Takers," *Wall Street Journal*, 25 October 2019.

5. I here build on the distinction between practice and policy made by Wood (2018, 4) with respect to wartime rape, and Adhikari (2020b)'s work on civilian-driven violence in settler genocides.

6. Of course, as with all typologies, this distinction should not be taken too literally. The history of most countries is characterized by instances of both settler or state-led colonization. For instance, both the eastern United States and Australia have cases of directed migration that were organized by the state, such as the Governor Brisbane's land grants of Wiradjuri country in the early 1820s and President Jackson's initiation of the Trail of Tears in the 1830s—though this latter case has been subject to much debate, with some historians contending that Jackson was actually seeking to protect the Cherokee from American colonists. See Satz (1992, 33) for a survey.

7. This has been true since antiquity. For instance, rising population pressure on land led to the Bantu migration to Southern Africa (1000 BCE–1100 CE) and the Yaoyi migration to Japan (300 BCE–300 CE), which were both violent processes that displaced hunter-gatherers.

8. Maxwell (1923, 172).

9. In order to assuage the fears of his settlers in Ulster, British King James I was forced to sell a number of Baronetcies in 1611 to fund a large standing army in Ireland's north. Thousands of settlers were still slaughtered there during the rebellion of 1641.

10. For instance, the Highland Clearances—the mass eviction of Scottish tenants from smallholdings and communal lands by large landowners—led to the emigration of hundreds of thousands of Scots to the New World. Similarly, as a result of the Irish famine in the late 1840s, approximately 1.5 million people emigrated from Ireland to other parts of the world.

11. For an excellent recent survey of this literature, see De Juan and Pierskalla (2017).

12. Likewse, Jharkhand—a state in eastern India—has experienced mass inward migration and displacement of its indigenous Adivasi population over the past century (Weiner, 1978). Stimulated in part by mineral discoveries, millions of Biharis emigrated to Jharkhand in the second half of the twentieth century. By 1981, indigenous peoples were a minority in Jharkhand.

13. Similarly, when London did stamp its authority on Rhodesia's settlers in the 1960s, setting the colony on the path to majority rule, Rhodesia unilaterally declared its independence from Britain in 1965.

14. This dilemma helps make sense of why only liberal European states like Britain and Spain (after the 1800s) tended to engage in settler colonialism in the eighteenth and nineteenth centuries, a puzzle raised by Lange, Mahoney, and Vom Hau (2006) and Mahoney (2010). The unfolding of historical events reveals that Britain only licensed settler colonialism in the face of settler expansionism; just like mercantilist Spain, Britain feared the costly implications of displacing indigenous peoples. The key reason why Britain and not Spain tended to engage in settler colonialism is the lesser degree of control that Britain exerted over its settlers— emigration to the Americas was tightly regulated by Spain until the 1820s. Lacking restrictions on labor mobility, liberal powers are more prone to settler-led colonization.

15. See Lustick (1993); Gerring et al. (2022); Acemoglu, Johnson, and Robinson (2001) for how differences in the extent of European colonization shaped the economic and political trajectories of states around the world.

16. Officials in Indonesia envisioned that the demobilized Javanese military families in Borneo in the 1970s could create a "security belt" to defend against perceived threats emanating from Indonesia's Chinese minority and Malaysia (Davidson, 2008, 96).

17. To keep settlers politically dependent on the central state, it is common for states to prevent settlers from selling their land, instead only gifting revocable leases or usufruct rights. See Albertus (2021).

18. See Mylonas (2012); Zhukov (2015); Balcells and Steele (2016); Hägerdal (2019); Blaydes (2017). Ethnicity is, of course, no guarantee that settlers will remain loyal to the state. Settlers are likely to remain fiercely loyal to the metropole only so long as they—and the state—continue to face a shared threat from the displaced indigenous group or external power, who seek to expel the settlers. See McNamee (2018) for this dynamic in post-independence Rwanda.

19. Ethnicity is not the only heuristic states can use. For instance, during the Spanish Civil War competing groups cleansed areas stereotypically associated with their opponents based on recent election results. As such, Balcells and Steele (2016) suggest that ethnic cleansing should be considered just one type of a broader category: political cleansing.

20. For the role of tying hands and sinking costs in interstate bargaining, see Fearon (1997).

21. Commonwealth of Australia Parliamentary Debates, House of Representatives, 10 October 1961

22. See, for instance, the reply by Henry Bate MP, Commonwealth of Australia Parliamentary Debates, House of Representatives, 10 October 1961.

23. As Kontogiorgi (2003, 74) summarizes, "Overall the settlement project imposed a financial burden on Greece that the economy proved unable to sustain."

24. Belshaw, Swan, and Spate (1953, 21–22).

186 NOTES TO CHAPTER 2

25. Report of the Parliamentary Select Committee on Aboriginal Tribes (British settlements), Great Britain House of Commons, 20 February 1837, p. 31

26. More broadly, coercive internal migration often leads to so-called "sons of the soil" conflicts, which are civil wars between settlers and indigenous groups (Weiner, 1978; Fearon and Laitin, 2011; Cote and Mitchell, 2018; Bhavnani and Lacina, 2018). Sons of the soil conflicts—whether between Sinhalas and Tamils in Sri Lanka, Arabs and Kurds in Kurdistan, or Thais and Malays in southern Thailand—are more deadly and last much longer than other forms of civil war (Fearon, 2004). So, even though states can faciliate colonization for clientelistic reasons (in order to build regime support among a core ethnic base)—as in late-twentieth century Mindanao and Casamance in Senegal—this is aberrant because such a move creates the conditions for protracted civil war.

27. "Pakistan Hits Back at India Over Kashmir Move, Targeting Bilateral Trade," *New York Times*, 7 August 2019

28. The strategy to manipulate births, whether through pronatalism or encouraging interethnic marriages, has also historically been an important tool for demographic engineering. Trying to change births and marriages, however, shares the disadvantage of a long lag time with other assimilationist policies and so I would theorize pronatalism similarly with assimilation.

29. Most famously, the French state eliminated internal linguistic differences in the early 1900s through the extension of state schooling and mass conscription (Weber, 1976).

30. For instance, after winning civil wars, states often try to reeducate children in restive areas to foster a sense of national identity (Paglayan, 2018). If there is absolutely no threat to the state, however, then I expect even assimilationist strategies to be absent or mild. This is consistent with Darden and Mylonas (2016)'s compelling comparison of nation-building strategies in Indonesia and Congo/Zaire.

31. Relatedly, a large literature has shown that more concentrated minority groups pose a greater risk of engaging in civil war as concentration facilitates collective action (Horowitz, 1985; Cornell, 2002; Toft, 2003; Weidmann, 2009; Morelli and Rohner, 2015). So, by demographically diluting a disloyal minority in a contested area, states can impede successful insurgencies.

32. To be sure, ethnic cleansing can often shade into killing, but the key distinction is whether indiscriminate violence is designed to displace or entirely eliminate a targeted population.

33. The way in which rising military threat leads to ever more coercive strategies for demographic engineering builds upon the "law of coercive responsiveness" proposed by Davenport (2007). And this prediction is consistent with a bellicist understanding of state building (Tilly, 1992; Centeno, 1997; Herbst, 2000; Thies, 2005). For instance, Thies (2005) and Lu and Thies (2013) find that models of state building that rely on international and domestic *rivalry* rather than war do a much better job at accounting for the development of state capacity, and Bulutgil (2016) finds that that historically most ethnic cleansing occurred outside of war or after conquest. Settler colonialism and ethnic cleansing are most likely to occur in the context of territorial insecurity but not necessarily of outright war.

34. Though I build upon Mylonas (2012)'s compelling theory of fifth column exclusion here, this prediction slightly differs from Mylonas' because he theorizes forced migration and internal colonization as *substitute* strategies for eliminating fifth columns. Given that expulsions

and colonization both dilute the demographic predominance of a fifth column, however, I predict that they are rather *complementary* strategies deployed together. I also extend this framework to include purely domestic civil wars against rebellious minorities.

35. Minority access to a foreign state also changes the nature of the military conflict, as it converts unconventional, guerilla conflicts into conventional conflicts where insurgents and the central state have clearly defined zones of control along either side of a border. In guerilla wars characterized by "fragmented" zones of control (Kalyvas, 2006), states use counterinsurgency strategies designed to identify the disloyal within their midst, such as forced relocation of civilians into new dwellings. So, forced relocation tends to occur in the context of irregular, guerilla warfare (Lichtenheld, 2020) whereas mass displacement tends to occur in conventional military conflicts where states are seeking to clear contested territories.

36. One may wonder why minorities and states can't simply try to strike a bargain, allocating a greater share of resource revenues to the minority group. Often states do precisely this, but a lack of transparency over the "true" extent of resource extraction can nonetheless lead to conflict (Ross, 2013).

37. It is worth noting that these are not the only relevant factors for understanding which ethnic groups become secessionist. Walter (2006) notably finds that both structural factors such as central government weakness as well as strategic factors such as successful secessions by other ethnic groups affect the decision of an ethnic group to seek secession. Consistent with this, in the absence of a foreign base or resources, rebellious minorities subject to colonization, such as the Tamils of Sri Lanka, tend to possess both a clearly defined homeland and a reasonable prospect for secession given the weakness of the central state.

38. In this sense, settler colonialism is an example of what political economists call a "principal agent problem." Failed colonization is the result of a binding incentive compatibility constraint.

39. The reader may have in mind the possibility that states could use coercion to "solve" the problem of settler abstention. Sometimes entire regions such as Van Diemen's Land (Tasmania) and Xinjiang can double as penal colonies. Yet, in order to permanently settle frontier regions, states must ultimately induce convicts and their descendants to remain in the settled locale. For this reason, upon their release, the Qing Dynasty provided two acres of land to convicts in the nineteenth century who stayed in Xinjiang (Millward, 1998).

40. Pertamina, Indonesia's national oil company, had a policy of non-employment of Melanesians given their perceived disloyalty (Budiardjo and Liong, 1988).

41. Similarly, Morocco's efforts to settle the contested Western Sahara since the 1970s have centered around drawing poor Arab laborers to work in the Sahara's lucrative phosphate industry.

42. Although I am cognizant that all social boundaries are constructed by humans and are thus non-natural in some basic sense (e.g., Fall 2010), I distinguish between "non-natural" and "natural" borders because geography plays a central role in military strategy and agriculture.

43. Natural borders that follow rivers and watersheds have also been shown to be less subject to dispute due to their focality (Goemans and Schultz, 2016). However, in this framework, which focuses on military strategy and not focality, the naturalness of a border should be considered a continuous function of the ease of its crossing. Specifically, given the greater difficulty of crossing mountains relative to rivers, mountain borders should therefore be considered more

"natural" than river borders and higher mountain ranges more "natural" borders than lower ones.

44. As Rosecrance (1986, 48) elegantly put it, "Land, which is fixed, can be physically captured, but labor, capital, and information are mobile and cannot be definitively seized; after an attack, these resources can slip away like quicksilver."

45. Consistent with these empirical findings, rationalist theories of war predict that as the value of territory falls, the prospect for peaceful territorial bargains increases (Fearon, 2018).

46. To be sure, the United States did create a number of military bases in areas such as Guam and Okinawa, allowing it to project power from afar. But these new territories were not permanently occupied by American settlers but by professional military personnel on a rolling basis.

47. *Speech of the Honorable William A. Jones in the House of Representatives* (Washington: U.S. Government Printing Office, 1913), pp. 23.

48. On disengagement as a strategic response to resistance in early twentieth century French West Africa, generally loss-making colonies, see McAlexander and Ricart-Huguet (2021). On fiscal pressures as a solvent of the French and British empires in the 1950s, see Cooper (1996); Gardner (2012).

49. "About 11% of Land in Japan Is Unclaimed," *Bloomberg*, 30 November 2017. In a remarkable cycle of history, one rural locality experiencing severe depopulation in Hokkaido—a northern island settled by Japan in the 1800s—has recently announced a policy of providing free land to try to stem the population outflow.

50. "A White Man's Country," *Mindanao Herald*, 8 April 1905, as quoted in Charbonneau (2019, 307).

51. Japan's GDP per capita was $2,000 in 1913 whereas the United States' was $8000—roughly equivalent to the difference between Moldova and Madagascar today. These GDP figures are taken from the Maddison Historical Statistics Project.

52. On Japanese settlement in Mindanao, see Goodman (1967); Yu-Jose (1996); Jose and Dacudao (2015).

53. *New York Times*, 11 February 1931.

54. Similarly, China subsidizes cotton production in Xinjiang and invests heavily in road and pipeline infrastructure there today. See Chapter 6.

55. On the endogenous emergence of a core-periphery economic structure due to transportation costs, see Paul Krugman's Nobel Prize-winning book *Geography and Trade* (Krugman, 1993). The positive economic feedback loops created by settlers is also a major theme of Belich (2009)'s study of the dynamics of European settler colonialism over the nineteenth century.

56. See, for instance, the representative survey conducted by Peace Now of 3,200 families outside the Green Line in 2002. Associated reporting at https://www.haaretz.com/1.5185962, accessed 2 February 19. There are, of course, religiously motivated settlers, and this is an idiosyncratic facet of the Israeli-Palestinian conflict. On how Zionists alter the settlement dynamics in the West Bank, see Haklai (2015), and on Israel as a clear empirical outlier, see Chapter 7.

57. This road was named for Avigdor Lieberman, a resident of the area, who was Minister of Transportation when construction began.

58. "Lieberman Road: The Impact of Bypass Roads on the Settlements, 2015," *Peace Now*, available at http://peacenow.org.il/wp-content/uploads/2016/01/leiberman-road-report.pdf, accessed 26 October 2021.

59. "Waiting for a miracle," *The Economist*, 15 August 2005.

60. To be sure, a number of other possibly important factors can be subsumed into my framework insofar as they emphasize other factors that affect the value of territory. For example, other economic factors affecting the calculus for territorial expansion including domestic labor mobility (Friedman, 1977), global growth (Bergesen and Schoenberg, 1980; Boswell, 1989) and the openness of international trade (Alesina and Spolaore, 1997). As these factors increase the willingness of states to take control over new territory rather than engage in trade from a distance (increasing the benefits of mercantilism relative to free trade), they plausibly increase state willingness to fund colonization. Low economic growth also makes it more likely that states will scapegoat minorities for domestic purposes (Adida, 2014).

61. Similarly, Michael Mann (2005, 4) contends that full democracies are less likely than either authoritarian regimes to commit ethnic cleansing due to constitutional guarantees for minorities. However, Mann also argues that ethnic cleansing is more likely in partial democracies than in stable autocracies, which have no need to appeal to the masses.

62. And this commitment has not been entirely toothless. For instance, to stop ethnic cleansing in East Timor in 1997, a multinational peacekeeping force led by Australia facilitated East Timor's independence. On the constraining effects of norms against civilian targeting, see Stanton (2016).

63. This assumption dovetails with constructivist approaches to international relations (e.g., Wendt 1992; Hopf 1998).

64. Also commonly cited is the notion of terra nullius—the idea, progressively formalized in British law, that land populated by hunter-gatherers is "empty" and can be legally alienated through settlement and cultivation alone. Wolfe (1994, 123), for instance, calls terra nullius the "ideological foundation of settler-colonisation."

65. See Goldstein and Keohane (1993) and Yee (1996) for when ideas causally affect policies.

66. Steinmetz shows how German treatment of the Chinese in Qingdao was shaped by the changing geopolitical orientation of Germany toward China, and how the 1904 Herero rebellion shaped the subsequent Herero genocide.

Chapter 3. Hit the Road, Jakarta: Indonesia's Colonization of West Papua

1. Figure based on original data collection—see data section. Absent any transmigration, I estimate that the proportion of Muslims in West Papua in 1999 would have been approximately 10% rather than 21%.

2. West Papua has changed names several times. Though it is anachronistic, to minimize confusion, I will use the term West Papua to refer to the area that encompasses the western half of the island of New Guinea. The area was known as West New Guinea during the Dutch colonial era. It was then renamed West Irian (Irian Barat) under Indonesian rule, and was renamed again Victorious Irian (Irian Jaya) in 1973, until 2002, when it was renamed Papua. I follow the practice of independence activists who call the area West Papua (MacLeod, 2015).

3. As a subsequent International Commission of Jurists (1985, 14) investigation summarized, "there is strong evidence that a fairly widespread plan had been made by ethnic Melanesians to attempt to take over the administration by force and that it was aborted. There followed fairly substantial disturbances at widely scattered places along the border by members of O.P.M. and by Indonesian armed forces."

4. This statement may have been coerced or sardonic, as in November 1984 the Governor was questioned by security forces—the government apparently believed him to be a potential OPM supporter (Osborne, 1985, 140). Indonesia formally announced in 1984 a sevenfold increase in the target transmigrant numbers to West Papua over the next five years (to 140,000 families), which meant that West Papua immediately became the single largest provincial destination for transmigrants in the country (Manning and Rumbiak, 1989, 47).

5. Fearing immediate dissolution, President Sukarno described transmigration "a matter of life and death for the Indonesian nation" (Fearnside, 1997, 554) and his successor, President Suharto, reportedly shared his "obsessional interest in transmigration" (Budiardjo, 1986, 114).

6. "Hand in Glove: How Suharto's Circle, Mining Firm Did So Well Together," Peter Waldman, *Wall Street Journal*, 29 September 1998. Available at https://www.wsj.com/articles /SB907020100505646000.

7. Papuan regency boundaries have changed substantially since they were first standardized in 1969. However, because new regencies have only ever been created through subdivision, it was relatively straightforward to aggregate the data to reflect consistently the regency boundaries from 1969. The data on transmigration prior to 1969 was reported at the project level, which, combined with information on where the projects were located, allowed me to recover total transmigrant numbers for each regency between 1964 and 69.

8. In the course of tracking these yearbooks down, I found that the only library worldwide that possesses most of them is the National Library of Australia. I also travelled to the archives at the Library of Congress, Washington D.C. in 2019 to complete the set.

9. The demographic data were compiled by village heads in West Papua (*kepala desa*). Villages are the smallest administrative unit in Indonesia and contain on average several thousand people. The village head is mandated to maintain a logbook of people's activities, including population changes, and reports these figures annually to the local full-time government official, the sub-district administrator (*camat*), who in turn reports the figures to higher levels.

10. This figure and the precise religious composition of transmigrants is only available from the first decade of the program (Herdito, 1973), but all subsequent yearbooks show that by far the great majority of transmigrants were from the island of Java, where the vast bulk of the population is Muslim. There are, of course exceptions, such as the some 1,500 Christians from Flores who were resettled to Merauke in 1987.

11. As many economic migrants to West Papua since the 1990s from nearby provinces are Christian, the proportion of Muslims actually underestimates the settler population in West Papua; approximately two-thirds of the non-indigenous population in West Papua are Muslim (McGibbon, 2004).

12. 1972 is the earliest date with regency-level religious data.

13. Given that only 10,000 refugees were recorded as entering Papua New Guinea over 1984 (International Commission of Jurists, 1985), I estimate that approximately 16,000 Papuans were killed, forced to flee to the forest (where they would not have been recorded in the statistical data), or forced to flee to other regencies of West Papua.

14. Indeed, during the 1960s and early 1970s, many transmigrant farms across Indonesia failed due to poor drainage, erosion, lack of water, and inadequate transportation infrastructure (Arndt, 1984). As the state began to invest far more money into detailed surveys of potential farmland and agricultural training, the estimated costs of resettlement per transmigrant family rose tenfold to $5,000 per family by 1981 (Van Der Wijst, 1985).

15. As Elmslie (2002) notes, copper is highly toxic to fish and marine invertebrates, and copper concentrations in the sediment around Timika during the 1990s were reported at thirty-eight times the level at which the Australia and New Zealand National Health and Medical Research Council recommend that a site be declared contaminated.

16. Tembagapura means "Copper Town" and was created by Freeport to house the workers on the mine.

17. See Elmslie (2002), Upton (2009), Ananta, Utami, and Handayani (2016), and Elmslie (2017) for notable exceptions that rely primarily on decennial census data. There have also been a number of extraordinary ethnographies based on legally risky fieldwork (e.g., Monbiot 1989; King 2004; Kirksey 2012; MacLeod 2015).

Chapter 4. White Australia or White Elephant? Australia's Failed Colonization of Papua New Guinea and the Northern Territory

1. The distribution of early European settlement in Australia was extremely geographically lopsided, with the vast bulk of settlement (and associated ethnic cleansing of indigenous Australians) occurring in the climatically mild southern colonies of Victoria and New South Wales. The capital of these two colonies—Melbourne and Sydney—began to industrialize and experience rapid population growth from the 1870s. By the 1890s, Melbourne was the largest city in the British Empire after London and one of the richest cities per capita in the world.

2. Of course, I do not mean to imply there have been no other relevant studies on the history of the Northern Territory or PNG in the twentieth century (e.g., Davidson 1965; Joyce 1971; Hastings 1969; Donovan 1984; Griffin et al. 1979; Thompson 1990; Nelson 2000; O'Brien 2009; Ling 2010; Denoon 2012; Hunt 2017). Rather, I only wish to highlight that previous studies have not reconstructed these settlement schemes and, crucially, why they failed. On debates over settling Papua New Guinea prior to the twentieth century, see Eves (2005).

3. A British protectorate had been originally been proclaimed over Papua in 1884. Australian settlers had been alarmed by the German annexation of northeastern New Guinea that same year and pressured Britain to secure a territorial buffer against further German expansion. Australian elites at Federation expressed interest in eventually exerting control over all the islands of the South Seas, including New Guinea, the Cook Islands, and Fiji.

4. See Prime Minister Barton's statement to Parliament in Commonwealth of Australia Parliamentary Debates, House of Representatives, 12 November 1901.

5. The commitment of Australia's policymakers to incorporating Papua was sincere. For instance, Barton spoke of the "long centuries for which I hope [Papua] is to be a territory, perhaps a State of this Commonwealth." Commonwealth of Australia Parliamentary Debates, House of Representatives, 12 November 1901. And Australia changed its national flag in 1909 to add an additional symbol for Papua and other future territories.

6. Through leasing rather than selling land, the government could prevent settlers from speculating by subjecting renewal of the lease to improvement conditions.

7. Lieutenant Governor of Papua. 1907. *Papua: Annual Report for the Year Ending 30th June.* p. 5. Melbourne, Australia: Commonwealth of Australia. The 1910 report also noted that the Papuan administration exempted all agricultural and pastoral inputs from taxation and charged no wharfage or harbour dues (p. 26).

8. E.g., Lieutenant Governor of Papua. 1910. Papua: Annual Report for the Year Ending 30th June. p. 26. Melbourne, Australia: Commonwealth of Australia.

9. Commonwealth of Australia Parliamentary Debates, House of Representatives, 14 September 1920.

10. This is not to deny the importance of other factors. For instance, the Australian government had prioritized awarding expropriated German properties to former servicemen. But with neither sufficient capital to develop these properties nor any knowledge about tropical agriculture, ex-servicemen proved poor farmers (Thompson, 1990).

11. Likewise, he stated in his annual report to Canberra that year that "it is not anticipated that there will be any further agricultural development of importance until the shipping arrangements are improved." Lieutenant Governor of Papua. 1920. Papua: Annual Report for the Year Ending 30th June. p. 7. Melbourne, Australia: Commonwealth of Australia.

12. Lieutenant Governor of Papua. 1922. *Papua: Annual Report for the Year Ending 30th June.* p. 6. Melbourne, Australia: Commonwealth of Australia. These costs were exacerbated by the application of the Navigation Act to Papua in the early 1920s, which meant that agricultural products had to be first shipped to Sydney before going overseas. The removal of Papua from the Navigation Act in the mid-1920s helped ameliorate freight costs but still failed to revitalize Papuan agriculture.

13. Lieutenant Governor of Papua. 1907. Papua: Annual Report for the Year Ending 30th June. p. 20. Melbourne, Australia: Commonwealth of Australia.

14. See Lieutenant Governor of Papua. 1929. Papua: Annual Report for the Year Ending 30th June. Melbourne, Australia: Commonwealth of Australia for a discussion of these schemes.

15. For example, Sangara Sugar Estates Ltd. started a large sugar plantation in the Northern District after trials in the 1920s revealed good yields. However, the plantation was abandoned by 1935 due to crippling transportation and labor costs (McKillop and Firth, 1980).

16. Throughout the interwar period, indigenous plantations made up only only a small fraction of Papuan commercial agriculture (Harris, 1980).

17. Lieutenant Governor of Papua. 1933. Papua: Annual Report for the Year Ending 30th June. p. 14. Melbourne, Australia: Commonwealth of Australia.

18. Copra is the chief ingredient in coconut oil, and producers of copra struggled with a relatively small market and high shipping costs. As one review later summarized, "Delays through breakdowns and other causes were frequent; ships' crews were difficult to get and retain, and the ships available were not always of the size most suitable to shift expeditiously and economically the copra awaiting transport" (Bureau of Agricultural Economics, 1953, 21).

19. Lieutenant Governor of Papua. 1934. Papua: Annual Report for the Year Ending 30th June. p. 10. Melbourne, Australia: Commonwealth of Australia. Murray had the previous year's annual report and also asked for funds to manufacture coconut oil in Papua in order to "save much of the heavy freights that cripple our industries . . . perhaps turning the cultivation of coconuts into a really profitable business" (p. 14).

20. Commonwealth of Australia Parliamentary Debates, House of Representatives, 1 June 1950

21. As Belshaw, Swan, and Spate (1953, 10) summarized: "Given difficulties of access and lack of amenity in the Territory, this is likely to be a serious inhibition as regards the more solid European capitalist, who could almost certainly find better prospects elsewhere."

22. Commonwealth of Australia Parliamentary Debates, House of Representatives, 22 August 1962.

23. Commonwealth of Australia Parliamentary Debates, House of Representatives, 12 March 1968.

24. Figures from the Northern Territory census, 1901, National Archives of Australia: F108, Volume 1. The indigenous population of the Northern Territory was not enumerated until 1971.

25. Quoted in McGregor (2016, 11)

26. Commonwealth of Australia Parliamentary Debates, House of Representatives, 13 April 1921.

27. E.g., Commonwealth of Australia Parliamentary Debates, House of Representatives, 10 February 1926, Commonwealth of Australia Parliamentary Debates, House of Representatives, 13 July 1923.

28. Commonwealth of Australia Parliamentary Debates, House of Representatives, 10 February 1926.

29. For further detail on these schemes, see Payne and Fletcher (1937); Powell (1982); Donovan (1984); Ling (2010).

30. Report on the Administration of the Northern Territory for the Year ending 30th June 1932, p. 5, as quoted in Ling and the National Archives of Australia (2011).

31. National Archives of Australia: A659, 1939/1/8371, Report of Development Branch, development of the Northern Territory, 25 February 1935, as quoted in Ling (2010, 101).

32. Payne and Fletcher (1937, xi).

33. Reflecting the uncertainty of the battle outcome, one Minister upon hearing news of the invasion force was heard saying, "it appears that we shall soon be the slaves of a foreign foe." Commonwealth of Australia Parliamentary Debates, House of Representatives, 28 August 1952.

34. Blamey to John Curtin, 21 December 1944, National Archives of Australia, A9816, 1945/20 Part 1. As quoted in McGregor (2013).

35. Commonwealth of Australia Parliamentary Debates, House of Representatives, 28 August 1952.

36. See McGregor (2016), Ch. 10, "The Divisive North."

37. Commonwealth of Australia Parliamentary Debates, House of Representatives, 12 March 1968.

38. Little has changed with respect to the challenge of keeping people in the Northern Territory. Darwin, for example, has been generally characterized by net negative internal migration since the 1980s and its total population declined over 2017/8 (Taylor and Carson, 2017). "Darwin only capital city in the nation where population is dropping," *ABC News*, 27 March 2019.

39. On the endogenous emergence of a new core by settlers creating markets for their own goods in southern Australia, see Belich (2009).

40. Commonwealth of Australia Parliamentary Debates, House of Representatives, 6 October 1953.

41. Here I draw on Belshaw, Swan, and Spate (1953, 21), who estimate that the government would have had to spend $1,000,000 per settler in subsidies to settle demobilized soldiers in Papua New Guinea after World War II.

42. In a similar vein, Australia and Forster (1960, 209) questioned the wisdom of spending money on settling the Northern Territory, querying whether "it [would] not be wise to spend the same amount of money which is needed in the Northern Territory to develop other parts of the Commonwealth, say Northern Queensland?"

Chapter 5. Best Friends Make the Worst Enemies: Demographic Engineering during the Sino-Soviet Split

1. This chapter is equally co-authored between Anna and myself. We were partners in data collection, research design, analysis, and writing.

2. These figures and others in this section based stem from original data collection. See Data section.

3. On the use of forced migration as a weapon of war more generally, see Greenhill (2011).

4. We primarily test these hypotheses in the context of China due to data availability, but we will also detail how similar patterns of demographic change can be observed in the former USSR.

5. The pre-1963 Xinjiang yearbooks do not contain county-level data. As such, there is a nine-year gap in our Xinjiang county panel between 1953 and 1962.

6. This is because new counties were created through subdivision. For example, county A would be subdivided into counties B and C in later years of the panel and then populations would be reported separately for counties B and C. By aggregating the populations of B and C, we can track population change across all the years of the data using county A's borders.

7. Chief among which is that the data does not capture flows of military personnel.

8. The results are unchanged if we look at different measures of proximity to Xinjiang's non-natural border, such as whether a county lies in northern Xinjiang or the distance of all counties to Xinjiang's northern border with the USSR. Northern counties of Xinjiang lie in the Dzungar Basin and southern counties in the Tarim Basin—the two are separated by a mountain range widely recognized as a politically significant divider between northern and southern Xinjiang.

9. Between 1982 and 1987, the number of Russians in Shawan increased tenfold to approximately 400.

10. Due to the extreme sensitivity of this topic and repressive context, we cannot provide quotes.

11. Oblast-level demographic data do not exist for the Central Asian republics, so they are excluded from the analysis. The available years with standard oblast boundaries are 1939, 1959, 1970, 1979, and 1989. Data source: Russian State Archive of Economy, accessed from http://www.demoscope.ru/weekly/ssp/census.php?cy=2 12 February 2017.

Chapter 6. Belt and Road to Nowhere: China's Ongoing Struggle to Colonize Xinjiang

1. Observations based on fieldwork. See also Human Rights Watch (2018); Zenz (2019); Leibold (2020).

2. As described in the previous chapter, the bingtuan are a military-agricultural colonizing force founded in 1950s with the responsibility to "open up wasteland and defend the frontier" in Xinjiang. As Millward (1998, 50) summarizes, "the settlement of soldiers and civilians on

reclaimed land to grow their own food has long been a staple element of Chinese frontier strategy."

3. The Population of China into the 21st Century—Xinjiang Volume (*Kua shiji de zhongguo renkou – Xinjiang fence*), China Statistics Press 1994, p. 418.

4. The discrimination on the part of the bingtuan toward Han is not a secret (Yin, 2015); for instance, the Corps publicized an explicit quota of 95% Han in its 2006 recruitment round for new officials. Civil Servant Recruitment in Xinjiang Favors Han Chinese, Congressional-Executive Commission on China. 25 July 2006. Available at https://www .cecc.gov/publications/commission-analysis/civil-servant-recruitment-in-xinjiang-favors-han -chinese, accessed 26 May 2020.

5. Likewise, a document issued by the Standing Committee of the Politburo in 1996 stated that the "Corps is an important force that can be trusted to guarantee the stability, build and defend the security of the border. . . . It is necessary to seize the opportunity for the country to develop southern Xinjiang and to expand and reinforce the Corps" (Becquelin, 2000, 79).

6. Wang Lequan, Xinjiang Party Secretary, Address to Chinese People's Political Consultative Conference, 27 March 1996, *Xinjiang Ribao*, from Seymour (2000)

7. This was budgeted at an extraordinary 10.7 billion yuan in 2002, reflecting the unprofitability of water-intensive agriculture in southern Xinjiang (Cliff, 2009).

8. "China's drive to settle new wave of migrants in restive Xinjiang," *South China Morning Post*, 8 May 2015.

9. Minority informants complained that they have been unable to obtain a Kashgar *hukou* despite repeated attempts whilst any Han migrant is readily able to do so. A report has an official in Xinjiang on record as saying that "Han applicants simply need to provide proof of address to obtain residential status. . . . But [granting hukous] is not applicable to people from southern Xinjiang. We don't know why it is like this. This is an order from the top." "Loosened 'Hukou' Restrictions in Xinjiang Benefit Hans, Not Uyghurs," *Radio Free Asia*, 10 June 2015.

10. Xinjiang local governments also benefited from preferential tax policies (*youhui zhengce*) allowing them to keep a much higher share of local taxes after 1992 (Becquelin, 2000).

11. On the Open Up The West program, see Goodman (2004).

12. See petroleum energy production statistics in the Xinjiang Statistical Yearbooks.

13. "Rich Province Poor Province," *The Economist*, 1 October 2016. The worldwide average in 2015 was 23% and in China as a whole was a still very high 44%. See Gross Fixed Capital Formation (% of GDP). Statistics drawn from the World Bank's online Data Bank.

14. There is also evidence that Beijing concluded that Xinjiang's Muslim population was becoming increasingly vulnerable to "infection" from ISIS and other transnational jihadist networks over this period (Greitens, Lee, and Yazici, 2020).

15. "'Absolutely No Mercy': Leaked Files Expose How China Organized Mass Detentions of Muslims" *New York Times*, 16 November 2019.

16. I exclude the county bordering India given India is not a Muslim-majority state. Its inclusion does not change the results. Unfortunately, I cannot test for heterogeneity in settler colonialism across natural and non-natural border zones in the south as the southern border of Xinjiang is entirely mountainous.

17. The results are unchanged when I model perceived threat by whether a county lies in southern Xinjiang, and the distance of all counties to Pakistan and Afghanistan. This last

measure accounts for the fact that the political dominance of Islamists in Afghanistan and northwest Pakistan in the 1990s was substantially greater relative to the ex-Soviet states that joined with China in seeking to restrict Islamist activity. The "Shanghai Five" of China, Kazakhstan, Kyrgyzstan, Russia, and Tajikistan was formed in 1996 and eventually transformed into the Shanghai Cooperation Organization in 2001. One of its first acts was to adopt the Shanghai Covenant on the Suppression of Terrorism, Separatism and Religious Extremism, which, as Clarke (2010) puts it, "declared the organization's intent to establish a regional response to the perceived threat of radical Islam to their states" (p. 20).

18. The results are unchanged when looking at the Uyghur population only, as Uyghurs are by far the most populous Muslim-majority ethnic group. The Uyghurs are approximately 45% of Xinjiang's population, the Kazakhs 7%, the Hui 5%, and the Kyrgyz 1%. Anna and I were not able to collect data on the number of Tajiks, but Tajiks are less than 0.1% of Xinjiang's population in any case.

19. This is admittedly not consistent with my theoretical predictions. But it is consistent with the cross-national patterns I find in the next chapter. Ethnic cleansing is more likely to occur to fifth columns like ethnic Russians during the Sino-Soviet split than to rebellious minorities, as fifth columns have a "home" state they can be expelled to. China has instead attempted to forcibly assimilate its Muslim minorities by encouraging intermarriage, suppressing minority births, establishing "reeducation" centers and, only very recently, internally deporting Muslims to eastern China. See "'If the others go I'll go': Inside China's scheme to transfer Uighurs into work," *BBC News*, 3 March 2021.

20. "Petroleum Topography: Tarim Basin," CNPC News, 1 October 2019. Available at http://center.cnpc.com.cn/bk/system/2019/01/10/001716533.shtml, accessed 24 February 2020.

21. See, for instance, the recent paean by the CNPC to Du Xiaorong, who graduated from Sichuan Gas Transmission Technical School in July 1992 and worked on Lunnan Oilfield for 27 years thereafter, http://news.cnpc.com.cn/system/2019/08/29/001742844.shtml, accessed 24 May 2019.

22. Oil companies were exempt from the requirement on the part of large state owned enterprises in Xinjiang to have at least 25% of their workforce be ethnic minority, given that they tended to hire only from petroleum technical schools.

23. See Chapter 2 for more on this distinction. Han migration to oil-rich regions of Xinjiang is a form of colonization because it is coercive and undesired by the native population. For instance, reflecting the perception that Han migrants have monopolized white-collar jobs in Xinjiang, a survey conducted at the turn of the millennium found that 60% of Uyghurs regarded Han migrants as either unwelcome or declined to comment (Yee, 2003)—the latter category being a telling response to an extremely sensitive question (Finley, 2013, 48).

24. Lelyveld, Michael, "China Pipelines Sold Far Below Cost," *Radio Free Asia*, 28 December 2015.

25. Jiao Ran and Xu Junfeng, "A Great Feat and a World Wonder," Xinhua Domestic Service, 18 August 1996, FBIS Internet Edition, 23 August 1996.

26. On phantom urbanization in China generally, see Sorace and Hurst (2016).

27. For example, one Han businessman who travels frequently in Xinjiang noted that he used to feel welcome in the south but "now it has all changed. They are not afraid. But they are

resentful. They look at me as if they are wondering what I am doing in their country." "China has turned Xinjiang into a police state like no other," *The Economist*, 31 May 2018.

28. As one Han shop assistant in southern Xinjiang explained to Joniak-Lüthi (2013, 166), "I came to Korla from Jiangsu one and a half years ago. I'm here with my husband. Our daughter is home in Changzhou with my parents and my older brother. We came here only because of money. We always return home during the Spring Festival. . . . I didn't transfer my household registration to Korla, it is in Changzhou. We plan to go back after some years. Our daughter goes to this famous school in Changzhou, we need to earn money to pay for it."

29. On the similar derision of economic Han migrants by the descendants of bingtuan in the southwest, see Hansen (1999).

30. "Xinjiang security crackdown sparks Han Chinese exodus." *Financial Times*. 21 December 2019.

31. "China's Nightmare Homestay," *Foreign Policy*, 26 October 2018.

32. E.g., Gladney 1998; Seymour 2000; Shichor 2005; Toops 2018; Anand 2019.

33. This has been recently echoed by Cliff (2016, 184), who contends that the "rising proportion of Han in South Xinjiang is helping to drive the region's progression . . . toward a "frontier of settlement" (Han civilian occupation)."

34. E.g., Sautman 2000; Hao 2000; Sautman 2006; Zhu and Blachford 2012; Yin 2015. For instance, Zhu and Blachford (2012, 721) assert that "Self-initiated/market-driven migration has a very direct impact on both demographic and employment situations in ethnic minority areas [but such] migration is mainly induced by market demand and for the most part is not under the government's direct control."

35. E.g., Bovingdon (2002, 45), Shichor (2005, 121), Clarke (2003, 218), Toops (2018), Liu and Peters (2017, 269).

36. "Xinjiang security crackdown sparks Han Chinese exodus." *Financial Times*. 21 December 2019.

37. Becquelin (2000, 83). The bingtuan has recently faced pressure to cut cotton prices by the central government. China's National Development and Reform Commission stated in 2015 that it would begin to phase out acquiring bingtuan cotton at artificially high prices, which led to a significant fall in worldwide cotton prices. "Top China cotton producer resists reforms in restive Xinjiang," *Reuters*, 20 February 2015.

38. These same points can be made for Tibet. Tibet has been characterized by little demographic change as measured by permanent residents, but much uneconomic government investment and seasonal Han migration since the 1990s (Yeh, 2013, 99–107).

39. For more representatives of this school of thought, see Pannell and Laurence (1997); Joniak-Lüthi (2013); Yeh (2013); Zhang (2020).

Chapter 7. Settler Colonialism around the World in the Late Twentieth Century

1. MAR tracks politically active minority groups in countries with a population greater than 500,000 and only if that minority numbered at least 100,000 or exceeded 1% of the population in a country.

2. Political scientists generally measure military clashes through the presence of a Militarized Interstate Dispute or MID. (See data description in the Appendix for more detail.)

3. The only areas of intense interstate territorial conflict without substantial ethnic cleansing or mass resettlement in Eurasia were the South China Sea and Korea. These conflictual areas lack partitioned groups or ethnically distinct states and so lack any structural imperative on behalf of states to change their demographic composition.

4. As a telling exception, this is not the case in Western Sahara and the Horn of Africa, which were both characterized by both substantial territorial conflict and demographic engineering.

5. The average GDP per capita of Indonesia in 1990 was $681.

6. Likewise, if and when China moves to settle Hong Kong with mainlanders, we should expect that it will have much greater success than in Xinjiang given Hong Kong's unusual status as a wealthy but contested city.

7. See Haklai (2015) for more on how Zionists alter the settler-state-indigene triangle in the West Bank.

8. As scholars have shown, war often leads to the election of ethno-national radicals empowered to undertake collective targeting in defence of the state (Snyder, 1989; Vasquez, 1993; Uzonyi, 2018). As such, we should be wary of conflating the proximate causes of state violence—the leadership of ethno-national radicals—for underlying causes, as the emergence of radical leaders is often produced by war and conflict (Bulutgil, 2016, 10).

9. "UN human rights chief points to "textbook example of ethnic cleansing" in Myanmar," *UN News*, 11 September 2017.

10. Poppy et al., S. Lewis, T. T. Aung, S. Naing, Z. Siddiqui, "Special Report: Myanmar's moves could mean the Rohingya never go home." *Reuters* (18 December 2018)

11. "Transcript: Aung San Suu Kyi's speech at the ICJ in full," *Al Jazeera*, 12 December 2019. Italics added for emphasis.

12. US Secretary of State Blinken recently acknowledged that ethnic cleansing had occurred in Tigray, a statement noteworthy for its criticism of an important US ally. "Blinken: Acts of 'ethnic cleansing' committed in Western Tigray," *CNN*, 10 March 2021.

13. This logic of this strategy was well known at the time. In December 1984, a high-ranking official in the Derg frankly admitted to a U.S. Government representative that "food is a major element in our strategy against the secessionists," and that the Ethiopian army "tries to cut the rebels off from food supplies" (Korn, 1986, 137).

14. "Thousands of Uyghur workers in China are being relocated in an effort to assimilate Muslims, documents show," *Globe and Mail*, 2 March 2021. For the most comprehensive study of Uyghur forced labor to date, see Xu et al. (2020).

15. As discussed in the Appendix, the proportion of a country's labor force that a state devotes to self-defence is a useful proxy for territorial insecurity.

16. Mann (2005) theorized that anocracies—neither full autocracies nor full democracies—would be most likely to engage in ethnic cleansing specifically. Consistent with Mann's argument, the greatest likelihood of ethnic cleansing occurs when a country is an anocracy, i.e., its Polity2 score is approximately 0. However, this is not true for settler colonialism—anocracies are actually the least likely type of regime to engage in settler colonialism. So, the evidence in favor of the importance of anocracy is also mixed.

17. Indeed, any international norm preventing violence against minorities would be expected to apply more strongly to ethnic cleansing than to dispossession.

Chapter 8. Conclusion: Decolonization, the Highest Stage of Capitalism

1. E.g., Wolfe (1999); Scott (2009); Veracini (2010); Brown (2014); Coulthard (2014); Hirano (2015); Glenn (2015); Lloyd and Wolfe (2016).

2. See Rostow (1960), Lerner (1958), and Lipset (1959) for early and influential formulations of modernization theory, and Gilman (2003) for a critical review.

3. For these and other critiques, see Huntington (1968); Hechter (1975); Wallerstein (1976); Chakrabarty (2000).

4. See Przeworski and Limongi (1997); Boix and Stokes (2003); Boix (2011); Acemoglu and Robinson (2018) for this debate. The major outlier remains China (Mattingly, 2019).

5. An exception is the large literature on the politics of national and ethnic identity formation including Horowitz (1985); Laitin (1992, 1998); Posner (2005); Wimmer (2012); Darden and Mylonas (2016); Fouka (2019) but this literature tends to be bracketed from demography.

6. For instance, see Adamson and Tsourapas (2019) for how diplomacy and interstate barganining affect international migration flows. Aside from recent work theorizing internal displacement (Steele, 2011; Balcells and Steele, 2016; Mylonas, 2012; Lichtenheld, 2020) and forced expulsions (Greenhill, 2011; Adida, 2014), internal migration tends to be treated as an explanatory factor for other outcomes like conflict (e.g., Fearon and Laitin 2011; Bhavnani and Lacina 2015; Pepinsky 2016; Gaikwad and Nellis 2017; Bhavnani and Lacina 2018). See Wallace (2014) and Whitaker and Giersch (2021) for noteworthy exceptions theorizing the causes of internal migration restrictions in China and the United States respectively.

7. See, among others, Ashcroft, Griffiths, and Tiffin (1991); Chakrabarty (2000). On the etymology of "decolonization," see Betts (2012).

8. Declaration on the Granting of Independence to Colonial Countries and Peoples, UN General Assembly resolution 1514 (XV).

9. See, for instance, the various unconvincing rationales that Jansen and Osterhammel (2017, 18) offer for excluding the breakup of the USSR from the study of decolonization, despite the long history of Russian colonization in Central Asia, which persisted well into the late twentieth century (see Chapter 5). On Russian colonialism in Central Asia and its afterlife, see Laitin (1998).

10. See, for instance, the rationalizations made by prominent Marxist and anti-colonial intellectual Vijay Prashad for the mass internment of Uyghurs in Xinjiang in "What Should the Left Do About China?" by David Klion, The Nation, 11 January 2022. In a similar vein, W.E.B. Du Bois was a surprisingly staunch defender of Japan's colonization of Manchuria in the 1930s, brushing aside the question of consent as "immaterial" in light of its economic benefits (Kearney, 1995). This stemmed from the belief that coercive modernization by non-white states was qualitatively different from European colonialism.

11. "But when dominions are acquired in a province differing in language, laws, and customs, the difficulties to be overcome are great, and it requires good fortune as well as great industry to retain them. . . . Plant colonies in one or two of those places which form as it were

the keys of the land, for it is necessary to either do this or to maintain a large force of armed men" (Machiavelli, 1950, 8–9).

12. "PM Sharon addresses the nation," 15 August 2005, available at https://mfa.gov.il/mfa /pressroom/2005/pages/pm%20sharon%20addresses%20the%20nation%2015-aug-2005.aspx, accessed 16 November 2021.

13. "Sharon maintains control in face of demographic shift," *The Irish Times*, 20 August 2005.

14. The persistent underdevelopment of the Global South was long explained by scholars of dependency theory as the result of power imbalances in the international system. For a summary and critique of dependency theory, see Ahiakpor (1985).

15. On the nonetheless strong appeal of nationalism as a form of political dignity see, among others, Lawrence (2013); Fukuyama (2018); Greenfeld (2019); Ding, Slater, and Zengin (2021).

16. For more on how genocide was a response to persistent Uyghur demographic dominance in southern Xinjiang, see Zenz (2021). See also Chapter 7 and the discussion of Ethiopia in the 1980s for more on why internal deportation is an ineffective strategy for demographic engineering in the absence of borders or settlers, which both effectively prevent indigenes from returning home.

Appendix

1. One cannot use data after 2003 because MAR's data coding subsequently changed substantially. Its website currently states, "Project staff are reviewing past coding systematically in order to release a single, integrated dataset coded on an annual basis from 1980 through 2006. Furthermore, the project is no longer updating the MARGene data generation program." http://www.mar.umd.edu/mar_data.asp, accessed 2 February 2019.

2. I do not use the newly released AMAR dataset (Birnir et al., 2018), which overcomes this selection issue because AMAR does not have my outcomes of interest.

3. To reduce measurement error, I calculate distances from the geographic center of the group polygons.

4. I use the updated list of rivals from Thompson and Dreyer (2011).

5. Rivals are a powerful framework for understanding international relations as interstate rivals fight each other much more than other states (Goertz and Diehl, 1993), particularly over territory (Lektzian, Prins, and Souva, 2010), and tend to elect more radical and ethno-nationally exclusionary governments (Snyder, 1989; Vasquez, 1993; Uzonyi, 2018).

6. 1990 is the earliest these data are available from EPR. Relative population density is the key predictor of interest, so I control for each country's overall population density per 1,000 square kilometers; data from the World Bank.

7. Domestic political competition has no relationship with ethnic cleansing overall and is associated with higher levels of land dispossession. More salient ethnic cleavages as proxied by greater land equality also decrease the probability of both settler colonialism and ethnic cleansing. I was unable to use Bulutgil (2016)'s third measure of cross-cutting cleavages, the vote share of left wing parties, because these data were not available around the world for this time period.

8. As fifth column status was coded from variables only found in the MAR data, it was not possible to code fifth column status for EPR ethnic groups.

BIBLIOGRAPHY

Abdelgadir, Aala and Vasiliki Fouka. 2020. "Political secularism and Muslim integration in the West: Assessing the effects of the French headscarf ban." *American Political Science Review* 114(3):707–723.

Abinales, Patricio N. 2000. *Making Mindanao: Cotabato and Davao in the Formation of the Philippine Nation-State*. Ateneo University Press.

Ablavsky, Gregory. 2021. *Federal Ground: Governing Property and Violence in the First US Territories*. Oxford University Press, USA.

Acemoglu, Daron and James A. Robinson. 2018. "Beyond modernization theory." *Annals of Comparative Democratization* 16(3):26–31.

Acemoglu, Daron, Simon Johnson, and James A. Robinson. 2001. "The colonial origins of comparative development: An empirical investigation." *American Economic Review* 91(5): 1369–1401.

Adamson, Fiona B. and Gerasimos Tsourapas. 2019. "Migration diplomacy in world politics." *International Studies Perspectives* 20(2):113–128.

Adhikari, Mohamed. 2020a. *Civilian-Driven Violence and the Genocide of Indigenous Peoples in Settler Societies*. University of Cape Town Press.

Adhikari, Mohamed. 2020b. " 'We will utterly destroy them … and we will go in and possess the land': Reflections on the role of civilian-driven violence in the making of settler genocides." *Acta Academica* 52(1):142–164.

Adida, Claire L. 2014. *Immigrant Exclusion and Insecurity in Africa*. Cambridge University Press.

Ahiakpor, James C. W. 1985. "The success and failure of dependency theory: The experience of Ghana." *International Organization* 39(3):535–552.

Albertus, Michael. 2021. *Property Without Rights: Origins and Consequences of the Property Rights Gap*. Cambridge University Press.

Alesina, Alberto and Enrico Spolaore. 1997. "On the number and size of nations." *Quarterly Journal of Economics* 112(4):1027–1056.

Allegra, Marco. 2013. "The politics of suburbia: Israel's settlement policy and the production of space in the metropolitan area of Jerusalem." *Environment and Planning A* 45(3):497–516.

Allen, Theodore W. 1994. *The Invention of the White Race*. Vol. 2. Verso.

Amnesty International. 2018. *Don't Bother, Just Let Him Die: Killing with Impunity in Papua*. Jakarta, Indonesia: Amnesty International Indonesia.

An, Tai-sung. 1973. *The Sino-Soviet Territorial Dispute*. Philadelphia, PA: The Wesminster Press.

Anand, Dibyesh. 2019. "Colonization with Chinese characteristics: Politics of (in) security in Xinjiang and Tibet." *Central Asian Survey* 38(1):129–147.

Ananta, Aris, Dwi Retno Wilujeng Wahyu Utami, and Nur Budi Handayani. 2016. "Statistics on ethnic diversity in the land of Papua, Indonesia." *Asia & the Pacific Policy Studies* 3(3): 458–474.

Anderson, Benedict. 1983. *Imagined Communities: Reflections on the Origin and Spread of Nationalism*. London: Verso Books.

Anderson, Kjell. 2015. "Colonialism and cold genocide: The case of West Papua." *Genocide Studies and Prevention: An International Journal* 9(2):5.

Antoniou, Dimitris. 2005. "Western Thracian Muslims in Athens. From economic migration to religious organization." *Balkanologie. Revue d'études pluridisciplinaires* 9(1-2).

Appiah, Anthony. 1993. *In My Father's House: Africa in the Philosophy of Culture*. Oxford University Press.

Arndt, Heinz Wolfgang. 1984. "Transmigration in Indonesia." Working Paper No. 146, Research School of Pacific Studies, Australian National University.

Ashcroft, Bill, Gareth Griffiths and Helen Tiffin. 1991. *The Empire Writes Back: Theory and Practice in Post-colonial Literatures*. Routledge.

Asian-African Conference. 1955. *Asia-Africa Speaks from Bandung*. Jakarta: Ministry of Foreign Affairs, Republic of Indonesia.

Australia and H. C. Forster. 1960. *Agriculture in the Northern Territory: Forster Committee report*. Canberra, Australia: Australian Government Publishing Service.

Australian Council for Overseas Aid. 1995. *Trouble at Freeport: Eyewitness Accounts of West Papuan Resistance to the Freeport-McMoran Mine in Irian Jaya, Indonesia and Indonesian Military Repression: June 1994–February 1995*. Canberra, Australia: Australian Council for Overseas Aid.

Baaz, Maria Eriksson and Maria Stern. 2013. *Sexual Violence as a Weapon of War?: Perceptions, Prescriptions, Problems in the Congo and Beyond*. Zed Books Ltd.

Balcells, Laia and Abbey Steele. 2016. "Warfare, political identities, and displacement in Spain and Colombia." *Political Geography* 51:15–29.

Ballard, Chris. 2002. The Signature of Terror: Violence, Memory, and Landscape at Freeport. In *Inscribed Landscapes: Marking and Making Place*, ed. Bruno David and Meredith Wilson. University of Hawai'i Press.

Ballard, Chris and Glenn Banks. 2003. Between a rock and a hard place: Corporate strategy at the Freeport mine in Papua, 2001–2006. In *Working with Nature against Poverty: Development, Resources and the Environment in Eastern Indonesia*, ed. Budy P. Resosudarmo and Frank Jotzo. Singapore: Institute of Southeast Asian Studies.

Bannon, Alicia L. 2005. "The responsibility to protect: The UN world summit and the question of unilateralism." *Yale Law Journal* 115:1157.

Bao, Yajun. 2018. "The Xinjiang Production and Construction Corps: An Insider's Perspective." Blavatnik School of Government Working Paper WP No. 23.

Barkey, Karen. 1994. *Bandits and Bureaucrats: The Ottoman Route to State Centralization*. Cornell University Press.

Barkley, Andrew P. 1990. "The determinants of the migration of labor out of agriculture in the United States, 1940–85." *American Journal of Agricultural Economics* 72(3):567–573.

Barta, Tony. 2008. "'They appear actually to vanish from the face of the Earth.' Aborigines and the European project in Australia Felix." *Journal of Genocide Research* 10(4):519–539.

Barter, Shane Joshua and Isabelle Côté. 2015. "Strife of the soil? Unsettling transmigrant conflicts in Indonesia." *Journal of Southeast Asian Studies* 46(1):60–85.

Bastos, Cristiana. 2008. "Migrants, settlers and colonists: The biopolitics of displaced bodies." *International Migration* 46(5):27–54.

Bateman, Fiona and Lionel Pilkington. 2011. Introduction. In *Studies in Settler Colonialism: Politics, Identity and Culture,* ed. Fiona Bateman and Lionel Pilkington. Springer.

Bates, Robert H. 1974. "Ethnic competition and modernization in contemporary Africa." *Comparative Political Studies* 6(4):457–484.

Bazzi, Samuel, Arya Gaduh, Alex Rothenberg, and Maisy Wong. Forthcoming. "Unity in diversity? How intergroup contact can foster nation building." *American Economic Review.*

Bazzi, Samuel, Arya Gaduh, Alexander D. Rothenberg, and Maisy Wong. 2016. "Skill transferability, migration, and development: Evidence from population resettlement in indonesia." *American Economic Review* 106(9):2658–2698.

Beadles, John A. 1968. "The Debate in the United States concerning Philippine independence; 1912–1916." *Philippine Studies* 16(3):421–441.

Becquelin, Nicolas. 2000. "Xinjiang in the nineties." *The China Journal* 44:65–90.

Belich, James. 2009. *Replenishing the Earth: The Settler Revolution and the Rise of the Anglo-World.* Oxford University Press.

Belshaw, Cyril S., Trevor W. Swan and Oskar Hermann Khristian Spate. 1953. *Some Problems of Development in New Guinea: Report of a Working Committee of the Australian National University.* Canberra, Australia: ANU Press.

Bender, Gerald J. 1972. "The limits of counterinsurgency: an African case." *Comparative Politics* 4(3):331–360.

Bender, Gerald J. and P. Stanley Yoder. 1974. "Whites in Angola on the eve of independence: The politics of numbers." *Africa Today* 21(4):23–37.

Bender, Gerald Jacob. 1978. *Angola under the Portuguese: The Myth and the Reality.* Berkeley, CA: University of California Press.

Bergesen, Albert and Ronald Schoenberg. 1980. Long waves of colonial expansion and contraction, 1415–1969. In *Studies of the Modern World-System,* ed. Albert Bergesen. New York: Academic Press pp. 231–278.

Berkhofer, Robert F. 1972. "Jefferson, the Ordinance of 1784, and the Origins of the American Territorial System." *The William and Mary Quarterly: A Magazine of Early American History* pp. 231–262.

Betts, Raymond F. 2012. Decolonization: A brief history of the word. In *Beyond Empire and Nation,* ed. Els Bogaerts and Remco Raben. Brill pp. 23–37.

Bhavnani, Rikhil R. and Bethany Lacina. 2015. "The effects of weather-induced migration on sons of the soil riots in India." *World Politics* 67(04):760–794.

Bhavnani, Rikhil R. and Bethany Lacina. 2018. *Nativism and Economic Integration across the Developing World: Collision and Accommodation.* Cambridge University Press.

Birnir, Jóhanna K., David D. Laitin, Jonathan Wilkenfeld, David M. Waguespack, Agatha S. Hultquist, and Ted R. Gurr. 2018. "Introducing the AMAR (All Minorities at Risk) data." *Journal of Conflict Resolution* 62(1):203–226.

Blaydes, Lisa. 2017. "State building in the Middle East." *Annual Review of Political Science* 20: 487–504.

Boix, Carles. 2011. "Democracy, development, and the international system." *American Political Science Review* 105(4):809–828.

Boix, Carles, Michael Miller, and Sebastian Rosato. 2013. "A complete data set of political regimes, 1800–2007." *Comparative Political Studies* 46(12):1523–1554.

Boix, Carles and Susan C Stokes. 2003. "Endogenous democratization." *World Politics* 55(4):517–549.

Bolt, Jutta, Robert Inklaar, Herman de Jong, and Jan Luiten van Zanden. 2018. "Rebasing 'Maddison': New income comparisons and the shape of long-run economic development." Maddison Project Database, version 2018. Maddison Project Working paper 10.

Bonilla-Silva, Eduardo. 2006. *Racism without Racists: Color-blind Racism and the Persistence of Racial Inequality in the United States*. Rowman & Littlefield Publishers.

Bonwick, James. 1883. *Port Phillip Settlement*. Sampson Low, Marston, Searle, & Rivingston.

Boswell, Terry. 1989. "Colonial empires and the capitalist world-economy: A time series analysis of colonization, 1640–1960." *American Sociological Review* pp. 180–196.

Bovingdon, Gardner. 2002. "The not-so-silent majority: Uyghur resistance to Han rule in Xinjiang." *Modern China* 28(1):39–78.

Boyce, James. 2011. *1835: The Founding of Melbourne & the Conquest of Australia*. Collingwood, Australia: Black Inc. Books.

Braim, Thomas Henry. 1846. *A History of New South, Wales: From Its Settlement to the Close of the Year 1844*. Vol. 1 London, UK: Bentley.

Braithwaite, Alex. 2010. "MIDLOC: Introducing the militarized interstate dispute location dataset." *Journal of Peace Research* 47(1):91–98.

Breustedt, Gunnar and Thomas Glauben. 2007. "Driving forces behind exiting from farming in Western Europe." *Journal of Agricultural Economics* 58(1):115–127.

Brooks, Stephen G. 1999. "The globalization of production and the changing benefits of conquest." *Journal of Conflict Resolution* 43(5):646–670.

Brooks, Stephen G. 2005. *Producing Security: Multinational Corporations, Globalization, and the Changing Calculus of Conflict*. Princeton University Press.

Brown, Nicholas A. 2014. "The logic of settler accumulation in a landscape of perpetual vanishing." *Settler Colonial Studies* 4(1):1–26.

Brown, Richard. 1966. Aspects of the Scramble for Matabeleland. In *The Zambesian Past: Studies in Central African History*, ed. Eric Stokes and Richard Brown. Manchester, UK: Manchester University Press.

Budiardjo, C. 1986. "The politics of transmigration." *The Ecologist* 16:111–116.

Budiardjo, Carmel and Liem Soei Liong. 1988. *West Papua: The Obliteration of a People*. Tapol Thornton Heath.

Bulutgil, H. Zeynep. 2016. *The Roots of Ethnic Cleansing in Europe*. Cambridge University Press.

Bureau of Agricultural Economics. 1953. *An Economic and Cost Survey of the Copra Industry in the Territory of Papua and New Guinea*. Canberra, Australia: Department of Commerce and Agriculture, Commonwealth of Australia.

Burke, Roland. 2006. "The compelling dialogue of freedom: Human rights at the Bandung Conference." *Human Rights Quarterly* 28:947–965.

Butt, Ahsan I. 2017. *Secession and Security: Explaining State Strategy Against Separatists*. Cornell University Press.

Cain, Allan. 2013. Angola: Land Resources and Conflict. In *Land and Post-Conflict Peacebuilding*, ed. Jon Unruh and Rhodri Williams. Routledge p. 177.

Castles, Stephen. 1992. "The Australian model of immigration and multiculturalism: Is it applicable to Europe?" *International Migration Review* 26(2):549–567.

Cavanagh, Edward and Lorenzo Veracini. 2016. *The Routledge Handbook of the History of Settler Colonialism*. Taylor & Francis.

Centeno, Miguel Angel. 1997. "Blood and debt: War and taxation in nineteenth-century Latin America." *American Journal of Sociology* 102(6):1565–1605.

Césaire, Aimé. 2000. *Discourse on Colonialism*. New York, NY: Monthly Review Press.

Chakrabarty, Dipesh. 2000. *Provincializing Europe: Postcolonial Thought and Historical Difference*. Princeton University Press.

Chandra, Kanchan. 2007. *Why Ethnic Parties Succeed: Patronage and Ethnic Head Counts in India*. Cambridge University Press.

Chang, Felix K. 2001. "Chinese energy and Asian security." *Orbis* 45(2):211–240.

Charbonneau, Oliver. 2019. "'A New West in Mindanao': Settler fantasies on the US imperial fringe." *The Journal of the Gilded Age and Progressive Era* 18(3):304–323.

Charnysh, Volha. 2019. "Diversity, institutions, and economic outcomes: Post-WWII displacement in Poland." *American Political Science Review* 113(2):423–441.

Chatterjee, Partha. 1993. *The Nation and Its Fragments*. Princeton University Press.

Chen, Jian. 2010. *Mao's China and the Cold War*. Chapel Hill, NC: University of North Carolina Press.

Chesnais, Jean-Claude. 1993. "The demographic transition: Stages, patterns, and economic implications." Routledge.

Christoffersen, Gaye. 1993. "Xinjiang and the great Islamic circle: The impact of transnational forces on Chinese regional economic planning." *The China Quarterly* 133:130–151.

Clarke, Michael. 2003. "Xinjiang and China's relations with Central Asia, 1991-2001: Across the 'domestic-foreign frontier'?" *Asian Ethnicity* 4(2):207–224.

Clarke, Michael. 2004. In the eye of power: China and Xinjiang from the Qing conquest to the 'New Great Game' for Central Asia, 1759–2004. PhD thesis Griffith University.

Clarke, Michael. 2010. "China, Xinjiang and the internationalisation of the Uyghur issue." *Global Change, Peace & Security* 22(2):213–229.

Clendinnen, Inga. 2017. *Dancing with Strangers*. Text Publishing.

Cliff, Thomas Matthew James. 2009. "Neo Oasis: The Xinjiang bingtuan in the twenty-first century." *Asian Studies Review* 33(1):83–106.

Cliff, Tom. 2016. *Oil and Water: Being Han in Xinjiang*. University of Chicago Press.

Commonwealth Bureau of Census and Statistics. 1961. *Census Bulletin No. 23 Summary of Population for Australia, Census of the Commonwealth 30th June 1961*. Canberra, Australia: Australian Government Publishing Service.

Connor, John. 2002. *The Australian Frontier Wars, 1788–1838*. Sydney, Australia: University of New South Wales Press.

Cooper, Frederick. 1996. *Decolonization and African Society: The Labor Question in French and British Africa*. Cambridge University Press.

Cooper, Frederick. 2005. *Colonialism in Question: Theory, Knowledge, History*. Berkeley, CA: University of California Press.

Cornell, Svante E. 2002. "Autonomy as a source of conflict: caucasian conflicts in theoretical perspective." *World Politics* 54(2):245–276.

Cote, Isabelle and Matthew I. Mitchell. 2018. Demography, migration, conflict, and the state: The contentious politics of connecting people to places. In *People Changing Places: New Perspectives on Demography, Migration, Conflict, and the State*, ed. Isabelle Cote, Matthew I. Mitchell, and Monica Duffy Toft. Routledge.

Côté, Isabelle, Matthew I Mitchell, and Monica Duffy Toft. 2018. *People Changing Places: New Perspectives on Demography, Migration, Conflict, and the State*. Taylor & Francis.

Coulthard, Glen Sean. 2014. *Red Skin, White Masks: Rejecting the Colonial Politics of Recognition*. University of Minnesota Press.

Darden, Keith and Harris Mylonas. 2016. "Threats to territorial integrity, national mass schooling, and linguistic commonality." *Comparative Political Studies* 49(11):1446–1479.

Davenport, Christian. 2007. "State repression and political order." *Annual Review of Political Science* 10:1–23.

Davidson, Bruce Robinson. 1965. *The Northern Myth: A study of the Physical and Economic Limits to Agricultural and Pastoral Development in Tropical Australia*. Melbourne, Australia: Melbourne University Press.

Davidson, Jamie Seth. 2008. *From Rebellion to Riots: Collective Violence on Indonesian Borneo*. University of Wisconsin Press.

Davies, Maureen. 1989. Aspects of aboriginal rights in international law. In *Aboriginal Peoples and the Law*, ed. Bradford W. Morse. Ottowa, Canada: Carleton University Press.

De Juan, Alexander, Fabian Krautwald and Jan Henryk Pierskalla. 2017. "Constructing the state: Macro strategies, micro incentives, and the creation of police forces in colonial Namibia." *Politics & Society* 45(2):269–299.

De Juan, Alexander and Jan Henryk Pierskalla. 2017. "The comparative politics of colonialism and its legacies: An introduction." *Politics & Society* .

Demetriou, Olga. 2004. "Prioritizing 'ethnicities': The uncertainty of Pomak-ness in the urban Greek Rhodoppe." *Ethnic and Racial Studies* 27(1):95–119.

Denoon, Donald. 2012. *A Trial Separation : Australia and the Decolonisation of Papua New Guinea*. Canberra, Australia: ANU Press.

Ding, Iza, Dan Slater, and Huseyin Zengin. 2021. "Populism and the Past: Restoring, Retaining, and Redeeming the Nation." *Studies in Comparative International Development* 56(2): 148–169.

Donovan, Peter Francis. 1984. *At the Other End of Australia: The Commonwealth and the Northern Territory, 1911–1978*. Brisbane, Australia: University of Queensland Press.

Downes, Alexander B. 2006. "Desperate times, desperate measures: The causes of civilian victimization in war." *International Security* 30(4):152–195.

Downes, Alexander B. 2007. "Restraint or propellant? Democracy and civilian fatalities in interstate wars." *Journal of Conflict Resolution* 51(6):872–904.

Downes, Alexander B. 2008a. *Targeting Civilians in War*. Cornell University Press.

Downes, Erica. 2008b. Business Interest Groups in Chinese Politics: The Case of the Oil Companies. In *China's Changing Political Landscape: Prospects for Democracy*, ed. Cheng Li. Brookings Institution Press.

Downs, Erica S. 2004. "The Chinese energy security debate." *The China Quarterly* 177:21–41.

Dun, Zhichun and Wuguo Zhang. 2014. "1962 Xinjiang Yili-Tacheng incident: The Soviet Union instigated the escape of over 60,000 border residents." *Chinese Community Party History* .

Edmonds, Penelope and Jane Carey. 2016. Australian settler colonialism over the long nineteenth century. In *The Routledge Handbook of the History of Settler Colonialism*, ed. Edward Cavanagh and Lorenzo Veracini. Routledge.

Eilenberg, Michael. 2014. "Frontier constellations: Agrarian expansion and sovereignty on the Indonesian-Malaysian border." *Journal of Peasant Studies* 41(2):157–182.

Ekaney, Nkwelle. 1976. "Angola: Post-mortem of a conflict." *Presence Africaine Identite Culturelle Negro-Africaine* 98(2):211–233.

Elkins, Caroline and Susan Pedersen. 2005. *Settler Colonialism in the Twentieth Century: Projects, Practices, Legacies*. Routledge.

Elliott, Mark C. 2001. *The Manchu Way: The Eight Banners and Ethnic Identity in Late Imperial China*. Stanford University Press.

Elmslie, Jim. 2002. *Irian Jaya under the Gun: Indonesian Economic Development versus West Papuan Nationalism*. University of Hawaii Press.

Elmslie, Jim. 2017. "The great divide: West Papuan demographics revisited; settlers dominate coastal regions but the highlands still overwhelmingly Papuan." *Asia-Pacific Journal* 15(2).

Engerman, Stanley L. and Kenneth L. Sokoloff. 2002. Factor endowments, inequality, and paths of development among new world economies. Technical report NBER Working Paper 9259.

Espiritu, Evyn Lê. 2018. Archipelago of resettlement: Vietnamese refugee settlers in Guam and Israel-Palestine. PhD thesis University of California Berkeley.

Eves, Richard. 2005. "Unsettling settler colonialism: Debates over climate and colonization in New Guinea, 1875–1914." *Ethnic and Racial Studies* 28(2):304–330.

Fall, Juliet J. 2010. "Artificial states? On the enduring geographical myth of natural borders." *Political Geography* 29(3):140–147.

Falleti, Tulia G. and James Mahoney. 2015. The comparative sequential method. In *Advances in Comparative Historical Analysis*, ed. James Mahoney and Kathleen Thelen. Cambridge University Press pp. 211–239.

Fan, C. Cindy. 2007. *China on the Move: Migration, the State, and the Household*. Routledge.

Fanon, Frantz. 1963. *The Wretched of the Earth*. New York, NY: Grove Press.

Fearnside, Philip M. 1997. "Transmigration in Indonesia: Lessons from its environmental and social impacts." *Environmental Management* 21(4):553–570.

Fearon, James D. 1997. "Signaling foreign policy interests: Tying hands versus sinking costs." *Journal of Conflict Resolution* 41(1):68–90.

Fearon, James D. 2004. "Why do some civil wars last so much longer than others?" *Journal of Peace Research* 41(3):275–301.

Fearon, James D. 2018. "Cooperation, conflict, and the costs of anarchy." *International Organization* 72(3):523–559.

Fearon, James D. and David D. Laitin. 2011. "Sons of the soil, migrants, and civil war." *World Development* 39(2):199–211.

Ferree, Karen E. 2006. "Explaining South Africa's racial census." *The Journal of Politics* 68(4):803–815.

Finley, Joanne N. Smith. 2013. *The Art of Symbolic Resistance: Uyghur Identities and Uyghur-Han Relations in Contemporary Xinjiang*. Brill.

Forsyth, William Douglass. 1942. *Myth of Open Spaces*. Oxford University Press.

Fouka, Vasiliki. 2016. "Backlash: The unintended effects of language prohibition in US schools after World War I." *Stanford Center for International Development Working Paper* (591).

Fouka, Vasiliki. 2019. "How do immigrants respond to discrimination? The case of Germans in the US during World War I." *American Political Science Review* 113(2):405–422.

Fravel, M. Taylor. 2008. *Strong Borders, Secure Nation : Cooperation and Conflict in China's Territorial Disputes*. Princeton, NJ: Princeton University Press.

Fredrickson, George M. 1980. Comparative history. In *The Past before Us: Contemporary Historical Writing in the United States*, ed. Michael G. Kammen. Ithaca, NY: Cornell University Presa pp. 457–473.

Frieden, Jeffry A. 1994. "International investment and colonial control: A new interpretation." *International Organization* pp. 559–593.

Friedman, David. 1977. "A theory of the size and shape of nations." *Journal of Political Economy* 85(1):59–77.

Friedmann, J. and R. Wulff. 1975. *The Urban Transition: Comparative Studies of Newly Developing Societies*. London: Edward Arnold.

Frymer, Paul. 2017. *Building an American Empire: The Era of Territorial and Political Expansion*. Princeton University Press.

Fujikane, Candace and Jonathan Y, Okamura. 2008. *Asian Settler Colonialism: From Local Governance to the Habits of Everyday Life in Hawaii*. University of Hawaii Press.

Fukuyama, Francis. 1997. "The East Asian Prospect: The Illusion of Exceptionalism." *Journal of Democracy* 8(3):146–149.

Fukuyama, Francis. 2018. *Identity: The Demand for Dignity and the Politics of Resentment*. Farrar, Straus and Giroux.

Gaikwad, Nikhar and Gareth Nellis. 2017. "The majority-minority divide in attitudes toward internal migration: Evidence from Mumbai." *American Journal of Political Science* 61(2): 456–472.

Gardner, Leigh. 2012. *Taxing Colonial Africa: The Political Economy of British imperialism*. Oxford University Press.

Garnaut, Ross. 1976. *Neo-colonialism and Independence: Papua New Guinea's Economic Relations with Australia and Japan*. Canberra, Australia: ANU Press.

Gartzke, Erik and Dominic Rohner. 2010. "To conquer or compel: Economic development and interstate conflict." Working Paper No. 412, Department of Economics, University of Zurich, Zurich, Switzerland.

Gartzke, Erik and Dominic Rohner. 2011. "Prosperous pacifists: The effects of development on initiators and targets of territorial conflict." Working Paper No. 500, Institute for Empirical Research in Economics University of Zurich, Zurich, Switzerland.

Geddes, Barbara. 1990. "How the cases you choose affect the answers you get: Selection bias in comparative politics." *Political Analysis* 2:131–150.

Gerring, John, Brendan Apfeld, Tore Wig, and Andreas Tollefsen. 2022. *The Deep Roots of Modern Democracy*. Cambridge: Cambridge University Press.

Gerring, John, Daniel Ziblatt, Johan Van Gorp, and Julian Arevalo. 2011. "An institutional theory of direct and indirect rule." *World Politics* 63(3):377–433.

Gietzelt, Dale. 1989. "The Indonesianization of West Papua." *Oceania* 59(3):201–221.

Gilman, Nils. 2003. *Mandarins of the Future: Modernization Theory in Cold War America*. John Hopkins University Press.

Ginsburgs, George. 1978. *The Sino-Soviet Territorial Dispute, 1949–64*. New York, NY: Praeger Publishers.

Gipson, Lawrence Henry. 1950. "The American revolution as an aftermath of the Great War for the Empire, 1754–1763." *Political Science Quarterly* 65(1):86–104.

Gladney, Dru C. 1998. "Internal colonialism and the Uyghur nationality: Chinese nationalism and its subaltern subjects." *Cahiers d'Etudes sur la Méditerranée Orientale et le monde Turco-Iranien* (25).

Glenn, Evelyn Nakano. 2015. "Settler colonialism as structure: A framework for comparative studies of US race and gender formation." *Sociology of Race and Ethnicity* 1(1):52–72.

Global Witness. 2005. *Paying for Protection: The Freeport Mine and the Indonesian Security Forces*. Washington, DC: Global Witness.

Goemans, H. E. and Kenneth A. Schultz. 2016. "The politics of territorial disputes: A geospatial approach applied to Africa." *International Organization* 71(1):31–64.

Goertz, Gary and Paul F. Diehl. 1993. "Enduring rivalries: Theoretical constructs and empirical patterns." *International Studies Quarterly* 37(2):147–171.

Goldstein, Judith and Robert Owen Keohane. 1993. *Ideas and Foreign Policy: Beliefs, Institutions, and Political Change*. Cornell University Press.

Goldstone, Jack A., Eric P. Kaufmann and Monica Duffy Toft. 2012. *Political Demography: How Population Changes Are Reshaping International Security and National Politics*. Oxford University Press.

Goodman, David SG. 2004. "The campaign to 'Open up the West': National, provincial-level and local perspectives." *The China Quarterly* 178:317–334.

Goodman, Grant K. 1967. *Davao: A Case Study in Japanese-Philippine Relations*. University of Kansas, Center for East Asian Studies.

Greenfeld, Liah. 2019. *Nationalism: A Short History*. Brookings Institution Press.

Greenhill, Kelly M. 2011. *Weapons of Mass Migration: Forced Displacement, Coercion, and Foreign Policy*. Cornell University Press.

Greitens, Sheena Chestnut, Myunghee Lee, and Emir Yazici. 2020. "Counterterrorism and preventive repression: China's changing strategy in Xinjiang." *International Security* 44(3): 9–47.

Griffin, James, Hank Nelson, Stewart Firth, et al. 1979. *Papua New Guinea: A Political History*. Melbourne, Australia: Heinemann Educational.

Gurr, Ted Robert. 2000. "Ethnic warfare on the wane." *Foreign Affairs* pp. 52–64.

Hägerdal, Nils. 2019. "Ethnic cleansing and the politics of restraint: Violence and coexistence in the Lebanese Civil War." *Journal of Conflict Resolution* 63(1):9–84.

Haklai, Oded. 2015. The decisive path of state indecisiveness: Israeli settlers in the West Bank in comparative perspective. In *Settlers in Contested Lands: Territorial Disputes and Ethnic Conflicts*, ed. Oded Haklai and Neophytos Loizides. Stanford, CA: Stanford University Press.

Haklai, Oded and Neophytos Loizides. 2015. Settlers and conflict over contested territories. In *Settlers in Contested Lands: Territorial Disputes and Ethnic Conflicts*, ed. Oded Haklai and Neophytos Loizides. Stanford, CA: Stanford University Press.

Han, Enze and Harris Mylonas. 2014. "Interstate relations, perceptions, and power balance: Explaining China's policies toward ethnic groups, 1949–1965." *Security Studies* 23(1):148–181.

Handel, Ariel, Galit Rand, and Marco Allegra. 2015. "Wine-washing: Colonization, normalization, and the geopolitics of terroir in the West Bank's settlements." *Environment and Planning A* 47(6):1351–1367.

Hansen, Mette Halskov. 1999. "The call of Mao or money? Han Chinese settlers on China's south-western borders." *The China Quarterly* 158:394–413.

Hao, Yan. 2000. "Tibetan population in China: Myths and facts re-examined." *Asian Ethnicity* 1(1):11–36.

Hardjono, Joan M. 1977. *Transmigration in Indonesia.* Oxford University Press.

Hardt, Michael and Antonio Negri. 2000. *Empire.* Harvard University Press.

Hariri, Jacob Gerner. 2012. "The autocratic legacy of early statehood." *American Political Science Review* 106(3):471–494.

Harris, G. T. 1980. Papuan village agriculture 1884–1960. In *A Time to Plant and a Time to Uproot: A History of Agriculture in Papua New Guinea,* ed. Donald Denoon and Catherine Snowden. Port Moresby, Papua New Guinea: Institute of Papua New Guinea Studies.

Harvey, David. 2005. *The New Imperialism.* Oxford University Press.

Hastings, Peter. 1969. *New Guinea: Problems and Prospects.* Melbourne, Australia: The Australian Institute of International Affairs.

Hechter, Michael. 1975. *Internal Colonialism: The Celtic Fringe in Bristish National Development.* London, UK: Routledge and Kegan Paul.

Hechter, Michael. 2000. *Containing Nationalism.* Oxford University Press.

Herbst, Jeffrey. 1990. "War and the State in Africa." *International Security* 14(4):117–139.

Herbst, Jeffrey. 2000. *States and Power in Africa: Comparative Lessons in Authority and Control.* Princeton University Press.

Herdito, Irawan. 1973. *Pelaksanaan dan program transmigrasi di Irian Jaya dalam hubungannya dengan pembangunan pertanian.* Jakarta : Departemen Pertanian.

Hierman, Brent. 2007. "The pacification of Xinjiang: Uighur protest and the Chinese state, 1988–2002." *Problems of Post-Communism* 54(3):48–62.

Hirano, Katsuya. 2015. "Thanatopolitics in the making of Japan's Hokkaido: Settler colonialism and primitive accumulation." *Critical Historical Studies* 2(2):191–218.

Hobson, John Atkinson. 1902. *Imperialism: A Study.* Ann Arbor, MI: University of Michigan Press.

Hoey, Brian A. 2003. "Nationalism in Indonesia: Building imagined and intentional communities through transmigration." *Ethnology.*

Hole, Hugh Marshall. 2016. *The Making of Rhodesia.* Routledge.

Holsti, Kalevi J. 1991. *Peace and War: Armed Conflicts and International Order, 1648–1989.* Cambridge University Press.

Hopf, Ted. 1998. "The promise of constructivism in international relations theory." *International Security* 23(1):171–200.

Horowitz, Donald L. 1985. *Ethnic Groups in Conflict.* Berkeley, CA: University of California Press.

Hug, Simon. 2013. "The use and misuse of the 'minorities at risk' project." *Annual Review of Political Science* 16:191–208.

Human Rights Watch. 2018. "Eradicating ideological viruses": China's campaign of repression against Xinjiang's Muslims. Technical report Human Rights Watch.

Hunt, Bruce. 2017. *Australia's Northern Shield? Papua New Guinea and the Defence of Australia Since 1880*. Melbourne, Australia: Monash University Publishing.

Huntington, Samuel P. 1968. *Political Order in Changing Societies*. Yale University Press.

Hussain, Monirul. 2008. *Interrogating Development: State, Displacement and Popular Resistance in North East India*. SAGE Publications.

Indonesia, Ministry of Transmigration Staff. 1991. "Planning for population mobility: The Indonesian transmigration programme." Paper presented at the Pacific Rim conference on resource management, April 1991, Taipei, Taiwan.

International Commission of Jurists. 1985. *The Status of Border Crossers from Irian Jaya to Papua New Guinea*. Sydney: International Commission of Jurists.

Jansen, Jan C. and Jürgen Osterhammel. 2017. *Decolonization*. Princeton University Press.

Jenne, Erin K., Stephen M. Saideman, and Will Lowe. 2007. "Separatism as a bargaining posture: The role of leverage in minority radicalization." *Journal of Peace Research* 44(5):539–558.

Jian, Chen. 2006. "The Tibetan rebellion of 1959 and China's changing relations with India and the Soviet Union." *Journal of Cold War Studies* 8(3):54–101.

Joniak-Lüthi, Agnieszka. 2013. "Han Migration to Xinjiang Uyghur Autonomous Region: Between state schemes and migrants' strategies." *Zeitschrift für Ethnologie* pp. 155–174.

Jose, Lydia N. Yu and Patricia Irene Dacudao. 2015. "Visible Japanese and invisible Filipino narratives of the development of Davao, 1900s to 1930s." *Philippine Studies Historical & Ethnographic Viewpoints* pp. 101–129.

Joyce, R. B. 1971. Australian interests in New Guinea before 1906. In *Australia and Papua New Guinea*, ed. W. J. Hudson. Sydney, Australia: Sydney University Press pp. 8–31.

Kalyvas, Stathis N. 2006. *The Logic of Violence in Civil War*. Cambridge University Press.

Karskens, Grace. 2015. "Appin Massacre." Published as part of the Dictionary of Sydney, State Library of New South Wales.

Kearney, Reginald. 1995. "The Pro-Japanese Utterances of WEB Du Bois." *Contributions in Black Studies* 13(1):1–17.

Keegan, John. 1993. *A History of Warfare*. New York, NY: Knopf.

Keller, Edmond J. 1992. "Drought, war, and the politics of famine in Ethiopia and Eritrea." *The Journal of Modern African Studies* 30(4):609–624.

Kerr, David and Laura C. Swinton. 2008. "China, Xinjiang, and the transnational security of Central Asia." *Critical Asian Studies* 40(1):89–112.

Kiernan, Ben. 2007. *Blood and Soil: A World History of Genocide and Extermination from Sparta to Darfur*. Yale University Press.

King, Peter. 2004. *West Papua & Indonesia since Suharto: Independence, Autonomy or Chaos?* University of New South Wales Press.

King, Russell. 2012. "Geography and migration studies: Retrospect and prospect." *Population, Space and Place* 18(2):134–153.

King, Russell and Ronald Skeldon. 2010. "'Mind the gap!' Integrating approaches to internal and international migration." *Journal of Ethnic and Migration Studies* 36(10):1619–1646.

Kinzley, Judd C. 2018. *Natural Resources and the New Frontier: Constructing Modern China's Borderlands*. University of Chicago Press.

Kirksey, Eben. 2012. *Freedom in Entangled Worlds: West Papua and the Architecture of Global Power*. Duke University Press.

Knights, Michael and Ahmed Ali. 2010. Kirkuk in transition. Technical Report 102 The Washington Institute for Near East Policy, Policy Focus.

Kontogiorgi, Elisabeth. 2003. Economic consequences following refugee settlement in Greek Macedonia, 1923–1932. In *Crossing the Aegean. An Appraisal of the 1923 Compulsory Population Exchange between Greece and Turkey*, ed. Renée Hirschon. Berghahn: New York and Oxford.

Korn, David A. 1986. *Ethiopia, the United States and the Soviet Union*. Routledge.

Krinks, Peter A. 1970. Peasant colonisation in Mindanao, the Philippines. PhD thesis Australian National University.

Krugman, Paul R. 1993. *Geography and Trade*. MIT press.

Laidlaw, Zoë and Alan Lester. 2015. *Indigenous Communities and Settler Colonialism: Land Holding, Loss and Survival in an Interconnected World*. Springer.

Laitin, David D. 1992. *Language Repertoires and State Construction in Africa*. Cambridge University Press.

Laitin, David D. 1998. *Identity in Formation: The Russian-Speaking Populations in the Near Abroad*. Cornell University Press.

Lange, Matthew. 2012. *Comparative-Historical methods*. SAGE Publications.

Lange, Matthew, James Mahoney, and Matthias Vom Hau. 2006. "Colonialism and development: A comparative analysis of Spanish and British colonies." *American Journal of Sociology* 111(5):1412–1462.

Langton, Marcia. 2010. Ngura Barbagai: Country lost: "They made a solitude and called it peace." In *First Australians*, ed. Marcia Langton and Rachel Perkins. Melbourne, Australia: The Miegunyah Press (University of Melbourne) pp. 1–43.

Larin, Viktor. 2013. "External threat as a driving force for exploring and developing the Russian Pacific region." Carnegie Endowment for Peace.

Lattimore, Owen. 1962. *Studies in Frontier History: Collected Papers, 1928–1958*. London, UK: Oxford University Press.

Lawrence, Adria. 2013. *Imperial Rule and the Politics of Nationalism: Anti-colonial Protest in the French Empire*. Cambridge University Press.

Lawrence, Adria. 2016. "Colonial approaches to governance in the periphery: Direct and indirect rule in French Algeria." John Hopkins University. Working Paper.

Lechler, Marie and Lachlan McNamee. 2018. "Indirect colonial rule undermines support for democracy: Evidence from a natural experiment in Namibia." *Comparative Political Studies* 51(14):1858–1898.

Lee, Everett S. 1966. "A theory of migration." *Demography* 3(1):47–57.

Lee, Melissa M. 2018. "The international politics of incomplete sovereignty: How hostile neighbors weaken the state." *International Organization* .

Leibold, James. 2019. "Planting the seed: Ethnic policy in Xi Jinping's new era of cultural nationalism." *China Brief* 19(22).

Leibold, James. 2020. "Surveillance in China's Xinjiang region: Ethnic sorting, coercion, and inducement." *Journal of Contemporary China* 29(121):46–60.

Leith, Denise. 2002. "Freeport and the Suharto regime, 1965–1998." *The Contemporary Pacific* 14(1):69–100.

Lektzian, David, Brandon C. Prins and Mark Souva. 2010. "Territory, river, and maritime claims in the Western Hemisphere: Regime type, rivalry, and MIDs from 1901 to 2000." *International Studies Quarterly* 54(4):1073–1098.

Lenin, Vladimir Ilich. 2010. *Imperialism: The Highest Stage of Capitalism*. Penguin Classics.

Lerner, Daniel. 1958. *The Passing of Traditional Society: Modernizing the Middle East*. New York: Free Press.

Liao, Zhaoyu. 2016. "The belt and road: How by 'cultural science' we can achieve Xinjiang's long-term peace and good government." *Journal of Kashgar University* 04:46–50.

Lichtenheld, Adam. 2020. "Explaining population displacement strategies in civil war: A cross-national analysis." *International Organization*.

Lindberg, Staffan I., Michael Coppedge, John Gerring, and Jan Teorell. 2014. "V-Dem: A new way to measure democracy." *Journal of Democracy* 25(3):159–169.

Ling, Ted. 2010. Blame and martyrs: The Commonwealth Government's administration of the Northern Territory's pastoral industry, 1911–1978. PhD thesis Charles Darwin University.

Ling, Ted and the National Archives of Australia. 2011. *Commonwealth Government Records about the Northern Territory*. Canberra Business Centre, A.C.T: National Archives of Australia.

Lipset, Seymour Martin. 1959. "Some social requisites of democracy: Economic development and political legitimacy." *American Political Science Review* 53(1):69–105.

Liu, Amy H and Kevin Peters. 2017. "The Hanification of Xinjiang, China: The economic effects of the Great Leap West." *Studies in Ethnicity and Nationalism* 17(2):265–280.

Lloyd, Christopher, Jacob Metzer, and Richard Sutch. 2013. *Settler Economies in World History*. Brill.

Lloyd, David. 2012. "Settler colonialism and the state of exception: The example of Palestine/Israel." *Settler Colonial Studies* 2(1):59–80.

Lloyd, David and Patrick Wolfe. 2016. "Settler colonial logics and the neoliberal regime."

Lobao, Linda and Katherine Meyer. 2001. "The great agricultural transition: Crisis, change, and social consequences of twentieth century US farming." *Annual Review of Sociology* 27(1):103–124.

Love, Eric TL. 2005. *Race over Empire: Racism and US Imperialism, 1865–1900*. Univ. of North Carolina Press.

Lu, Lingyu and Cameron G Thies. 2013. "War, rivalry, and state building in the Middle East." *Political Research Quarterly* 66(2):239–253.

Lu, Sidney Xu. 2019. *The Making of Japanese Settler Colonialism*. Cambridge University Press.

Lujala, Päivi, Jan Ketil Rod, and Nadja Thieme. 2007. "Fighting over oil: Introducing a new dataset." *Conflict Management and Peace Science* 24(3):239–256.

Lustick, Ian. 1987. "Israeli state-building in the West Bank and the Gaza Strip: theory and practice." *International Organization* 41(1):151–171.

Lustick, Ian. 1993. *Unsettled States, Disputed lands: Britain and Ireland, France and Algeria, Israel and the West Bank-Gaza*. Ithaca NY: Cornell University Press.

Lustick, Ian. 2015. The political dynamics of settlement projects: The central state-settler-native triangle. In *Settlers in Contested Lands: Territorial Disputes and Ethnic Conflicts*, ed. Oded Haklai and Neophytos Loizides. Stanford, CA: Stanford University Press.

Lustick, Ian S. 1996. "History, historiography, and political science: Multiple historical records and the problem of selection bias." *American Political Science Review* 90(3):605–618.

Lustick, Ian S. 2019. *Paradigm Lost: From Two-State Solution to One-State Reality.* University of Pennsylvania Press.

Lüthi, Lorenz M. 2010. *The Sino-Soviet Split: Cold War in the Communist World.* Princeton, NJ: Princeton University Press.

Machiavelli, Niccolo. 1950. *The Prince.* New York, NY: Random House.

Macintyre, Stuart and Anna Clark. 2013. *The History Wars.* Melbourne, Australia: Melbourne University Publishing.

Mackay, James Alexander Kenneth, William Edward Parry-Okeden, and Charles Edward Herbert. 1907. *Report of the Royal Commission of Inquiry into the Present Conditions, Including the Method of Government, of the Territory of Papua, and the Best Means for their Improvement.* Melbourne, Australia: Commonwealth of Australia.

MacLeod, Jason. 2015. *Merdeka and the Morning Star: Civil Resistance in West Papua.* Brisbane, Australia: University of Queensland Press.

Maddison, Sarah. 2016. Settler Australia in the twentieth century. In *The Routledge Handbook of the History of Settler Colonialism*, ed. Edward Cavanagh and Lorenzo Veracini. Routledge.

Madley, Benjamin. 2004. "Patterns of frontier genocide 1803–1910: The Aboriginal Tasmanians, the Yuki of California, and the Herero of Namibia." *Journal of Genocide Research* 6(2): 167–192.

Madley, Benjamin. 2008. "From terror to genocide: Britain's Tasmanian penal colony and Australia's history wars." *Journal of British Studies* 47(1):77–106.

Magaloni, Beatriz, Jonathan Chu, and Eric Min. 2013. "Autocracies of the world, 1950–2012 (Version 1.0)." Stanford CA: Stanford University available at *http://cddrl.fsi.stanford.edu /research/autocracies_of_the_world_dataset/*, accessed 2 February 2019.

Mahoney, James. 2010. *Colonialism and Postcolonial Development: Spanish America in Comparative Perspective.* Cambridge University Press.

Mahoney, James and Kathleen Thelen, eds. 2015. *Advances in Comparative-Historical Analysis.* Cambridge University Press.

Mamdani, Mahmood. 1998. "When does a settler become a native? Reflections of the colonial roots of citizenship in Equatorial and South Africa." Text of Inaugral Lecture as A. C. Jordan Professor of African Studies, University of Cape Town available at https:// citizenshiprightsafrica.org/wp-content/uploads/1998/05/mamdani-1998-inaugural-lecture .pdf, accessed 14 April 2020.

Mamdani, Mahmood. 2020. *Neither Settler nor Native.* Harvard University Press.

Mann, Michael. 2005. *The Dark Side of Democracy: Explaining Ethnic Cleansing.* Cambridge University Press.

Manning, Chris and Michael Rumbiak. 1989. *Economic Development, Migrant Labour and Indigenous Welfare in Irian Jaya, 1970–84.* Number 20 National Centre for Development Studies, Research School of Pacific Studies.

Mao, Huahe. 2019. *The Ebb and Flow of Chinese Petroleum: A Story Told by a Witness.* Brill.

Mao, Zedong. 1974. *Mao Tse-tung Unrehearsed: Talks and Letters, 1956–71.* London: Penguin books.

Mar, Tracey Banivanua and Penelope Edmonds. 2010. *Making Settler Colonial Space: Perspectives on Race, Place and Identity.* Springer.

Markowitz, Jonathan, Christopher Fariss, and R. Blake McMahon. 2018. "Producing goods and projecting power: How what you make influences what you take." *Journal of Conflict Resolution* pp. 1–35.

Marshall, Monty G. and Keith Jaggers. 2007. *Polity IV Project: Dataset Users' Manual*. George Mason University and Center for Systemic Peace. http://www.systemicpeace.org/inscr/p4manualv2006.pdf.

Matteson, David M. 1933. George Washington every day. In *History of the George Washington Bicentennial Celebration*, ed. Sol Bloom. Vol. 3 Washington, D.C. United States George Washington Bicentennial Commission.

Mattingly, Daniel C. 2019. *The Art of Political Control in China*. Cambridge University Press.

Maxwell, Constantia. 1923. "The Plantation in Ulster at the Beginning of James I's Reign." *The Sewanee Review* 31(2):164–177.

May, Ron J. 1998. From promise to crisis: A political economy of Papua New Guinea. In *Governance and Reform in the South Pacific*, ed. P. Larmour. Vol. 23 Canberra, Australia: Asia Pacific Press p. 154.

McAlexander, Richard J. and Joan Ricart-Huguet. 2021. "State disengagement: Evidence from French West Africa." *International Studies Quarterly* .

McCulloch, Lesley. 2003. Trifungsi: The role of the Indonesian military in business. In *The Military as an Economic Actor: Soldiers in Business*, ed. Jörn Brömmelhörster; Wolf-Christian Paes. Palgrave Macmillan.

McGarry, John. 1998. "'Demographic engineering': The state-directed movement of ethnic groups as a technique of conflict regulation." *Ethnic and Racial Studies* 21(4):613–638.

McGibbon, Rodd. 2004. "Plural society in peril: Migraton, economic change, and the Papua conflict." *Policy Studies* (13):I.

McGrath, Frank Roland. 2000. Intentions of the framers of the Commonwealth of Australia constitution. PhD thesis University of Sydney.

McGregor, Russell. 1997. *Imagined Destinies: Aboriginal Australians and the Doomed Race Theory, 1880–1939*. Melbourne University Press.

McGregor, Russell. 2012. "A dog in the manger: White Australia and its vast empty spaces." *Australian Historical Studies* 43(2):157–173.

McGregor, Russell. 2013. "Developing the north, defending the nation? The Northern Australia Development Committee, 1945–1949." *Australian Journal of Politics & History* 59(1):33–46.

McGregor, Russell. 2016. *Environment, Race, and Nationhood in Australia*. Springer.

McKillop, R. and S. G. Firth. 1980. Foreign intrusion: The first fifty years. In *A Time to Plant and a Time to Uproot: A History of Agriculture in Papua New Guinea*, ed. Donald Denoon and Catherine Snowden. Port Moresby, Papua New Guinea: Institute of Papua New Guinea Studies.

McNamee, Lachlan. 2018. "Mass resettlement and political violence: Evidence from Rwanda." *World Politics* 70(4):595–644.

McNamee, Lachlan. 2020. "Colonial legacies and comparative racial identification in the Americas." *American Journal of Sociology* 126(2):318–353.

Mealey, George A. 1996. *Grasberg: Mining the Richest and Most Remote Deposit of Copper and Gold in the World, in the Mountains of Irian Jaya, Indonesia*. Freeport-McMoRan Copper & Gold New Orleans, USA.

Memmi, Albert. 2006. *Decolonization and the Decolonized*. University of Minnesota Press.

Memmi, Albert. 2010. *The Colonizer and the Colonized*. London, UK: Souvenir Press.

Millward, James. 1998. *Beyond the Pass: Economy, Ethnicity, and Empire in Qing Central Asia, 1759-1864*. Stanford University Press.

Minorities at Risk Project. 2009. "Minorities at Risk dataset." Published by College Park, MD: Center for International Development and Conflict Management. Retrieved from http://www.mar.umd.edu/ on: 2 February 2019.

Mollah, Wayne S. et al. 1982. *Humpty Doo: Rice in the Territory*. Brinkin, NT: The Australian National University, North Australia Research.

Monbiot, George. 1989. *Poisoned Arrows: An Investigative Journey through Indonesia*. London, UK: Michael Joseph Ltd.

Morelli, Massimo and Dominic Rohner. 2015. "Resource concentration and civil wars." *Journal of Development Economics* 117:32–47.

Morgensen, Scott Lauria. 2011. "The biopolitics of settler colonialism: Right here, right now." *Settler Colonial Studies* 1(1):52–76.

Moses, A Dirk. 2000. "An antipodean genocide? The origins of the genocidal moment in the colonization of Australia." *Journal of Genocide Research* 2(1):89–106.

Moses, A. Dirk. 2011. "Official apologies, reconciliation, and settler colonialism: Australian indigenous alterity and political agency." *Citizenship Studies* 15(02):145–159.

Mufti, Hania. 2004. *Claims in Conflict: Reversing Ethnic Cleansing in Northern Iraq*. Human Rights Watch.

Mundy, Jacob and Stephen Zunes. 2015. Moroccan settlers in Western Sahara : Colonists or fifth column? In *Settlers in Contested Lands: Territorial Disputes and Ethnic Conflicts*, ed. Oded Haklai and Neophytos Loizides. Stanford University Press.

Murray, Hubert, Atlee Hunt and Walter Lucas. 1920. *Interim and Final Reports of the Royal Commission of Late German New Guinea*. Melbourne, Australia: Commonwealth of Australia.

Mylonas, Harris. 2012. *The Politics of Nation-Building: Making Co-nationals, Refugees, and Minorities*. New York, NY: Cambridge University Press.

Mylonas, Harris. 2015. "Methodological problems in the study of nation-building: Behaviorism and historicist solutions in political science." *Social Science Quarterly* 96(3):740–758.

Mylonas, Harris and Marko Žilović. 2019. "Foreign policy priorities and ethnic return migration policies: Group-level variation in Greece and Serbia." *Journal of Ethnic and Migration Studies* 45(4):613–635.

Nelson, Hank. 2000. "Liberation: The end of Australian rule in Papua New Guinea." *Journal of Pacific History* 35(3):269–280.

Notestein, Frank W. 1945. Population: The long view. In *Food for the World*, ed. Theodore W. Schultz. Chicago: University of Chicago Press.

O'Brien, Patricia. 2009. "Remaking Australia's colonial culture? White Australia and its Papuan frontier 1901–1940." *Australian Historical Studies* 40(1):96–112.

O'Leary, Brendan. 2001. The elements of right-sizing and right-peopling the state. In *Right-sizing the State: The Politics of Moving Borders*, ed. Brendan O'Leary, Ian Lustick, and Thomas Callaghy. Oxford University Press pp. 15–73.

Operations Evaluation Department, World Bank. 1994. *Indonesia Impact Evaluation Report No. 12874-IND*. Washington, D.C.: The World Bank.

Osborne, Robin. 1985. *Indonesia's Secret War: The Guerilla Struggle in Irian Jaya*. Allen & Unwin Sydney.

Osterhammel, Jürgen. 1997. *Colonialism: A Theoretical Overview*. Markus Wiener Publishers.

Pagden, Anthony. 2007. *Peoples and Empires: A Short History of European Migration, Exploration, and Conquest, from Greece to the Present*. New York, NY: Modern Library.

Paglayan, Agustina. 2018. "Civil war, state consolidation, and the spread of mass education." Presented at the 2018 American Political Science Association (APSA) annual meeting.

Panncll, Clifton W. and J. C. Ma Laurence. 1997. "Urban transition and interstate relations in a dynamic post-Soviet borderland: The Xinjiang Uygur Autonomous Region of China." *Post-Soviet Geography and Economics* 38(4):206–229.

Pateman, Carole. 2007. The Settler Contract. In *Contract and Domination*, ed. Charles W. Mills. Cambridge: Polity pp. 35–78.

Payne, William and John Fletcher. 1937. *Report of the Board of Inquiry Appointed to Inquire into the Land and Land Industries of the Northern Territory of Australia, Dated 10th October, 1937*. Canberra, Australia: Australian Government Publishing Service.

Penvenne, Jeanne Marie. 2005. Settling against the tide: The layered contradictions of twentieth-century Portuguese settlement in Mozambique. In *Settler Colonialism in the Twentieth Century: Projects, Practices, Legacies*, ed. Caroline Elkins and Susan Pedersen. Routledge.

Pepinsky, Thomas B. 2016. "Colonial migration and the origins of governance: Theory and evidence from Java." *Comparative Political Studies* 49(9):1201–1237.

Perdue, Peter C. 2009. *China Marches West: The Qing Conquest of Central Eurasia*. Harvard University Press.

Pinker, Steven. 2012. *The Better Angels of Our Nature: Why Violence Has Declined*. Penguin.

Pitcher, M Anne. 1991. "Sowing the seeds of failure: Early Portuguese cotton cultivation in Angola and Mozambique, 1820–1926." *Journal of Southern African Studies* 17(1):43–70.

Polanyi, Karl. 1944. *The Great Transformation*. Farrar & Rinehart.

Posner, Daniel N. 2005. *Institutions and Ethnic Politics in Africa*. Cambridge University Press.

Pounds, Norman. 1972. *Political Geography*. New York NY: McGraw-Hill Inc.

Povinelli, Elizabeth A. 2002. *The Cunning of Recognition: Indigenous Alterities and the Making of Australian Multiculturalism*. Duke University Press.

Powell, Alan. 1982. *Far Country*. Melbourne University Press.

Power, Samantha. 2002. *"A Problem from Hell": America and the Age of Genocide*. New York, NY: Public Affairs.

Pratsinakis, Manolis. 2014. "Resistance and compliance in immigrant–native figurations: Albanian and Soviet Greek immigrants and their interaction with Greek society." *Journal of Ethnic and Migration Studies* 40(8):1295–1313.

Preece, Jennifer Jackson. 1998. "Ethnic cleansing as an instrument of nation-state creation: changing state practices and evolving legal norms." *Human Rights Quarterly* 20:817.

Przeworski, Adam and Fernando Limongi. 1997. "Modernization: Theories and Facts." *World Politics* 49(2):155–183.

Qi, Qingshun. 2002. "Analysis of A Few Issues on Xinjiang in the 'Sino-Soviet Treaty of Friendship, Alliance and Mutual Assistance.'" *Xinjiang University Academic Journal* (4): 58–67.

Raczka, Witt. 1998. "Xinjiang and its Central Asian borderlands." *Central Asian Survey* 17(3): 373–407.

Rahmato, Dessalegn. 2003. *Resettlement in Ethiopia: the Tragedy of Population Relocation in the 1980s*. Addis Adaba, Ethiopia: Forum for Social Studies.

Ravenstein, Ernst Georg. 1885. "The laws of migration." *Journal of the Statistical Society of London* 48(2):167–235.

Reno, William. 1997. "War, markets, and the reconfiguration of West Africa's weak states." *Comparative Politics* pp. 493–510.

Reynolds, Henry. 1976. "The other side of the frontier: Early Aboriginal reactions to pastoral settlement in Queensland and Northern New South Wales." *Historical Studies* 17(66): 50–63.

Reynolds, Henry. 2006. *The Other Side of the Frontier: Aboriginal Resistance to the European Invasion of Australia*. Sydney, Australia: University of New South Wales Press.

Robinson, Thomas W. 1972. "The Sino-Soviet border dispute: Background, development, and the March 1969 clashes." *American Political Science Review* 66(4):1175–1202.

Rosecrance, Richard N. 1986. *The Rise of the Trading State: Commerce and Conquest in the Modern World*. New York: Basic Books.

Ross, Michael L. 2004. "How do natural resources influence civil war? Evidence from thirteen cases." *International Organization* 58(1):35–67.

Ross, Michael L. 2013. *The Oil Curse: How Petroleum Wealth Shapes the Development of Nations*. Princeton University Press.

Rostow, Walt Whitman. 1960. *The Stages of Economic Growth: A Non-Communist Manifesto*. Cambridge University Press.

Rotberg, Robert I. 1988. *The Founder: Cecil Rhodes and the Pursuit of Power*. Oxford University Press.

Rowse, Tim. 2014. "Indigenous heterogeneity." *Australian Historical Studies* 45(3):297–310.

Rummel, Rudolph J. 1995. "Democracy, power, genocide, and mass murder." *Journal of Conflict Resolution* 39(1):3–26.

Ryan, Lyndall. 2010. "Settler massacres on the Port Phillip frontier, 1836–1851." *Journal of Australian Studies* 34(3):257–273.

Rynhold, Jonathan and Dov Waxman. 2008. "Ideological change and Israel's disengagement from Gaza." *Political Science Quarterly* 123(1):11–37.

Sahlins, Peter. 1989. *Boundaries: The Making of France and Spain in the Pyrenees*. University of California Press.

Said, Edward. 2000. Reflections on exile. In *Reflections on Exile and Other Essays*. Cambridge MA: Harvard University Press pp. 172–186.

Salehyan, Idean. 2009. *Rebels without Borders*. Ithaca, NY: Cornell University Press.

Satz, Ronald N. 1992. Rhetoric Versus Reality: The Indian Policy of Andrew Jackson. In *Cherokee Removal: Before and After*, ed. William L. Anderson. University of Georgia Press.

Sautman, Barry. 2000. "Is Xinjiang an internal colony?" *Inner Asia* 2(2):239–271.

Sautman, Barry. 2006. 'Demographic annihilation' and Tibet. In *Contemporary Tibet: Politics, Development, and Society in a Disputed Region*, ed. June Teufel Dreyer. ME Sharpe New York pp. 230–257.

Schiavo-Campo, Salvatore and Mary P. Judd. 2005. The Mindanao conflict in the Philippines: Roots, costs, and potential peace dividend. Technical report Conflict Prevention & Reconstruction Paper No. 24, World Bank.

Schumpeter, Joseph. 1942. *Capitalism, Socialism and Democracy*. Harper & Brothers.

Scott, James C. 1998. *Seeing Like a State: How Certain Schemes to Improve the Human Condition Have Failed*. Yale University Press.

Scott, James C. 2009. *The Art of Not Being Governed: An Anarchist History of Upland Southeast Asia*. Yale University Press.

Sen, Maya and Omar Wasow. 2016. "Race as a bundle of sticks: Designs that estimate effects of seemingly immutable characteristics." *Annual Review of Political Science* 19.

Seymour, James D. 2000. "Xinjiang's production and construction corps, and the Sinification of Eastern Turkestan." *Inner Asia* 2(2):171–193.

Seymour, James D. and Michael R. Anderson. 2015. *New Ghosts, Old Ghosts: Prisons and Labor Reform Camps in China: Prisons and Labor Reform Camps in China*. Routledge.

Shichor, Yitzhak. 2005. "Blow up: Internal and external challenges of Uyghur separatism and Islamic radicalism to Chinese rule in Xinjiang." *Asian Affairs: An American Review* 32(2): 119–136.

Shipway, Martin. 2007. *Decolonization and Its Impact: A Comparative Approach to the End of the Colonial Empires*. Wiley.

Shiraishi, Takashi and Saya S. Shiraishi. 2018. *The Japanese in Colonial Southeast Asia*. Cornell University Press.

Shoemaker, Nancy. 2015. "A typology of colonialism." *Perspectives on History* 53(7):29–30.

Sicular, Terry and Yaohui Zhao. 2004. Earnings and labor mobility in rural China: Implications for China's accession to the WTO. In *China and the WTO: Accession, Policy Reform and Poverty Reduction Strategies*, ed. D. Bhattasali, S. Li and W. J. Martin. New York, NY: Oxford University Press pp. 239–260.

Simpson, Audra. 2016. "Whither settler colonialism?" *Settler Colonial Studies* 6(4):438–445.

Singh, Bilveer. 2017. *Papua: Geopolitics and the Quest for Nationhood*. Routledge.

Skeldon, Ronald. 2012. "Migration transitions revisited: Their continued relevance for the development of migration theory." *Population, Space and Place* 18(2):154–166.

Slater, Dan and Daniel Ziblatt. 2013. "The enduring indispensability of the controlled comparison." *Comparative Political Studies* 46(10):1301–1327.

Smith, Darren P. and Russell King. 2012. "Editorial introduction: Re-making migration theory." *Population, Space and Place* 18(2):127–133.

Snyder, Jack. 1989. "International leverage on Soviet domestic change." *World Politics* 42(1):1–30.

Snyder, Jack. 1991. *Myths of Empire: Domestic Politics and International Ambition*. Ithaca, NY: Cornell University Press.

Sorace, Christian and William Hurst. 2016. "China's phantom urbanisation and the pathology of ghost cities." *Journal of Contemporary Asia* 46(2):304–322.

Staniland, Paul. 2012. "States, insurgents, and wartime political orders." *Perspectives on Politics* 10(2):243–264.

Stanton, Jessica A. 2016. *Violence and Restraint in Civil War: Civilian Targeting in the Shadow of International Law*. Cambridge University Press.

Stedman, Stephen John and Fred Tanner. 2004. *Refugee Manipulation: War, Politics, and the Abuse of Human Suffering*. Brookings Institution Press.

Steele, Abbey. 2011. "Electing displacement: Political cleansing in Apartadó, Colombia." *Journal of Conflict Resolution* 55(3):423–445.

Steinmetz, George. 2007. *The Devil's Handwriting: Precoloniality and the German Colonial State in Qingdao, Samoa, and Southwest Africa*. University of Chicago Press.

Steinmetz, George. 2008. "The colonial state as a social field: Ethnographic capital and native policy in the German overseas empire before 1914." *American Sociological Review* 73(4):589–612.

Strakosch, Elizabeth. 2016. Beyond colonial completion: Arendt, settler colonialism and the end of politics. In *The Limits of Settler Colonial Reconciliation: Non-Indigenous People and the Responsibility to Engage*, ed. Sarah Maddison, Tom Clark and Ravi de Costa. Springer pp. 15–33.

Strang, David. 1990. "From dependency to sovereignty: An event history analysis of decolonization 1870-1987." *American Sociological Review* pp. 846–860.

Straus, Scott. 2015. *Making and Unmaking Nations: War, Leadership, and Genocide in Modern Africa*. Cornell University Press.

Sukarno. 1961. *The People's Command for the Liberation of West Irian: Given by the President/Supreme Commander of the Armed Forces of the Republic of Indonesia, Commander-in-Chief of the Supreme Command for the Liberation of West Irian, at a Mass Meeting in Jogjakarta, on 19th December 1961*. Department of Information, Republic of Indonesia.

Swan, Quito. 2018. "Blinded by Bandung? Illumining West Papua, Senegal, and the Black Pacific." *Radical History Review* 2018(131):58–81.

Tarrow, Sidney. 2010. "The strategy of paired comparison: Toward a theory of practice." *Comparative Political Studies* 43(2):230–259.

Taylor, Andrew and Dean Carson. 2017. *Synthesising Northern Territory Population Research: A Report to the Northern Territory Department of the Chief Minister*. Charles Darwin University: Northern Institute.

Teitelbaum, Michael S. 2015. "Political demography: Powerful trends under-attended by demographic science." *Population Studies* 69(sup1):S87–S95.

Thacker, W. 1854. *Papers Relating to the Settlement of Europeans in India*. Thacker, Spink and Co.

Ther, Philipp. 2014. *The Dark Side of Nation-States: Ethnic Cleansing in Modern Europe*. Berghahn Books.

Thies, Cameron G. 2005. "War, rivalry, and state building in Latin America." *American Journal of Political Science* 49(3):451–465.

Thomas, Martin. 2014. *Fight or flight: Britain, France, and Their Roads from Empire*. Oxford University Press.

Thompson, Roger G. 1990. "Making a mandate: The formation of Australia's New Guinea policies 1919-1925." *The Journal of Pacific History* 25(1):68–84.

Thompson, William and David Dreyer. 2011. *Handbook of International Rivalries*. CQ Press.

Thompson, William R. 2001. "Identifying rivals and rivalries in world politics." *International Studies Quarterly* 45(4):557–586.

Tilly, Charles. 1975. Reflections on the history of European state-making. In *The Formation of National States in Western Europe*, ed. Charles Tilly. Princeton, NJ: Princeton University Press.

Tilly, Charles. 1985. War making and state making as organized crime. In *Bringing the State Back In*, ed. T. Skocpol, P. Evans and D. Rueschemeyer. Cambridge MA: Cambridge University Press.

Tilly, Charles. 1992. *Coercion, Capital and European States: AD 990–1990*. Cambridge MA: Basil Blackwell.

Todaro, Michael P. 1969. "A model of labor migration and urban unemployment in less developed countries." *American Economic Review* 59(1):138–148.

Toft, Monica Duffy. 2003. *The Geography of Ethnic Violence: Identity, Interests, and the Indivisibility of Territory*. Princeton University Press.

Tong, Yufen. 1994. "The Prediction Results of Xinjiang Population Interprovincial Migration System Model." Research report published by the Xinjiang University Population Research Institute.

Toops, Stanley. 2004. "Demographics and development in Xinjiang after 1949." Working Paper No. 1, May 2000, East-West Center Washington.

Toops, Stanley. 2018. "Spatial results of the 2010 census in Xinjiang." URL: https://theasia dialogue.com/2016/03/07/spatial-results-of-the-2010-census-in-xinjiang/

Transparency International. 2004. *Global Corruption Report*. London, UK: Pluto Press.

Tuck, Eve and K. Wayne Yang. 2012. "Decolonization is not a metaphor." *Decolonization: Indigeneity, Education & Society* 1(1).

Uchida, Jun. 2011. *Brokers of Empire: Japanese Settler Colonialism in Korea, 1876–1945*. Harvard University Press.

Upton, Stuart. 2009. The impact of migration on the people of Papua, Indonesia. PhD thesis University of New South Wales.

Uzonyi, Gary. 2018. "Interstate rivalry, genocide, and politicide." *Journal of Peace Research* 55(4):476–490.

Valentino, Benjamin A. 2004. *Final Solutions. Mass Killings and Genocide in the 20th Century*. Ithaca, NY: Cornell University Press.

Valentino, Benjamin, Paul Huth and Dylan Balch-Lindsay. 2004. "'Draining the sea': mass killing and guerrilla warfare." *International Organization* 58(2):375–407.

Van Der Wijst, Ton. 1985. "Transmigration in Indonesia: An evaluation of a population redistribution policy." *Population Research and Policy Review* 4(1):1–30.

Vasquez, John A. 1993. *The War Puzzle*. Cambridge, UK: Cambridge University Press.

Veracini, Lorenzo. 2007. "Settler colonialism and decolonisation." *Borderlands* 6(2).

Veracini, Lorenzo. 2010. *Settler Colonialism: A Theoretical Overview*. New York, NY: Palgrave Macmillan.

Veracini, Lorenzo. 2011. "Introducing: Settler colonial studies." *Settler Colonial Studies* 1(1):1–12.

Veracini, Lorenzo. 2014. "Defending settler colonial studies." *Australian Historical Studies* 45(3):311–316.

Voutira, Eftihia. 2003. When Greeks meet other Greeks: Settlement policy issues in the contemporary Greek context. In *Crossing the Aegean. An Appraisal of the 1923 Compulsory Population Exchange between Greece and Turkey*, ed. Renée Hirschon. Berghahn: New York and Oxford.

Wallace, Jeremy. 2014. *Cities and Stability: Urbanization, Redistribution, and Regime Survival in China*. Oxford University Press.

Wallerstein, Immanuel. 1976. Modernization: Requiescat in pace. In *The Uses of Controversy in Sociology*, ed. Otto Larsen and Lewis A. Coser. New York, NY: Free Press pp. 131–35.

Walling, Carrie Booth. 2000. "The history and politics of ethnic cleansing." *The International Journal of Human Rights* 4(3-4):47–66.

Walter, Barbara F. 2006. "Information, uncertainty, and the decision to secede." *International Organization* 60(1):105–135.

Wang, Haijiang Henry. 1999. *China's Oil Industry and Market*. Elsevier.

Wang, Xiyu and Jianpo Chen. 1996. Channel the migrants and establish agriculture in the desert (Yinru yimin, jianli huangmo nongye). In *China Development Research (Zhongguo Fazhan Yanjiu)*, ed. Hong Ma and Shangqing Sun. Beijing: China Development Publisher (Zhongguo Fazhan Chubanshe).

Weber, Eugen. 1976. *Peasants into Frenchmen: The Modernization of Rural France, 1870–1914*. Stanford University Press.

Webster, David. 2001. "'Already sovereign as a people': A foundational moment in West Papuan nationalism." *Pacific Affairs* pp. 507–528.

Weidmann, Nils B. 2009. "Geography as motivation and opportunity: Group concentration and ethnic conflict." *Journal of Conflict Resolution* 53(4):526–543.

Weiner, Myron. 1978. *Sons of the Soil: Migration and Ethnic Conflict in India*. Princeton, NJ: Princeton University Press.

Weiner, Myron and Michael S Teitelbaum. 2001. *Political Demography, Demographic Engineering*. Berghahn Books.

Weinstein, Jeremy M. 2006. *Inside Rebellion: The Politics of Insurgent Violence*. Cambridge University Press.

Wendt, Alexander. 1992. "Anarchy is what states make of it: The social construction of power politics." *International Organization* 46(2):391–425.

Wernstedt, Frederick L. and Paul D. Simkins. 1965. "Migrations and the settlement of Mindanao." *The Journal of Asian Studies* 25(1):83–103.

West, Francis. 1957. "The beginnings of Australian rule in Papua." *Political Science* 9(1): 38–50.

Whitaker, Beth Elise and Jason Giersch. 2021. "Strategic calculations? Partisan differences in support for Puerto Rican migration to the mainland USA." *Migration Studies*.

White, Lynn T. 1979. "The road to Urumchi: Approved institutions in search of attainable goals during pre-1968 rustication from Shanghai." *The China Quarterly* 79:481–510.

White, Richard. 2010. *The Middle Ground: Indians, Empires, and Republics in the Great Lakes Region, 1650–1815*. Cambridge University Press.

Whitten, Anthony J. 1987. "Indonesia's transmigration program and its role in the loss of tropical rain forests." *Conservation Biology* 1(3):239–246.

Whitten, Anthony J., J. H. Haeruman, H. S. Alikoddra, and M. Thohari. 1987. *Transmigration and the Environment in Indonesia: The Past, Present, and Future*. IUCN.

Williams, Eric. 1944. *Capitalism & Slavery*. Chapel Hill, NC: University of North Carolina Press.

Wimmer, Andreas. 2002. *Nationalist Exclusion and Ethnic Conflict: Shadows of Modernity*. Cambridge University Press.

Wimmer, Andreas. 2012. *Waves of war: Nationalism, state formation, and ethnic exclusion in the modern world*. Cambridge University Press.

Wimmer, Andreas. 2015. "Race-centrism: A critique and a research agenda." *Ethnic and Racial Studies* 38(13):2186–2205.

Wimmer, Andreas, Lars-Erik Cederman, and Brian Min. 2009a. "Ethnic politics and armed conflict: A configurational analysis of a new global data set." *American Sociological Review* 74(2):316–337.

Winant, Howard. 2015. "Race, ethnicity and social science." *Ethnic and Racial Studies* 38(13): 2176–2185.

Windschuttle, Keith. 2000. "The myths of frontier massacres in Australian history, Part 1: The invention of massacre stories." *Quadrant* 44(10):9–14.

Wolfe, Patrick. 1994. "Nation and miscegenation: Discursive continuity in the post-Mabo era." *Social Analysis: The International Journal of Social and Cultural Practice* (36):93–152.

Wolfe, Patrick. 1999. *Settler Colonialism and the Transformation of Anthropology: The Politics and Poetics of an Ethnographic Event.* London, UK: Cassell.

Wolfe, Patrick. 2001. "Land, labor, and difference: Elementary structures of race." *American Historical Review* 106(3):866–905.

Wolfe, Patrick. 2006. "Settler colonialism and the elimination of the native." *Journal of Genocide Research* 8(4):387–409.

Wood, Elisabeth Jean. 2010. "Rape is not inevitable in war." *Yale Journal of International Affairs* 5:161.

Wood, Elisabeth Jean. 2018. "Rape as a practice of war: Toward a typology of political violence." *Politics & Society* 46(4):513–537.

World Bank. 2012. *World Development Indicators.* Washington, D.C.: The World Bank. Retrieved from http://data.worldbank.org/data-catalog/world-development-indicators 2 February 2019.

Wucherpfennig, Julian, Nils B. Weidmann, Luc Girardin, Lars-Erik Cederman, and Andreas Wimmer. 2011. "Politically relevant ethnic groups across space and time: Introducing the GeoEPR dataset." *Conflict Management and Peace Science* 28(5):423–437.

Xinjiang Provincial Government. 1998. *General Chronicles of Xinjiang - Xinjiang Production and Construction Corps.* Vol. 37 Urumchi: Xinjiang People's Publishing House.

Xu, Vicky Xiuzhong, Danielle Cave, James Leibold, Kelsey Munro, and Nathan Ruser. 2020. "Uyghurs for sale." *Australian Strategic Policy Institute.*

Ye, Ruiping. 2017. Colonisation and Aboriginal land tenure: Taiwan during the Qing Period (1684-1895) and the Japanese period (1895–1945). PhD thesis Victoria University Wellington.

Yee, Albert S. 1996. "The causal effects of ideas on policies." *International Organization* 50(1): 69–108.

Yee, Herbert S. 2003. "Ethnic relations in Xinjiang: A survey of Uyghur-Han relations in Urumqi." *Journal of Contemporary China* 12(36):431–452.

Yeh, Emily T. 2013. *Taming Tibet: Landscape transformation and the gift of Chinese development.* Cornell University Press.

Yin, Weiwen. 2015. "The natural resource curse in Xinjiang." *CEU Political Science Journal* 10 (01-02):112–140.

Youé, Chris. 2018. "Settler colonialism or colonies with settlers?" *Canadian Journal of African Studies/Revue canadienne des études africaines* 52(1):69–85.

Yu-Jose, Lydia N. 1996. "World War II and the Japanese in the prewar Philippines." *Journal of Southeast Asian Studies* pp. 64–81.

Zelinsky, Wilbur. 1971. "The hypothesis of the mobility transition." *Geographical Review* pp. 219–249.

Zenz, Adrian. 2019. "'Thoroughly reforming them towards a healthy heart attitude': China's political re-education campaign in Xinjiang." *Central Asian Survey* 38(1):102–128.

Zenz, Adrian. 2021. "'End the dominance of the Uyghur ethnic group': An analysis of Beijing's population optimization strategy in southern Xinjiang." *Central Asian Survey* .

Zenz, Adrian and James Leibold. 2019. "Securitizing Xinjiang: Police recruitment, informal policing and ethnic minority co-optation." *The China Quarterly* pp. 1–25.

Zhang, Anfu. 2014. "The northwestern frontier during the Sino-Soviet military standoff: Xinjiang production and construction corp to enhance military stock." *Contemporary Studies of Chinese History* .

Zhang, Anna. 2020. "Stay west young Han: State response to sons of the soil riots." Available at https://www.annazhang.org/research.html.

Zhang, Feng. 2010. One mouth, different tunes: Newspaper representations of migrants to Xinjiang 1949–2004. In *Western Development and Socio-economic Change: China-Canada Comparative Studies*. Beijing: Intellectual Property Press.

Zhao, Suisheng. 2016. "Xi Jinping's Maoist revival." *Journal of Democracy* 27(3):83–97.

Zhu, Yuchao and Dongyan Blachford. 2012. "Economic expansion, marketization, and their social impact on China's ethnic minorities in Xinjiang and Tibet." *Asian Survey* 52(4): 714–733.

Zhu, Yuchao and Dongyan Blachford. 2016. "'Old bottle, new wine'? Xinjiang bingtuan and China's ethnic frontier governance." *Journal of Contemporary China* 25(97):25–40.

Zhukov, Yuri M. 2015. "Population resettlement in war: Theory and evidence from Soviet archives." *Journal of Conflict Resolution* 59(7):1155–1185.

INDEX

Page numbers in *italics* refer to figures and tables.

GPSR Authorized Representative: Easy Access System Europe - Mustamäe tee
50, 10621 Tallinn, Estonia, gpsr.requests@easproject.com

www.ingramcontent.com/pod-product-compliance
Lightning Source LLC
Chambersburg PA
CBHW031126270326
41929CB00011B/1521